JavaServer Pages™

JavaServer Pages™

Larne Pekowsky

ADDISON–WESLEY

Boston • San Francisco • New York • Toronto • Montreal
London • Munich • Paris • Madrid
Capetown • Sydney • Tokyo • Singapore • Mexico City

The publisher offers discounts on this book when ordered in quantity for special sales. For more information, please contact:

Pearson Education Corporate Sales Division
One Lake Street
Upper Saddle River, NJ 07458
(800) 382-3419
corpsales@pearsontechgroup.com

Visit AW on the Web: www.awl.com/cseng/

Library of Congress Cataloging-in-Publication Data

Pekowsky, Larne
    JavaServer Pages / Larne Pekowsky
        p.   cm.
    Includes bibliographical references and index.
    ISBN 0-201-70421-8
    1. JavaServer pages 2. Web sites—Design.   I. Title

    TK5105.8885.J38 P45 2000
    005.7'2—dc21   00-021302

ISBN 0201704218
Text printed on recycled and acid-free paper.

2 3 4 5 6 7 8 9 10 –CRS– 04 03 02 01 00
Second printing, May 2000

*Once again, for all my crescent
fresh friends on Handlink.*

CONTENTS

PREFACE

This is a book about how to create dynamic, interactive web sites using an exciting new technology called JavaServer Pages™. As its name implies, this technology is based on the Java Programming Language and inherits many of the language's features and benefits. Most notably, Java makes JSPs available on almost every kind of computer and operating system, and certainly those in most common use.

Anyone who is reasonably comfortable with HTML can learn to write JavaServer Pages by using a few new tags and small packages of code called JavaBeans. This allows for a very productive working relationship between HTML experts who build pages and programmers who build beans.

Both kinds of developer will find material of interest here. Chapter 1 gives a brief history of the Web, to provide some context for understanding what JavaServer Pages are and why they work the way they do. Chapters 2 and 3 introduce JSPs, which leads into the introduction of beans in Chapter 4. These chapters require absolutely no knowledge of programming or Java.

Chapter 5 introduces a little of the Java language, enough to put sophisticated control into pages. Chapter 6 describes how to use this information to build more sophisticated pages. Chapter 7 discusses more advanced ways to use beans in JSPs. Chapter 8 shows programmers how to create new beans.

The next several chapters focus on some important real-world issues that most sites face sooner or later and how JavaServer Pages can help. Chapter 9 introduces databases, which every sufficiently large or complex site will need. Chapter 10 shows how JSPs and databases can be used to build a fully functional news site with many advanced features. Chapter 11 covers personalization, which allows users of a site to tailor it to their own tastes. Chapter 12 describes e-commerce and ad targeting—two ways that sites can support themselves.

The remainder of the book covers advanced topics. Chapter 13 presents servlets and how they interact with JSPs. Chapter 14 covers some advanced features of the JSP specification.

Readers who are not interested in the programming side of life will get the most out of this book by reading straight through, possibly skipping Chapters 8 and 13. Chapter 5 introduces enough elements of the Java Programming Language to follow the examples through the rest of the book.

Readers already familiar with Java who are interested in JSPs will want to move quickly through Chapters 2 and 3 to get a feel for the JSP syntax. Chapter 4 shows how JSPs use beans, which will help programmers use the information in Chapter 8. Chapter 9 shows how to export database functionality through beans. Programmers may then wish to skim the examples in Chapters 10, 11, and 12 to see some more complex uses of JavaServer Pages and will then want to read about servlets and advanced JSP features in Chapters 13 and 14. The Custom Tags section of Chapter 14 is likely to be of particular interest.

Although still fairly young, JSP technology has already generated a lot of excitement, and many companies are planning or deploying web sites based on it. This is because the JSP specification is both simple and powerful. Fortunately, the Apache/Jakarta project puts JSPs within the reach of any web site, no matter how large or small. It is my hope that this book will help you get the most out of this revolutionary new method for building compelling, exciting web sites.

ACKNOWLEDGMENTS

JavaServer Pages™ didn't spring fully formed from my head; many people contributed in many ways to its existence.

I would like to start by thanking my first book's coauthors, Dan Woods and Tom Snee, for proving that writing a book was possible, and Dan especially for coming up with the idea in the first place.

It has been my very great pleasure to work with some of the brightest and most dedicated people in New York, both at Time Inc. New Media and at CapitalThinking. Although there are too many to name, I want to thank them all for helping to keep technology fun and exciting enough to write about. Almost every real-world consideration regarding server-side Java that appears in this book came out of projects my colleagues and I worked on.

Many thanks and high praise to everyone at Sun behind the Jakarta and the JavaServer Web Development Kit. The decision to open the source to Jakarta and Tomcat deserves a round of applause from every Java and JSPs developer.

All the code in this book was developed on a PPC system running Linux, which was only possible because of the Herculean efforts of the Blackdown Java–Linux and PowerPC JDK teams. Steve Byrne, Kevin B. Hendricks, Juergen Kreileder, and everyone else involved in the Linux ports are true unsung heros.

I would also like to thank everyone who took the time to read over the manuscript and make suggestions. The final result is definitely better for their efforts.

This book would be nothing but a collection of unread bits on my hard drive if not for everyone at Addison Wesley Longman, especially Mary O'Brien, Marilyn Rash, and Mariann Kourafas, who continue to be an unending source of patience and assistance.

Finally, I would like to thank the artists who created the music that kept me company as I was writing. Many of their names appear in examples scattered throughout the text.

CHAPTER 1
Introduction

The Web is a paradox. On one hand, it changes so fast that it is impossible to keep up with all the new sites, new technologies, and new paradigms. On the other, all too many web sites themselves are static and may remain unchanged for weeks or months.

In a way this is understandable, since to a large extent people are still trying to figure out what the Web is. Some treat it like a kind of newspaper or magazine, where content gets "published," people read it, and then it moves into some long-term archive where it may be searched much as one might search through a library's back issues.

Others want the Web to be television or radio, where users turn on their computers and receive "broadcast" content. Often referred to as "push," this model was very much in vogue a couple of years ago but has recently fallen into disfavor.

Both schools of thought have their merits and may be perfectly appropriate for some things. However, both are missing worlds of possibilities that the Web offers as a unique medium. The "archivists" are missing out on the possibilities of *dynamic* or *interactive* content—pages that change not just once a week or a couple of times a day but constantly. The "broadcasters" assume that users are passive participants and miss out on the chance for *personalization* by not allowing them to mix, match, and adjust as they see fit. Neither side is using the Web to its best effect.

This is truly regrettable, since in the end both camps are doing a disservice to themselves and their users. Flat pages or a flood of streaming images may be interesting the first time, and such sites might be worth revisiting as their content changes. But how much more compelling a site could be if it changed all the time, reacted to the user, and allowed the user to adjust it to suit her needs.

A Brief History of the Web

Before the Web there were a number of ways to get data from one computer to another. The first was called UNIX-to-UNIX copy, or UUCP, which acted like a mail order company. A user could enter a command to request a "catalog" of files from a remote system. Once the catalog was received, another command could be entered that would order a particular file. This process was not at all interactive; a user would enter a command, and some time later the files would show up. Although this didn't take the typical "4 to 6 weeks for delivery," sometimes a request could take several hours to a day to be satisfied. This makes a five-minute wait for a big web page seem pretty trivial by comparison!

The next development was the File Transfer Protocol, or *FTP*, which is still in wide use today. FTP works more like the filesystem on a PC. Once an FTP client program has connected to the FTP server on a remote computer, a user can get a listing of a remote directory, move into a subdirectory, and copy files back to his computer. In fact, many client programs available for the PC make using FTP look exactly like browsing through local files.

UUCP and FTP are both very much tied to files, and they both lack a means to organize and present information beyond hierarchies of directories; both mechanisms are missing a sophisticated way to organize and present data. Enter HTTP, which handles the former, and HTML, which handles the latter. HTTP abstracts content away from files on a disk to arbitrary URLs, which can be any type of resource. HTML can specify how data should look through a wide variety of tags, images, and tables and many other techniques of questionable value. It also links one document to many others, which in turn can link to still others, and so on—hence a rapidly growing "web" of connections.

In principle this new kind of document could still have existed in the context of UUCP or FTP. A user could request an HTML document via FTP, which would contain both the content and links, and the links could simply reference other documents available via FTP. But this is cumbersome, so HTML quickly spawned two new programs, the Web Browser and the Web Server, which talk to each other via HTTP.

Web browsers, as everyone knows by now, are large, complex programs that display HTML and render links as images or text that can be clicked. That's a polite way to describe them. Internet legend James "Kibo" Parry

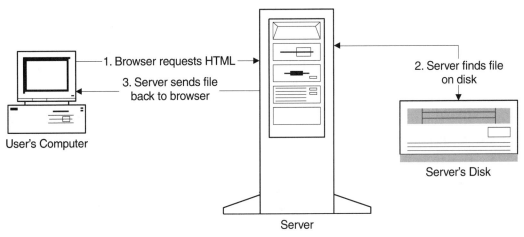

Figure 1.1   The Relationship between Browser and Server

describes web browsers less kindly but more accurately as "fragile assemblies of bugs, held together with Hello Kitty stickers." This is due in large part to rapid development, the race to add new features, and poor adherence to standards.

In any case, when a link is clicked the browser contacts the appropriate web server and asks for the page that was referenced. The server responds by finding the page on its local disk and sending it back to the browser. This whole process is shown in Figure 1.1, which shows how the early Web worked and how much of it still does. Of course, there have been lots of changes on the browser side. Browsers can now handle animated images, Java applets, JavaScript, streaming audio and video, and a wide variety of other data, much of which, again, is of questionable value.

There have also been many improvements on the server side, but one bears special mention. Today a web server can do other things besides send a file in response to a request. It can also *run a program* and send the output of that program to the user. This process is shown in Figure 1.2. The web browser does not care where the data came from; the HTML file it receives could have come from a file, a database, or a program. As long as what the browser gets looks like HTML, it will be able to display the page properly.

Notwithstanding, this move from files to programs makes a huge difference in what the Web can do. Here are just a few of the things this makes possible:

1. There are lots and lots of web sites that publish stock quotes, and they are used by uncountable numbers of people. If all web servers could do

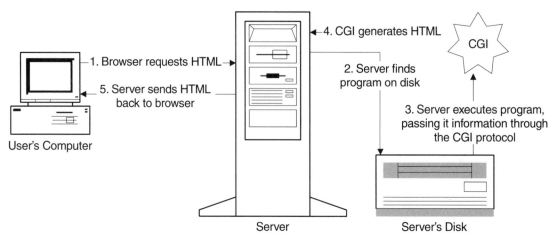

Figure 1.2   How a Server Generates Dynamic Content

was send files around, every site would need a separate file for every imaginable stock. This would mean a huge set of files that would be impossible to keep updated. Stock quotes on the Web would always be at least a couple of hours old, making them pretty useless.

2. More and more commercial sites allow users to shop for items online. The "electronic shopping cart," now commonplace, would be completely impossible without the ability to run programs on the server. Sure, a site could still put its catalog online as a collection of files, but it takes a program to keep track of the items ordered as well as to connect with the shipping and inventory systems to actually send the merchandise to the user.

3. Now that the Web is so big, a search engine is the only way to find a particular piece of information. Some companies, notably Yahoo, build huge, well-ordered, catalogs of web sites, and these can be regular HTML pages. For a user to enter arbitrary text in an entry box and obtain a list of files that contain that word requires a program to actually look through the files and find ones that match.

4. Games! Users love web sites where they can vote for their favorite celebrity, manage a virtual stock portfolio, or compete against other users in a match of wits and knowledge.

All of these are examples of dynamic content that immediately reacts to the user's needs. Clearly, dynamic content offers a lot of benefits, either in conjunction with static content or on its own. The question is, then, why is there still so little of it on the Web? There are two short answers. Dynamic web sites typically have been much harder to build than static ones, and serving a dynamic site requires a much bigger, faster, and more expensive computer.

A Brief History of Dynamic Content

As shown in Figure 1.2, the server and the program communicate via something called the Common Gateway Interface, or *CGI*. The programs that generate dynamic content consequently became known as "CGI programs" or sometimes simply "CGIs."

The earliest CGIs were written in a language called C. C programs run very fast, because C is *compiled*. That is, after it is written it is converted from a form that humans can understand into the computer's "native language." Most compilers will also turn it into a form that is as efficient as possible.

There are two downsides to this approach. First, it makes it relatively difficult to change programs. Instead of just editing a file containing the program, the programmer must recompile the program after each change. Depending on the size and complexity of the program, this may take a while. Compilation will save time in the long run by producing programs that run quickly, but in exchange there is a one-time penalty whenever the program is changed.

The second problem is that C is relatively "low-level." Although there are many utility libraries available for C, it is still difficult to manipulate large blocks of text. This is especially a problem in CGIs, where the goal is to transform the text representing the user's request into the HTML representing the response.

C was rapidly overtaken as the CGI language of choice by Perl. Perl is extremely good at manipulating text. Moreover, unlike C, Perl programs do not need to be recompiled every time they are changed because Perl is an *interpreted* language. Every time a Perl program runs, another program called the Perl interpreter starts up, reads the program, and internally translates it into instructions the computer can understand. This translation obviously takes some time, which means that Perl has made the opposite tradeoff to the one C made—it sacrifices speed at runtime in favor of faster development and changes.

Today it is possible to write CGIs in almost every language available, some interpreted, some compiled. It is even possible to write CGIs in Java. However, the CGI model itself has a number of intrinsic problems, regardless of any language-specific issues.

The first is speed. Even for a compiled language like C, having the web server simply locate and start up the CGI program may take a long time. This penalty must be paid for every request, since once a CGI program has completed processing one it exits and disappears from the computer's memory as if it had never existed. The next time the web server needs the program, it must be restarted from scratch. This is a particular problem for complex CGIs that may need to access a database or some other system resource. Not only do these programs need to start up fresh each time, they also need to reopen their connections to the database or access the other resource.

The transient nature of CGI programs also limits what they can do, at least without help. The shopping cart is a classic example of this. Clearly a shopping cart will need to remember what items a user has selected, but it cannot do this alone if it is going to evaporate after each item is added. In more technical terms, CGI programs are *stateless,* meaning that they cannot keep track of any data between requests. Most CGIs get around this problem by saving all necessary information to a database before they exit, but this can be slow and, again, requires that the connection to the database be opened each time the program is started.

Perhaps the most serious problem with CGIs is the way they mesh presentation with logic. The presentation of a page is expressed as HTML and is typically written by designers and/or expert HTML authors. Program logic—such as what to do on a stock page if the request symbol does not exist—lives in the program code and is written by programmers. There are exceptions to this, of course, but generally HTML coding and programming are such complex and specialized activities that it is rare to find someone skilled at both.

The problem here is that at some point the HTML must be incorporated into the program. This is because the program must ultimately generate the output, and to do this it must have all the HTML that will go on the page. This is bad for both programmers and HTML authors. When the design changes, or new pages are designed, the authors cannot change the HTML directly because it is buried in the program. They present the new designs to the programmers, who must then incorporate the changes into their code without breaking anything. The authors then try out the program to ensure that the HTML that comes out is identical to the HTML that went in and so on. Hours of company time can be lost this way, and all too frequently animosity can develop between the programming and production groups.

The problems of speed, lack of data persistence, and development have been addressed in a number of ways.

Speeding up CGIs

As we observed, one of the biggest problems with CGIs is that a whole new program must be started up for every request. A number of approaches have been taken to keep the program continuously running.

One approach is called Fast CGI, in which, instead of restarting each time, stays running. The web server passes the CGI requests to the program over a communication channel called a socket, reads the HTML back over the same channel, and then passes it on to the user. This gives the situation illustrated in Figure 1.3.

In addition to some of the speed problems, Fast CGI also solves the problem of keeping state. Because the CGI program never exits, it can hold onto information between requests. All that is needed now is some way for the CGI to recognize which user is accessing the page so it will be able to associate the right data with the right user. Typically this is accomplished by sending the user a cookie. Fast CGIs also allow programs to keep connections to a database open, eliminating the need to reopen them for each request. This speeds things up another notch.

There are still some problems with Fast CGIs. Most notably, each CGI program is now a separate process, and each will use up some portion of memory and some of the central processor. This drain can be alleviated by putting the CGIs on a different computer than the web server, but then the sockets must talk across the network, which slows things down. Even so, this is still faster than having to start a new program each time.

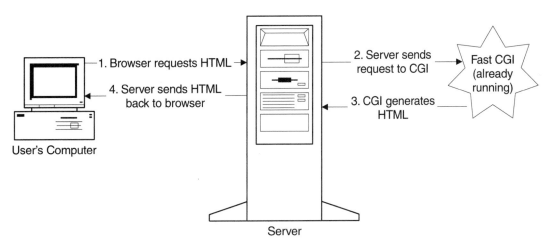

Figure 1.3 Fast CGI

Fast CGIs also introduce a new problem. Updating a regular CGI or adding a new one is a simple matter—the old version of the program is replaced with the new one. Updating a Fast CGI is a bit more involved, since the old version needs to be shut down and the new one started, and the web server needs to close down the socket and open another one. Installing a new Fast CGI is even harder and typically requires some change to the web server's configuration, describing where the Fast CGI process is running and providing other information. Most Fast CGI implementations automate this process as much as possible, but it may still require special system privileges to make all the changes happen.

Fast CGIs can be written in C, Perl, or numerous other languages. The programs look just like regular CGIs, with perhaps some additional code at the beginning. This makes it easy for programmers to learn how to write Fast CGIs, but it leaves all the same problems regarding the intermingling of program code and HTML.

Since the development of Fast CGIs, a couple of improvements have been made. Most of the popular web servers can deal with too many separate processes by allowing new dynamic functionality to be added to the web server itself. The idea is that when the web server sees a request that formerly it would have passed off to a CGI, it instead invokes the new functions (see Figure 1.4). This greatly enhances the speed of requests, since now everything stays in one process.

Apache, perhaps the most used and most extensible web server, took this idea a step further and actually incorporated the Perl interpreter. This extension, called mod_perl, allows any Perl program, with some minor modifications, to run as part of the web server.

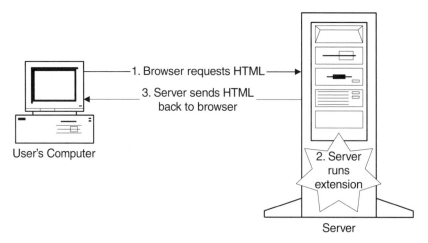

Figure 1.4 Web Server Extensions

Extending the web server this way is not for the fainthearted! It requires knowing a lot about how the web server works and also some very careful programming. If an error causes a CGI to exit prematurely, no harm is done since the next request will simply start a new one—even Fast CGIs can typically recover after a crash—but if an extension to the web server crashes, the whole server is likely to go down.

Updating extensions to the web server is even harder than updating a Fast CGI, and only a few system administrators in any given company will have the permissions to do so. This makes this kind of extension useful only for adding very fundamental functions, such as new registration or security features; it is not well suited to CGI-like applications.

Another approach to improving performance was taken by *application servers,* which combine the best features of Fast CGIs and server extensions. Like Fast CGIs, an application server runs as a separate process and stays running between requests, thus eliminating the cost of starting a new program each time. Like server extensions, application servers are extensible, allowing programmers to add new features as needed. This architecture is illustrated in Figure 1.5.

In a sense, application servers are enhanced Fast CGIs, where each extension acts as a separate Fast CGI but all sit in the same process. This has numerous benefits. For example, we mentioned that a Fast CGI can maintain an

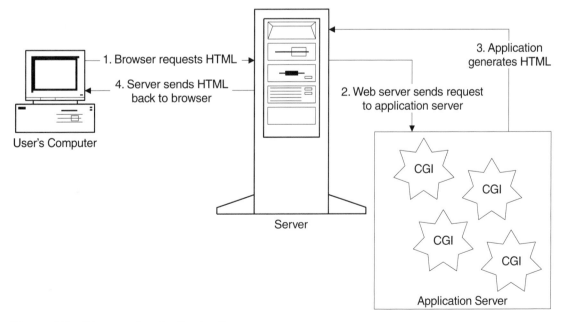

Figure 1.5   Diagram of an Application Server

open connection to a database. Clearly, though, each Fast CGI running individually will have to have its own connection. An application server can maintain a central "pool" of open connections and hand these connections off to each component as needed.

Most modern application servers also support some form of *load balancing*, which allows multiple instances of an application server to run, possibly on different computers. If one application server gets too busy, or one of the computers crashes, all requests can go to another server. The users should never notice the problem.

Templating

Parallel to the developments on the speed front is the progress being made on separating HTML from program logic. The motivation behind many of these approaches can be understood by considering the simplest possible CGI first and building up the complexity from there.

The simplest possible CGI is one that has no logic but simply prints out a lot of HTML. In this case all the HTML can be pulled out of the CGI and placed in a separate file, which the CGI opens, reads, and prints. Now the HTML author can edit the file without needing to touch the program code.

Once this mechanism has been built, it is easy to slowly extend it. For example, a CGI commonly has to put some data, such as a user's name, into the page, which frequently requires it to access some information sent by the browser or perhaps look up the name in a database.

However, the HTML author does not care where this data comes from. The design of the page requires only that the user's name show up where it belongs. The author can indicate this by a special tag, perhaps something like <USER_NAME_HERE>. If the CGI is written in Perl, this "tag" can even be a Perl variable, such as $USERNAME, in which case no special parsing is needed.

Now when the program reads the HTML and before it sends it to the user, it can look over the whole file for any occurrences of <USER_NAME_HERE>, do whatever it needs to do to get the user's name, replace the tag with the name anywhere the tag appears, and send the page along.

This idea can be extended by creating more tags to indicate other common behaviors. Essentially the new tags define a new language that both programmers and HTML authors agree to speak, and the CGI acts as a translator, converting tags into actions. Such a system is often called *templating*, since the HTML page with the special tags acts as a template, or blueprint, for all the pages built by the CGI.

Unfortunately, this scheme turns out to be not *quite* powerful enough to do all the things dynamic pages need to do. Or, rather, by the time it does become sufficiently powerful the set of tags will be as complicated as any programming language, and we will be back where we started. For this reason, most systems built around this idea have introduced a few mechanisms that allow the basic scheme to be dynamically extended.

The first is to allow the set of tags to be *extensible*. If an HTML author is creating a page for a music catalog, she might need a tag to represent the artist's name. In an extensible system she can communicate this need to someone on the programming staff, and the two can agree on a new tag. The author then starts using the tag, while the programmer writes the code that will respond to it.

There are other ways to extend the system. Programmers could create new *functions*, which may be thought of as small magic boxes with a slot to drop things into and a ramp on which things come out. An HTML author could, metaphorically, drop the name of a musical artist into the slot, and the names of all the artist's albums would come spilling down the ramp. Then tags could be used to specify where on the page the names of these albums should go.

Best of all, a templating system like this could be extended by the programmer providing new *objects*. Programming objects are much like physical objects in the real world. They have properties that can be obtained or changed, numerous complex ways they may relate to other objects, and so on. Thus, in the previous example, instead of providing a function the programmer could provide an artist object, one property of which would be a list of albums, that an HTML-like tag could request. However, now each album would also be an object and some of its properties would be things like the year it was recorded and the tracks. In other words, the artist object would encapsulate all the relevant information in one neat bundle. Again, tags could be created to access the information from this object and the other objects it contains.

New tags, functions, and objects can greatly extend the way templates get data, but they still do not allow much control over how that information is presented. For example, it is easy to create a tag that means "get all albums by this artist," but it is hard to express the concept "display all the albums where the first track was written by the lead singer." The necessary information might be present in the object, but combining it in arbitrary ways may be infeasible.

Consequently, most templating systems allow for some form of *scripting*. Scripting allows elements of a full programming language—usually the language in which the translation CGI is written—to be included in the page. All languages have some way to compare two pieces of text and do different things depending on whether or not they match. The example in the previous paragraph would require code that checked whether the name of the lead singer matched the name of the author of the first track.

Once again, this is mixing code with HTML, but since most of the hard work is done in the objects or functions, typically all that HTML authors need to know is some relatively simple control structures that do things like compare two values or that loop through a set of values, performing some action on each.

The Best of Both Worlds

So far, nothing has been said about performance. Not surprisingly, the speed of a templating system may be less than ideal. First, the CGI has to be started, then it has to read the template, then it has to look for all the special tags and process them, and so on. All other things being equal, a system like this is likely to be orders of magnitude slower than a CGI written entirely in C.

There is still hope for templating, however, in the performance improvement ideas discussed previously. In particular, it is possible to turn the templating CGI into an extension to the web server, which eliminates the need to start it up each time a template is needed. This also allows templates to save state information, use shared resources efficiently, and so on.

Many such templating systems are alive and well today, from PHP, a well-known "hypertext preprocessor" that mixes scripting commands with HTML, to WebSQL, a templating system that provides easy access to databases, and to osforms, a system built by Object Design to work with their object database.

Active Server Pages

Without doubt, the best known and most used of all templating systems is Microsoft's Active Server Pages, or ASPs. Even a casual web server will soon encounter a page ending in *.asp* instead of *.html*, and it may be doing anything from looking up baseball statistics to providing checkout services at an online mall.

ASPs are a classic example of the kind of templating system outlined above. They support scripting in both Visual Basic and JScript. They allow programmers to extend the system by creating Active X objects, which ASPs can access. Microsoft has spent a great deal of effort to make ASPs perform well by integrating them very tightly with IIS, their web server.

For all ASP's usefulness, it does have some important limitations. Despite Microsoft's efforts at performance, the fact remains that for every request the .asp file must be read and interpreted by the scripting engine. As previously noted, it is just not possible for this to compete with compiled CGIs.

Because ASPs are so tightly integrated with IIS and Active X, they are and will remain very much a Microsoft-only solution, limiting the ways in which a site can scale if it suddenly becomes very popular. There are sites that have scaled by adding hundreds of computers running NT, but some might prefer to use fewer, more powerful computers, such as high-end systems from Sun. If the site was built using IIS and ASP, this move will not be possible. If only the pages and code for a site could be written once and run anywhere. . . .

Servlets and JavaServer Pages

Let's rewind for a moment and reconsider some of the problems with CGIs. As previously noted, restarting a CGI program for each request is time consuming; because the program does not persist between connections, it is difficult to maintain state. It is possible to overcome this problem with Fast CGIs or server extensions, but these make adding new functionality relatively difficult.

Sun's approach is called *servlets*. Just as an applet is a small application that extends the functionality of a web browser, a servlet is a small piece of code that extends a server's functionality.

Technically a servlet is an object written in Java that is equipped to receive a request and build and send back a response. Written in Java a servlet inherits all of the language's strengths, including speed, since Java is compiled. Although Java programs typically are not as fast as corresponding C programs, they are faster than Perl or other interpreted languages. More important, Java is also truly cross platform, so it is possible to develop a servlet under Linux, deploy it on NT, and move to Solaris when the site grows—all without needing to change or recompile anything.

Of special interest to web developers is that Java is intrinsically dynamic and extensible. This neatly eliminates the problems inherent in extending a web server. If the server supports Java, it can load a new servlet just by being told to do so; there is no need to modify the server itself.

The servlet architecture is designed to eliminate the need to reload anything every time a request is made. Instead, the servlet is loaded once the first time it is needed; after that it stays active, turning requests into responses as fast as the web server can send them. This gives servlets all the speed of Fast

CGIs, with none of the hassles. In short, servlets can completely replace CGIs with no downside.

Servlets have one additional advantage. Because Java was designed from the ground up as a secure language, servlets can be run in a "secure sandbox," which prevents them from accessing any potentially sensitive system resources. It is certainly possible to write a CGI that has no security problems, and there are tools to assist in this endeavor. Nonetheless, most security breaches on web sites happen through CGIs.

The next logical step would be to build a templating system on top of servlets, in much the same way that ASPs are built on top of CGIs. However, a Boston company, the Art Technology Group (ATG), had a better idea. Instead of writing a servlet that reads a file, figures out what to do based on special tags, and then does it, why not *translate the special tags directly into Java and then compile and run the Java code?* In this way the first time a page was requested it would take a little longer to do the conversion, but the second and subsequent requests would be as fast as a servlet. This revolutionary concept, called *page compilation,* was introduced in Dynamo, ATG's application server. Sun was so impressed by the concept that they licensed the technology for inclusion in their own Java Web Server. The JHTML model is shown in Figure 1.6.

No idea is perfect on the first try, and there were problems with page compilation. Most significantly, the set of special tags that ATG had defined were somewhat cumbersome, somewhat limited, and completely unlike the tags that other templating systems were using. Over time, Sun has refined these tags to create JavaServer Pages.

JavaServer Pages, or JSPs, combine many of the best features just discussed. They are implemented in Java, so they are cross platform and inherit all of Java's other strengths. They are built on top of servlets, so they are fast and can be easily changed. They are extensible, and programmers can easily create new objects and functionality using Java beans, which page authors can use equally easily.

JSPs are generating a huge wave of interest. Sun considers them important enough to have included them as a formal part of the Java 2 Enterprise Edition, the standard version of Java for complex, performance-critical tasks. Every major vendor of application servers has announced support for JSPs, including ATG, BEA's WebLogic, IBM's Web Sphere, and many more. JSPs are truly becoming an industry standard.

Best of all, the power of JSPs is not limited to big enterprises or companies that can afford an application server. At the 1999 Java One conference, Sun announced a partnership with the makers of the Apache web server to provide full

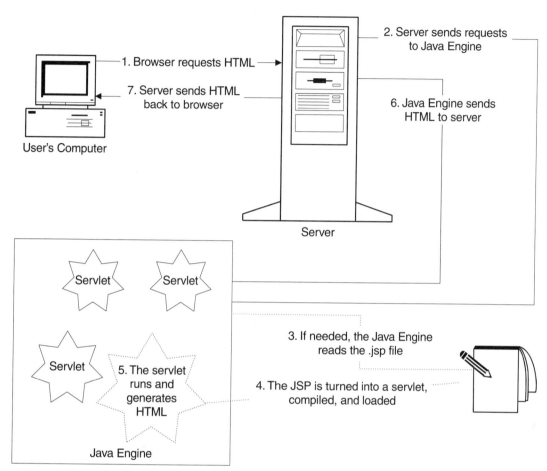

Figure 1.6 The Flow of Information through a JHTML Page

support for JSPs under Apache. The Jakarta project, as it has been named, will allow anyone with a computer to develop and deploy JSPs—completely free.

Welcome to "Java News Today"

Throughout this book we will be following the evolution of a fictional web site called "Java News Today." JNT is a startup company made up of Java enthusiasts who want to create a compelling, up-to-the-minute site covering all things Java. Because they want to attract and maintain an audience, their site will be as dynamic as possible. In addition to frequent content updating, they want the site to have games, polls, search functionality, and other interactive features. They also consider it very important to allow users to customize and adjust the site to fit their needs. The folks at JNT hope that lots of users will make JNT their home page, and no one will move into a home they cannot redecorate.

Everyone at JNT openly admits to being fans of the Slashdot site at

http://www.slashdot.org

and the Java Lobby at

http://www.javalobby.com

Readers familiar with those sites may notice some similarities in the features that JNT is trying to build, but, then, imitation is the sincerest form of flattery.

Trying the Examples

All the examples in this book have been included on the companion CD-ROM, so readers can see them in action and experiment with changes. Unfortunately, at the time of writing Jakarta was not yet available, so the current version of Tomcat, Sun's reference implementation and the JSP and Servlet engine behind Jakarta, has been included along with instructions for setting it up. Tomcat is the implementation against which all others are compared. Thus, as more and more vendors implement JSPs, they can check their versions against Tomcat; if their version produces the same output when given the same JSP, they know their implementation is correct.

Although Tomcat may be an ideal tool for developers to start building servlets and JSPs, it still has a few rough edges. These will be cleaned up in the production versions of Jakarta, and shortly after other companies will start providing JSP implementations optimized for speed and scalability. Keep watching for updates at

http://jakarta.apache.org and *http://java.sun.com*

CHAPTER 2

Simple JSPs

Chapter 1 presented the case for dynamic sites and surveyed a number of techniques for building them, focusing on the strengths of JavaServer Pages technology. Now that these preliminaries are out of the way, we can actually start creating some pages. This chapter will begin by introducing some of the simpler features of JSPs.

To begin, consider Java News Today (JNT), the mythical news site we discussed in Chapter 1. The company has set up Tomcat and is ready to start building their site. Beginning at the beginning is always a good idea, so they have decided to start with the new home page and, for the moment, not worry about the dynamic elements. Their first version is shown in Listing 2.1.

Listing 2.1   The JNT Index Page

```
<HTML>
<HEAD><TITLE>Java News Today!</TITLE>
<BODY BGCOLOR="#FFFFFF">
<TABLE BORDER="0" WIDTH="100%">
  <TR>
      <TD BGCOLOR="#0000FF" ALIGN="CENTER" COLSPAN="2">
      <!-- Begin Header -->
      <H1>Welcome To Java News Today</H1>
      <P>Your on-line home for up to the minute
      Java news</P>
      <!-- End Header -->
    </TD>
  </TR>
  <TR>
```

```
<TD ALIGN="LEFT" WIDTH="20%" BGCOLOR="#000077">
 <!-- Begin Navigation -->
 <FONT COLOR="FFFFFF">
 <FONT COLOR="#FF0000">&sect;</FONT>
 Home Page<BR>
 <FONT COLOR="#FF0000">&sect;</FONT>
 Industry news<BR>
 <FONT COLOR="#FF0000">&sect;</FONT>
 Enterprise Java<BR>
 <FONT COLOR="#FF0000">&sect;</FONT>
 Standard Edition Java<BR>
 <FONT COLOR="#FF0000">&sect;</FONT>
 Micro edition &amp; devices<BR>
 <FONT COLOR="#FF0000">&sect;</FONT>
 Beans<BR>
 <FONT COLOR="#FF0000">&sect;</FONT>
 Editorials<BR>
 </FONT>
 <!-- End Navigation -->
</TD>
<TD>
<!-- Content goes here -->
</TD>
</TR>
</TABLE>
</BODY>
</HTML>
```

OK, perhaps they should think about hiring a new design staff, but the basic elements are all there. Normally they would now name this file *index.html* and put it in their public HTML directory. However, this time they do something strange and magical—they name it *index1.jsp*. Assuming that they have set up their web server as described in the documentation on the companion CD-ROM, they can point their browsers at the following URL, and, as expected, the page in Figure 2.1 will show up:

http://localhost:8080/jspbook/ch01/index1.jsp

Like the best magic, this change from HTML to JSP is simple and quite subtle at first glance. With an HTML file, the web server would simply have read the contents and sent them to the browser. With a JSP file, the web server instead asks the JSP Engine program for the page. The JSP Engine does not directly send out the page either, but first converts the file into a special Java program called a servlet (covered in more detail in Chapter 13). It then sends the request to the servlet, and the servlet generates a response, which includes the page text, and sends it back to the browser, as shown in Figure 1.6.

In this particular case, all this extra work has not really accomplished anything. Still, the translation has not been at all pointless since it has created a

Figure 2.1   The JNT Home Page, as Seen in a Browser

program from HTML. This is why JSP authors generally do not need to do much programming themselves. The JSP Engine is quite sophisticated, and it can turn a few simple tags into very complex code. The servlet generated and the environment in which this code runs are also very sophisticated, which removes even more of the programming burden.

Comments

All it takes is a small change to the example page to exhibit some of the things the JSP Engine can do. Note the HTML comments, such as

```
<!-- Start Header -->
```

Comments like these are often useful to people building and maintaining pages, since they identify exactly a block of otherwise indecipherable HTML. However, because this comment is a regular part of the document, it shows up if anyone uses the "view source" function in his or her browser. Usually this is not a problem, although it does mean some small amount of text is sent to the user that she will normally never see, which makes the download time a tiny fraction of a second longer. A more serious concern is that sometimes HTML comments contain implementation details that might be confidential, or a page author having a bad day might have some comment space to rant about his bosses, his relationships, or the state of the world. These comments can be quite embarrassing if anyone happens to see them.

Hence this dilemma: Comments are useful to authors but useless (or worse) for readers. JSP's solution is to replace the above HTML comment with a JSP comment, like so:

```
<%-- Start Header --%>
```

When the JSP Engine sees this tag, it recognizes it as a comment and does not put it into the servlet it builds. The comment will thus never be sent to the user and will not show up when the user does a view source. Again, this effect is subtle and frankly not that exciting. However, it does begin to show that what goes into a JSP file can and will be different from what comes out.

Templating

Since the JSP Engine can take things out of a JSP page, it only stands to reason that it can also put things in. This functionality is very useful for people building and maintaining sites.

The index page currently consists of three major sections: the header, the navigation, and the content area. Different pages have different content, but it is reasonable to expect that the header and navigation will be repeated all over the site. This can be a major headache because the author of each new page must remember to put these pieces in and will have to worry about getting everything right. Worst of all, sooner or later will come the hateful day when a new section is introduced and everyone has to go back and re-edit all their pages.

The cure for this nightmare scenario is called *templating*, although the word here is used slightly differently than it was in Chapter 1. Here a template is merely an HTML page with some "spaces" where text should be, plus some way to indicate where this text can be found. The advantage is that many pages can have the same spaces and all these spaces can be filled from the same place. This makes it possible to keep the header in exactly one file and let each page have a space that this file should fill.

JSP provides a mechanism for this kind of templating, called the *include directive*, which allows any JSP file to include other JSP or HTML files. Like pages the user asks for directly, HTML files can come from anywhere on the server. JSP files must come from a designated JSP directory. Since the elements we want to include are global, it makes sense to create a "global" directory under the top-level JSP directory.

Now it is only necessary to pull out the header and navigation and place them in separate files. These separate files can be either HTML or JSP, but it makes more sense to make them JSPs since the ultimate goal is to allow each piece to be dynamic. The contents of *global/header.jsp* are shown in Listing 2.2. Those of *global/navigation.jsp* are shown in Listing 2.3.

Listing 2.2   *header.jsp*

```
<%-- Begin Header --%>
<H1>Welcome To Java News Today</H1>
<P>Your on-line home for up to the minute
Java news</P>
<%-- End Header --%>
```

Listing 2.3   *navigation.jsp*

```
<%-- Begin Navigation --%>
<FONT COLOR="FFFFFF">
<FONT COLOR="#FF0000">&sect;</FONT>
Home Page<BR>
<FONT COLOR="#FF0000">&sect;</FONT>
Industry news<BR>
<FONT COLOR="#FF0000">&sect;</FONT>
Enterprise Java<BR>
<FONT COLOR="#FF0000">&sect;</FONT>
Standard Edition Java<BR>
<FONT COLOR="#FF0000">&sect;</FONT>
Micro edition &amp; devices<BR>
<FONT COLOR="#FF0000">&sect;</FONT>
Beans<BR>
<FONT COLOR="#FF0000">&sect;</FONT>
Editorials<BR>
</FONT>
<%-- End Navigation --%>
```

To be consistent, the rest of the HTML comments have been converted to JSP comments.

Now for the fun part. The header can be put back into the home page with the tag

```
<%@include file="global/header.jsp">
```

The tag for the navigation, as expected, is

```
<%@include file="global/navigation.jsp">
```

This leads to the second version of the home page, which will be called *index2.jsp* and is shown in Listing 2.4.

Listing 2.4   The Second Version of the Index Page

```
<HTML>
<HEAD><TITLE>Java News Today!</TITLE>
<BODY BGCOLOR="#FFFFFF">
<TABLE BORDER="0" WIDTH="100%">
  <TR>
    <TD BGCOLOR="#0000FF" ALIGN="CENTER" COLSPAN="2">
      <%@include file="global/header.jsp"%>
    </TD>
  </TR>
  <TR>
    <TD ALIGN="LEFT" WIDTH="20%" BGCOLOR="#000077">
      <%@include file="global/navigation.jsp"%>
    </TD>
    <TD>
      <!-- Content goes here -->
    </TD>
  </TR>
</TABLE>
</BODY>
</HTML>
```

All the table elements, the TRs and TDs, are still in the main file. Of course, it would have been possible to move them into the included files as well, but that might have limited the usefulness of the header and navigation. For example, Java News Today might wish to create a parallel version of the site for browsers or consumer devices that do not support tables. By not having any table structure in the included files, this is as easy as creating a new JSP, such as the one in Listing 2.5.

Listing 2.5   A Version of the Home Page without Tables

```
<HTML>
<HEAD><TITLE>Java News Today!</TITLE>
<BODY BGCOLOR="#FFFFFF">
<HR>
<%@include file="global/header.jsp"%>
</HR>
<!-- Content goes here -->
```

```
<HR>
<%@include file="global/navigation.jsp"%>
</BODY>
</HTML>
```

In general, this is a good rule to follow when templating: Leave the structural elements, such as tables, in one place and pull out only the minimal amount of content.

By the way, JSP templating looks a great deal like another common templating technique called a *server-side include,* in which the web server itself fills in the spaces. This works, but it puts too much burden on the server. Pages, and perhaps even the whole site, can begin to noticeably slow down with lots of server-side includes.

When Do Includes Happen?

As noted, each JSP goes through two distinct phases. The first, when the JSP Engine turns the file into a servlet, is called *"translation time."* The second, when the resulting servlet is run to actually generate the page, is called *"request time."* Different things happen in each phase, and the distinction is important.

The include directive is handled by the JSP Engine at translation time. Incidentally, it is called a "directive" because it directs the JSP Engine to do something—in particular to open the included file and place its contents directly into the servlet it builds. This has pros and cons. On the plus side, the servlet will not have to open and include the file each time it runs and so will run faster. On the minus side, if the included file changes, the servlet will have no way to know that it should update itself. In fact, this is not a serious problem, as it will always be possible to make the JSP Engine regenerate all the servlets that might include some other file. The details may vary between implementations. Under Tomcat it is just necessary to shut down and restart the server.

By the way, it is worth using the "view source" command from the browser and looking at the resulting HTML from this version. Notice that the text in the JSP comment tags is still gone.

This may not be surprising, but until now there was never any guarantee that comments would work the same in included files as they do in main files. That JSPs can actually guarantee this goes back to the distinction between translation time and request time. When the JSP Engine builds the servlet at translation time it also reads and translates the included file. Thus, not only comments but also the include directive will work inside included files. Yes, files can include files that can include files, and so on—potentially to infinity.

Errors

As smart as the JSP Engine is, it is very literal-minded. Like any other program ever written, the best it can manage is to "do what we say," which is not always the same as "do what we want." When a JSP page does not say what to do in exactly the right way, the JSP Engine sometimes has no alternative but to give up, return an error page, and ask for help.

Unfortunately, there are lots more ways to get a JSP tag wrong than there are to get one right. One common error is leaving out a closing tag, which might happen if a page author forgets that she is writing a JSP comment and tries to close it as if it were an HTML comment. Perhaps someone at JNT has decided to use a JSP comment in the index page to indicate the placement of the content and accidentally writes:

```
<%-- Content goes here -->
```

A user trying to access this page will receive a rather unsettling page that just says Error 500. No detailed message. Fortunately, the JSP Engine is more forthcoming with information for the page author. The exact nature and location of the error detail will be different from one implementation to the next. In Tomcat, a message similar to the one in Listing 2.6 appears in the browser.

Listing 2.6   An Error Message

```
com.sun.jsp.compiler.ParseException: Unterminated <%--
    at com.sun.jsp.compiler.Parser$Comment.accept(Parser.java:221)
    at com.sun.jsp.compiler.Parser.parse(Parser.java:564)
    at com.sun.jsp.compiler.Parser.parse(Parser.java:552)
    at com.sun.jsp.compiler.Main.compile(Main.java:218)
    at com.sun.jsp.runtime.JspLoader.loadJSP(JspLoader.java:117)
    [etc]
```

The bulk of this message is not important, although it does give us a glimpse into Tomcat's internals. The important line is right at the top, where it clearly states what the problem is. Unfortunately, it does not indicate what file, or what line within that file, is the problem's source.

Includes can make tracking down this kind of error somewhat harder. If, instead of breaking the content tag in *index2.jsp*, the page author had written

```
<%-- End Navigation -->
```

exactly the same error message would have been printed. The best way to find a problem like this is to start by testing the JSP pages that are used as components but that do not include any other JSPs. In this case, the author might start by using a browser to go to *global/header.jsp* directly. Until now this page was only used within the index page, but it is still a full-fledged JSP and can send a page to a browser just like any other. If *headline.jsp* checks out, the next page to be checked is *navigation.jsp*, where the fault is discovered.

Unclosed comment tags can be unpleasant, but at least the JSP Engine detects them and they are relatively easy to find and fix. However, there is an insidious variation of this problem. Consider what would happen if, instead of breaking the second comment in *navigation.jsp*, the first one was left unclosed. This time no error message would be generated but the navigation would simply and quietly disappear.

The reason for this vanishing act is not mysterious. When the JSP Engine sees the characters <%--, the start of a comment tag, it does exactly as it is told and throws away everything up to the next --%> it finds. If it does not find one, it knows something is wrong. In this case it *does* find one, right at the end of the second comment tag! It therefore discards everything between the start of the first comment tag and the end of the second.

This error is hard to find because the JSP Engine can provide no clues—as far as it is concerned, there is no problem. The best approach is still to look at each included piece individually to see which one the error shows up in. In this example there is an obvious place to start looking. Since it is the navigation that is missing, *navigation.jsp* is a likely culprit.

Includes can suffer from the same kinds of errors as comments do. First, tags can be broken, as with

```
<%@include file="global/header.jsp">
```

which is missing the closing percent sign. The JSP Engine will catch this error and report it as `Unterminated <%@`. It is also possible to attempt to include a file that does not exist, which is usually the fault of a typo, such as "headers.jsp" instead of "header.jsp." In this case, the JSP Engine will report `Can't read file headers.jsp`, which is easily fixed.

There is one other kind of error that results from includes. If a JSP file tries to include itself, or if a file includes another file that in turn includes the original file, the JSP Engine becomes permanently stuck. Remember that every time the JSP Engine sees an include, it not only includes the file but processes it as well. So if *index2.jsp* includes *header.jsp*, and *header.jsp* includes *index2.jsp*, the JSP Engine will process *index2*, see that it needs header, then process *header* and see that it needs *index2*, which needs *header*, and so on. In such a situation even trying files one at a time will not help, since the problem will be exactly the same whether *index2* or *header* is the first file accessed. The only solution is to carefully review all of the includes. It also pays to be very careful when including files that include other files.

Summary

This chapter started down the exciting road of writing JSPs. The two phases of a JSP's existence were discussed: translation, where JSP code is turned into a Java servlet; and request, where the servlet is run to produce HTML. Two translation-time tags were introduced, the comment tag `<%-- ... --%>`, which can include information for the page author that will not be seen by the user; and the include directive `<%@include file="..."%>`, which refers to another HTML or JSP page to include when building the servlet. The latter tag is useful for templating—that is, taking common elements of a site and moving them into separate files.

We have not even begun to scratch the surface of JSPs, so hold on if so far the effects they can produce seem less than thrilling. The next chapter will look at some of the things that can be done at request time, which is when the doorway to dynamic content opens wide.

CHAPTER 3

Request-Time Expressions

Chapter 2 showed some of the things that JavaSever Pages can do at translation time. This is when the JSP Engine turns the *.jsp* file into a servlet, a special kind of Java program.

The translation happens only once, the first time the page is requested by a user. This greatly limits the things that can happen at this point. In particular, it allows no dynamic content, since, by definition, for an element on a page to be dynamic it must be rebuilt each time the page is requested.

This chapter will look at the capabilities of request-time processing. Request time is the stage where the servlet is run and produces output. As such, it is a much more interesting realm since it is where true dynamic content really begins.

Expressions

The first dynamic element we will look at is called an *expression*—a small piece of Java code that, as the name implies, expresses something. When one is encountered in the servlet, it turns into something that can be put in a page. Expressions are indicated by placement in the special tag <%= %>. Listing 3.1 shows a very simple page called *example1.jsp* that contains an expression.

Listing 3.1   A Simple Expression

```
<HTML>
<BODY>
1 + 1 equals <%= 1 + 1 %>
</BODY>
</HTML>
```

When a browser accesses *example1.jsp*, the resulting page will contain

```
1 + 1 equals 2
```

Obviously, this is not a surprising result, but what is interesting here is the mechanism by which it is generated. As in many philosophies, sometimes it is the path that is important, not the destination.

Just like the examples from Chapter 2, the path here goes from the original JSP file through the JSP Engine to a servlet. But this servlet is doing something very different. All the servlets built from examples in the last chapter simply sent some HTML to the user; this one will first send out a block of HTML containing everything up to the expression. In other words,

```
<HTML>
<BODY>
1 + 1 equals
```

Next, it will *compute the value* of 1 + 1, turn the result into text, and send the text to the user. Then it will send the remaining HTML, consisting of

```
</BODY>
</HTML>
```

The same concept extends to multiple expressions on the same page. Listing 3.2 shows a variation of Listing 3.1 with two expressions.

Listing 3.2   A Page with Two Expressions

```
<HTML>
<BODY>
1 + 1 equals <%= 1 + 1 %> and
2 * 2 equals <%= 2 * 2 %>
</BODY>
</HTML>
```

Again, when a user first accesses *example2.jsp* the JSP Engine turns the page into a servlet. Then, and every subsequent time, the servlet will run and do the following things:

1. Send a chunk of HTML consisting of

```
<HTML>
<BODY>
1 + 1 equals
```

2. Compute the value of 1 + 1.

3. Turn the result of that computation into text and send it to the user.

4. Send another chunk of HTML, this time consisting of

```
and
2 * 2 equals
```

5. Compute the value of 2 * 2.

6. Turn the result of that computation into text and send it to the user.

7. Send the last chunk of HTML:

```
</BODY>
</HTML>
```

In other words, everything inside the <%= %> tag will be computed (or, more technically, *evaluated*). This concept may be new to readers who have not programmed before—how can something say "1 + 1" on a page and "2" in a browser? The answer is somewhat subtle and has to do with the difference between a *thing* and a *representation* of that thing.

This is a distinction we use so often in real life that most people never think about it. For example, when I say "Tori Amos" I am referring to a specific person, a female singer-songwriter with alarmingly red hair. The words "Tori Amos" are not this woman but merely a convenient way to represent her.

It is possible for one thing or person to have many representations. I could refer to Tori Amos by her previous name "Myra Ellen Amos" or as "the woman who recorded the album *Little Earthquakes*" or as "that person who performed at Jones Beach on September 1, 1999." That last may be a bad example, since it could equally well apply to Alanis Morissette.

In the same sense, the expression "1 + 1" is not the number 2 but just one way of representing that number. There are lots of other ways of expressing 2, such as "10/5," "the square root of 4," and so on.

What this boils down to is that the JSP Engine treats things outside of `<%= %>` tags as simple text to be sent back to the user. It treats things inside these tags as representations of something else, and it builds the servlet to find out what this something is. It is as if we could write a JSP page containing `<%= Tori Amos =>` and have her jump out of the browser when the page was accessed. Which would probably save a great deal of money in concert tickets, but that's besides the point.

The wonderful thing about this mechanism is that sometimes the same expression can refer to different things at different times. For example, the expression "Tori Amos's latest CD" represented "Under the Pink" in 1994 and "To Venus and Back" in 2000. Likewise, the expression "1 + 1" will always mean "2," and so `<%= 1 + 1 %>` will always do the same thing, but the expression "the name of the computer on which the user is viewing this page" will likely be different for each user. Of course, that expression is not written in Java, so the servlet cannot understand or evaluate it.

The next section will show how this can be written in Java, but the important point for now is that the `<%= %>` tag is the first ingredient of dynamic content. To make a page dynamic, the first step is often deciding what elements will change for each request or each user and constructing expressions that represent the information to fill those elements. Then, at request time, the servlet will use the expression to build or find the appropriate version of the information for the page and user in question.

Of course "constructing the expressions," is often easier said than done. It may be difficult to find an appropriate representation of some desired, changeable, information. In a sense, this is what programming is all about. However, JSPs provide a great deal of useful information that authors can use right away. It is packaged into what are called *implicit objects*. "Implicit" means that there is no need for page authors to explicitly declare that they will use these objects; they are automatically available.

The Implicit Objects

There are a number of implicit objects, and the first one we will look at is called "request." As might be expected, this object contains lots of information about the request the user's browser sent in to get the page, including the browser and computer being used; the page being requested, the kinds of information the browser will accept as a response, and so on.

Listing 3.3 shows a page called *example3.jsp* that includes the representation for "the name of the computer on which the user is viewing this page," as promised in the last section.

Listing 3.3   A Simple Expression Using the Request Object

```
<HTML>
<BODY>
Hello user!  You are using a computer
called <%= request.getRemoteHost() %>!
</BODY>
</HTML>
```

Conceptually, there is no difference between this and the simple arithmetic examples. The servlet will send some HTML, evaluate the expression `request.getRemoteHost()`, and then send the result followed by the remaining HTML.

The syntax of `request.getRemoteHost()` may look odd, but all will be explained in Chapter 5. The important thing is that this expression will get the implicit request object and then use its `getRemoteHost()` method to find the name of the remote computer.

The name `getRemoteHost()` might seem wrong. If Alice is sitting at her machine called *spacedog.someisp.com* (so named because Alice is also a Tori Amos fan), she will see this page on her browser:

```
<HTML>
<BODY>
Hello user!  You are using a computer called
spacedog.someisp.com!
</BODY>
</HTML>
```

Alice wouldn't think the method should be called `getRemoteHost()` because as far as she's concerned spacedog is local—in fact, it's right in front of her. However, remember that the JSP is running on the server, not the browser, so it is correct in treating the server as the local computer and all the users as being on remote systems.

In fact, the request object has information about both systems, and the example could be modified to include both, as in Listing 3.4.

Listing 3.4   Two Values from the Request Object

```
<HTML>
<BODY>
Hello user! I am on a computer called
<%= request.getServerName() %>, and you are using a computer
called <%= request.getRemoteHost() %>!
</BODY>
</HTML>
```

Table 3.1 Methods in the Request Object

Method	Purpose
getCharacterEncoding()	The character set in which this page is encoded (e.g., ISO)
getProtocol()	The protocol used for the request, such as HTTP/1.0
getScheme()	The "scheme" portion of the URL, such as HTTP
getServerName()	The name of the computer on which the server is running
getServerPort()	The port the server is listening to
getRemoteAddr()	The address of the computer the request came from
getRemoteHost()	The name of the computer the request came from
getAuthType()	The type of authorization used for this request (if the page is not protected, this will be null)
getHeader()	Any header sent by the browser
getMethod()	The method used for this request (usually GET or POST but also HEAD, PUT, DELETE, etc.)
getPathInfo()	The path info (if a JSP resides at */stories.jsp* and the browser requests */stories.jsp/story1*, the path info will be */story1*)
getPathTranslated()	The path to the requested file on the server's local filesystem
getQueryString()	The query string portion of the URL (i.e., anything after a question mark)
getRemoteUser()	The name the user logged in as (if this page is not protected, this will be null)
getRequestURI()	The full request URL of the JSP

There is much more information available from the request object. Table 3.1 lists some of the more common methods and what they are used for. It is not complete, but it is certainly enough to get started. Listing 3.5 is an example program that illustrates these methods in action.

Listing 3.5   A Sample of Methods in the Request Object

```
<HTML>
<HEAD><TITLE>Request fields</TITLE></HEAD>
<BODY BGCOLOR="#FFFFFF">
<TABLE BORDER="1">
<TR>
```

```
      <TD>You are using this authorization type:</TD>
      <TD><%= request.getAuthType() %></TD>
   </TR>
   <TR>
      <TD>You are using this request method:</TD>
      <TD><%= request.getMethod() %></TD>
   </TR>
   <TR>
      <TD>Characters are encoded using this scheme:</TD>
      <TD><%= request.getCharacterEncoding() %></TD>
   </TR>
   <TR>
      <TD>The protocol used for this request was:</TD>
      <TD><%= request.getProtocol() %></TD>
   </TR>
   <TR>
      <TD>The scheme used for this request was:</TD>
      <TD><%= request.getScheme() %></TD>
   </TR>
   <TR>
      <TD>The server's name is:</TD>
      <TD><%= request.getServerName() %></TD>
   </TR>
   <TR>
      <TD>The server is running on port:</TD>
      <TD><%= request.getServerPort() %></TD>
   </TR>
   <TR>
      <TD>Your computer's address is:</TD>
      <TD><%= request.getRemoteAddr() %></TD>
   </TR>
   <TR>
      <TD>Your computer's name is:</TD>
      <TD><%= request.getRemoteHost() %></TD>
   </TR>
   <TR>
      <TD>The path info portion of the URL is:</TD>
      <TD><%= request.getPathInfo() %></TD>
   </TR>
   <TR>
      <TD>The translated path is:</TD>
      <TD><%= request.getPathTranslated() %></TD>
   </TR>
   <TR>
      <TD>The QUERY_STRING portion of the URL is:</TD>
      <TD><%= request.getQueryString() %></TD>
   </TR>
   <TR>
      <TD>You have signed into this server using the name:</TD>
      <TD><%= request.getRemoteUser() %></TD>
   </TR>
   <TR>
```

```
   <TD>The full request URI is:</TD>
   <TD><%= request.getRequestURI() %></TD>
</TR>
<TR>
   <TD>You are using a browser called:</TD>
   <TD><%= request.getHeader("User-Agent") %></TD>
</TR>
<TR>
   <TD>Your browser accepts the following types of files:</TD>
   <TD><%= request.getHeader("Accept") %></TD>
</TR>
</TABLE>
</BODY>
</HTML>
```

Note that the same method is used to get the last two fields, *User-Agent* and *Accept.* Unlike all the other methods, which get a particular piece of information, getHeader() can get anything the browser sends. Some of these fields, like *User-Agent,* are pretty standard, but others are sent only by certain browsers. Chapter 6 will introduce another method that can be used to determine which headers have been sent.

Try this example from some different computers and browsers to see how the values change. In particular, note how the value of *User-Agent* reflects which browser is being used. One of the biggest problems facing HTML authors is that the same HTML or JavaScript frequently will not work the same on Netscape and Internet Explorer. The request object has information about which browser is being used, so it might seem that the JSP should be able to use this information to produce browser-specific HTML. In fact, this is possible, and Chapter 6 will discuss this as well.

Several fields will likely be returned as "null." Chapter 5 explains this value, in particular the difference between null and the empty string, "".

Finally, notice the query string in Listing 3.5. Query strings are one way to carry information from an HTML form to the program that handles that form. Listing 3.6 shows a sample HTML form that can be used to send data to the JSP in Listing 3.5.

The form asks a few questions regarding James Gosling, the principal architect of the Java language. Java News Today might run such a form as a survey following an interview with James Gosling, assuming they are ever lucky enough to get one. Note how the value of the query string changes as different values are entered. Also note that the URL itself changes, with the values entered from the form appearing after the question mark.

Listing 3.6   A Form That Sends Values to *request.jsp*

```
<HTML>
<HEAD><TITLE>A typical form entry page</TITLE></HEAD>
<BODY BGCOLOR="#FFFFFF">
<CENTER>
<FORM ACTION="request.jsp" METHOD="GET">
<P>A radio button:</P>
<TABLE BORDER="1" WIDTH="60%"><TR><TD>
<P>Have you ever met James Gosling?</P>
<INPUT TYPE="RADIO" NAME="met" VALUE="no" CHECKED>no<br>
<INPUT TYPE="RADIO" NAME="met" VALUE="yes">yes<br>
</TD></TR></TABLE>
<P>A menu, allowing multiple entries:</P>
<TABLE BORDER="1" WIDTH="60%"><TR><TD>
At which conferences have you heard him speak?<P>
<SELECT NAME="conferences" MULTIPLE="yes">
<OPTION NAME="Java One, 1996">Java One, 1996
<OPTION NAME="Java One, 1997">Java One, 1997
<OPTION NAME="Java One, 1998">Java One, 1998
<OPTION NAME="Java One, 1999">Java One, 1999
</SELECT>
</TD></TR></TABLE>
<P>A menu, with multiple answers:</P>
<TABLE BORDER="1" WIDTH="60%"><TR><TD>
<P>If you could ask Mr. Gosling one question, what would it be?
<INPUT TYPE="TEXT" NAME="question">
</TD></TR></TABLE>
<TABLE BORDER="1" WIDTH="60%"><TR><TD>
<INPUT TYPE="SUBMIT" NAME="go" VALUE="Go!">
</TD></TR></TABLE>
</FORM>
</CENTER>
</BODY>
</HTML>
```

Clearly, if JSPs are going to be able to react to user input, they must be able to get form variables. However, there are three problems with getting this information via `getQueryString()`:

1. As can be seen from the last example, all the values are bunched together, making it difficult, though not impossible, to pull out the response to a particular question.

2. All the spaces and other nonalphanumeric characters have been turned into other characters. This is necessary because the server and browser could be confused if, for example, a slash (/) were to appear in the query string. There would be no way to tell whether the slash was sent by a form or was part of a directory name.

3. There is another method for sending form information that does not use the query string at all. If method="GET" in the HTML page were changed to method="POST", the data would not show up in the URL nor would it be returned by getQueryString(). The POST method is often preferable to GET, both because it can handle large amounts of data and because it does not show up in the URL. If personal or confidential information is sent through a form, the user probably does not want anyone to be able to read his response just by looking at the URL on his browser.

Fortunately, the request object has a number of ways to make it much easier to get form variables. The first one is called getParameter() and it takes as an argument the name of the parameter to get. Listing 3.7 shows a JSP that processes the form submitted by the James Gosling questionnaire. To see it in action, simply change the action tag in Listing 3.6 to jganswers1.jsp.

Listing 3.7   A JSP That Responds to User Input

```
<HTML>
<BODY BGCOLOR="#FFFFFF">
<P>
You answered
"<%= request.getParameter("met") %>"
when asked if you've met Mr. Gosling.
</P>
<P>
Given the chance, you would ask the following question:
<%= request.getParameter("question") %>
</P>
</BODY>
</HTML>
```

Things get more difficult with the conferences question, which can have anything from zero to four responses. It is possible to simply add the following to Listing 3.7:

```
You heard him speak at
<%= request.getParameter("conferences") %>
```

If the user selects one or more conferences, the first one will show up. However, if no responses are selected, "null" will be printed. Null is a special value in some ways equivalent to "no answer," and we will discuss it in more detail in Chapter 5 when we introduce Java coding. Regardless of what it may mean to page designers, however, it will probably just confuse page users.

Of course, there are solutions to this problem, which will be presented in Chapter 6. Just to give a quick preview, a JSP can use *conditional expressions,* which allow it to determine whether or not a value has been provided as well as to tailor itself based on the answer given. Chapter 6 will also introduce *loops,* which allow a JSP to process as many responses as the user provides.

A First Application

Even without conditional expressions, there is enough power in the JSP constructs presented so far to write some simple applications that do something almost useful. We start with a very simple calculator that takes two numbers and computes their sum. First, users must have a way to enter values. Obviously a form is needed, and it is shown in Listing 3.8.

Listing 3.8   The Entry Form for the Calculator

```
<HTML>
<HEAD><TITLE>A simple calculator</TITLE></HEAD>
<BODY>
<P>
Enter two numbers and click the 'calculate' button.
</P>
<FORM ACTION="calculate.jsp" METHOD="GET">
<INPUT TYPE="TEXT" NAME="value1"><BR>
<INPUT TYPE="TEXT" NAME="value2"><BR>
<INPUT TYPE="SUBMIT" NAME="Calculate" VALUE="Calculate">
</FORM>
</BODY>
</HTML>
```

From here, constructing the result page would seem to be pretty simple— just use the request object to get the values and add them together, as shown in Listing 3.9. H. L. Mencken once said, "For every problem there is a solution which is simple, obvious, and wrong." Unfortunately, this JSP fits all of these criteria. If a user were to enter the values 8 and 53, the answer would come back as 853. If only deposits to bank accounts worked that way!

Listing 3.9   A Buggy Version of the Calculator

```
<HTML>
<HEAD><TITLE>A simple calculator: results</TITLE></HEAD>
<BODY>
<P>
```

```
The sum of your two numbers is
<%= request.getParameter("value1") +
    request.getParameter("value2") %>
</P>
</BODY>
</HTML>
```

The problem lies in the fact that getParameter() returns a string, not an integer. When Java sees two strings connected by the + operator, it assumes that what is wanted is the result of appending them. This may seem dumb on Java's part, but there is no alternative. Neither the JSP Engine nor the Java language can know what the page author wants to do with values from a form. They may be numbers, names, colors, or anything else. The only sensible possibility is to express these values in the most general form possible, which means strings.

By the way, this problem would have shown up differently if the calculator had tried to multiply the two numbers instead of adding them. The * operator can be applied only to numbers, so at translation time the JSP Engine would have detected and reported the problem.

As correct as Mencken's quote may be, it is also true that for many bugs there is a fix that is simple, somewhat obvious, and correct. In this case, it is only necessary to convert the strings to integers before proceeding, and there are a number of ways to do this. The simplest is to use Java's Integer class, which has a method called parseInt() that takes a string and returns an integer. The corrected version of the calculator is shown in Listing 3.10.

Listing 3.10   The Correct Version of the Calculator

```
<HTML>
<HEAD><TITLE>A simple calculator: results</TITLE></HEAD>
<BODY>
<P>
The sum of your two numbers is
<%= Integer.parseInt(request.getParameter("value1")) +
    Integer.parseInt(request.getParameter("value2")) %>
</P>
</BODY>
</HTML>
```

The real trick here is knowing about the Integer class and its methods. Even though JSPs remove much of the programming burden from page authors, it is still worth knowing at least some of the more common classes in the

Java core library. Think of these classes as tools. It will usually be possible to get the job done without them, but they can make life much easier. A good place to start is the documentation on the java.lang package, which can be found at

http://java.sun.com/products/jdk/1.2/docs/api/index.html

This fix works if the user provides values that can be converted to numbers. If the user enters something like 11amas into one of the fields, then she will get the Error: 500 page, and Tomcat will complain about a java.lang. NumberFormatException: 11ama. Again, it seems that what is needed is a way of checking user input. Again, the solution will need to wait for Chapter 6.

Back to Java News Today

Before moving on to Chapter 4 it is worth looking at how Java News Today might use some of the information from this chapter.

First, you need to remember that one of their goals is personalization, and that one of the easiest ways to achieve it is to include the user's name on every page, perhaps in the header. Right now Java News Today can try doing that with <%= request.getRemoteUser() %>; however, they are not yet ready to build the system that will allow a user to log on to the site. For the time being, they must content themselves with simply showing the name of the user's computer. Not quite as warm and personal as the user's name, but it is at least a start.

Because the header has already been made into an included file, placing this change there will make it automatically available to every other page. Listing 3.11 shows the new version of *header.jsp*.

Listing 3.11   A Slightly Personalized Header

```
<%-- Begin Header --%>
<H1>Welcome To Java News Today</H1>
<P>Your on-line home for up to the minute
Java news</P>
<CENTER>
  <FONT SIZE="-1">Welcome back, user from
  <%= request.getRemoteHost() %>!</FONT>
</CENTER>
<%-- End Header --%>
```

The next change is even more interesting. To keep the site compelling, JNT has decided to add a daily quiz—a simple multiple-choice question that shows up in every navigation bar. A correct answer gives the user a point, and over time high scores will appear on a separate page. Not only will this keep users coming back to see their name in lights, but if the question ties into one of the current stories, users will be inclined to read through more of the site to find the answers.

Again, since the question will appear on every navigation bar, the text will be included in the separate *navigation.jsp*. However, the quiz is not really a part of the navigation, and it might also appear somewhere else in the site. So the navigation JSP will simply include a new JSP, called *quiz.jsp,* shown in Listing 3.12. As noted in Chapter 2, because the JSP Engine processes all included files, there is no reason that an included file cannot include another file and so on.

Listing 3.12   The Navbar with a Quiz

```
<%-- Begin Navigation --%>
<FONT COLOR="FFFFFF">
<FONT COLOR="#FF0000">&sect;</FONT>
Home Page<BR>
<FONT COLOR="#FF0000">&sect;</FONT>
Industry news<BR>
<FONT COLOR="#FF0000">&sect;</FONT>
Enterprise Java<BR>
<FONT COLOR="#FF0000">&sect;</FONT>
Standard Edition Java<BR>
<FONT COLOR="#FF0000">&sect;</FONT>
Micro edition &amp; devices<BR>
<FONT COLOR="#FF0000">&sect;</FONT>
Beans<BR>
<FONT COLOR="#FF0000">&sect;</FONT>
Editorials<BR>
<HR>
Today's quiz:<BR>
<%@include file="global/quiz.jsp"%>
<%-- End Navigation --%>
```

Now for the quiz itself, just a simple form with the question and possible answers. This component has no dynamic elements, so it could be an HTML file instead of a JSP. However, there is no compelling reason to make it an HTML file, and nothing is lost by allowing for the possibility that it will be dynamic at some point in the future. Listing 3.13 shows the quiz.

Listing 3.13 The Quiz

```
<P>What is the Apache/JSP project called?</P>
<FORM ACTION="quizresult.jsp" METHOD="POST">
<INPUT TYPE="radio" NAME="guess" VALUE="Apache/JSP">
The Apache/JSP project<BR>
<INPUT TYPE="radio" NAME="guess" VALUE="Jakarta">
Jakarta<BR>
<INPUT TYPE="radio" NAME="guess" VALUE="JaSPer">
JaSPer<BR>
<INPUT TYPE="Submit" NAME="Go" VALUE="Go">
</FORM>
```

This element references another JSP, which tells the user whether or not he is right, adds up the score, and perhaps displays some additional information. JNT still doesn't have qbbuite enough information to do all this, but they can make a start on this page and at least have it display the user's selection. The quiz result page is shown in Listing 3.14.

Listing 3.14 The Quiz Result Page

```
<HTML>
<HEAD><TITLE>Java News Today: Quiz Result</TITLE>
<BODY BGCOLOR="#FFFFFF">
<TABLE BORDER="0" WIDTH="100%">
  <TR>
    <TD BGCOLOR="#0000FF" ALIGN="CENTER" COLSPAN="2">
      <%@include file="global/header.jsp"%>
    </TD>
  </TR>
  <TR>
    <TD ALIGN="LEFT" WIDTH="20%" BGCOLOR="#000077">
      <%@include file="global/navigation.jsp"%>
    </TD>
    <TD VALIGN="TOP">
      <P>
      The question was: What is the Apache/JSP project called?
      </P>
      <P>
      You responded "<%= request.getParameter("guess") %>"
      </P>
    </TD>
  </TR>
</TABLE>
</BODY>
</HTML>
```

Note that this page looks almost like the index page, except for the title and the fact that there is now something in the content area. However, the header and navigation are exactly that same, once again demonstrating the usefulness of templating. Not surprisingly, the user's selection is retrieved with a call to getParameter(). There is no need to worry about "null" here because the quiz will always send exactly one answer. Someone out on the Internet might try to access this page without going through the question page, but if they do they deserve all the nulls they get.

Request-Time Errors

Clearly, request-time processing is much more powerful than translation-time processing. Unfortunately, with this extra power come many more kinds of errors.

One possible error might arise from trying to use a value that is not provided. Consider trying to convert the name of a conference to upper case before displaying it. This could be done with the following code snippet:

```
<%= getParameter("conferences").toUpperCase() %>
```

(The exact meaning of this syntax will be discussed in Chapter 5.) If a user provides a value for conferences, all will be well, but if no value is provided, Tomcat will return a page that looks something like Listing 13.15.

Listing 3.15   A Request-Time Error Page

```
                                              Error: 500

Internal Servlet Error:
javax.servlet.ServletException
        at org.apache.jasper.runtime.PageContextImpl.
          handlePageException(367)
        at _0002ftest_00031_0002ejganswers2_jsp_1.
          _jspService(68)
```

This error message is fundamentally different from those in Chapter 2. First and foremost, it came from the servlet, not the JSP Engine, and so is aimed more at programmers, who usually are the ones to write servlets, rather than JSP authors, who usually write files for the JSP Engine.

This means that the error message itself is a good deal more cryptic. On the plus side, though, it clearly indicates what file the problem came from—in this case, *jganswers2_jsp*.

The line number provided is the line number of the servlet, not that of the JSP. This is unfortunate because it makes figuring out a fix harder, but it is still useful. Most JSP implementations allow developers to see the generated servlet code. So far this book has not done so, because for the most part the code hiding in the servlet is not fit for human consumption. Nonetheless, Tomcat places all the servlet code in the work directory. The error message there indicated that the problem came from *jganswers2_jsp_1.java:60*. The lines around 60 in *jganswers2_jsp_1.java* reveal the following:

```
// begin [file=/jspbook/examples/ch03/
// jganswers2.jsp;from=(13,3);to=(13,45)]
```

Now this is useful! It shows that the problem is in the file that is called */jspbook/examples/ch03/jganswers2.jsp* on line 13, between the characters 13 and 45. A look back at the original file shows that this is where the value of conferences was requested. We still do not know exactly what went wrong or how to fix it, but once the problem has been located this precisely the rest is relatively easy.

Summary

This chapter introduced expressions, which may be thought of as arbitrarily complex ways of naming or specifying some information. They may be simple arithmetic forms, such as $8 - 2$ or sophisticated calls to Java methods. One particularly useful expression gets a value from the request object, which provides information about the request ranging from data sent by the browser to form values sent by the user.

We have now well and truly entered the realm of dynamic pages. Many of the examples in this chapter changed from one request to the next, which, after all, is what dynamic pages do. However, at this point the dynamic behavior is limited to simple substitutions. Chapter 4 will show how to make pages even more dynamic by introducing *beans* that can react to the values in the request object as well as many other things.

CHAPTER 4

Using Beans

In Chapter 3 we saw some truly dynamic, although simple, pages that could change themselves in limited ways in response to user input or information sent by the browser. Still missing is a way for pages to *react* to these expressions. There is no HTML or JSP tag that can perform different actions on different inputs, so at this point some Java code is needed. Fortunately, one of the major strengths of JSPs is that the code can be kept out of the page and placed in a *bean,* which can then share data with one or more pages.

What Beans Are

Forget about Java for the moment and consider a real bean, which has certain characteristics, or *properties,* such as color, size, shape, species, and so on. Not all beans have the same properties. Coffee beans have a "grams of caffeine" property, which lima beans do not.

It is always possible to determine the value of these properties, although sometimes this requires careful chemical study. However, imagine if a bean could reveal the value of one of its properties just by being asked to do so. Furthermore, imagine if beans could change their properties at will so someone could order a bean to set its size to three feet or its color to blue and the bean would instantly comply.

Finally, consider a super "bean microscope" that could automatically list all of a bean's properties. Note that none of these activities—finding the current state of a property, changing a property, or discovering which properties are available—would require cutting the bean open or studying its metabolism or anything similarly complex.

This is a reasonably good metaphor for a Java bean. A Java bean has a set of properties that can be read or changed. It is also possible to discover the properties a bean has available, which well suits beans for modeling all kinds of real-world things that can also be described as a set of properties. A CD could be modeled as bean with properties representing the year it was released, the record company that produced it, the list of tracks, and so on. Likewise, each track could be modeled as a bean with properties representing its lyrics, key, length, and so forth.

Two things make beans especially useful. The first is that neither programmers nor JSP authors need to know anything in advance about a bean in order to use it. A CD bean could be purchased from a bean company, and it would need only to be installed on the local system for JSP authors to start using it immediately.

The second useful thing about beans is that it does not matter what they do to retrieve or alter a property. Maybe the request to get a property requires the bean to look up some information in a database. Perhaps when a bean's property is changed it sends some mail out to a system administrator. In fact, both accessing and changing properties can trigger arbitrarily complex actions, but the JSP author does not need to worry about this. In this sense, beans act as mysterious black boxes with switches and readouts. Page authors can turn the knobs to change properties and read the properties off the readouts without ever knowing what is really going on inside the box. This model of Java beans is illustrated in Figure 4.1.

This is what allows beans to separate programming from page authoring. The programmer puts all the logic into beans and defines properties that trigger this logic; the page author uses these properties and accesses values that may end up on pages. This access is through three new tags, presented in the next section.

Using Beans

JSPs provide three basic tags for working with beans: one to find and use the bean, one to get a property, and one to set one or more properties. There are many ways to use a bean, so the use tag has a number of variations. In the most basic form, a bean may be made available to a JSP with the following tag:

```
<jsp:useBean id="bean name" class="bean class" />
```

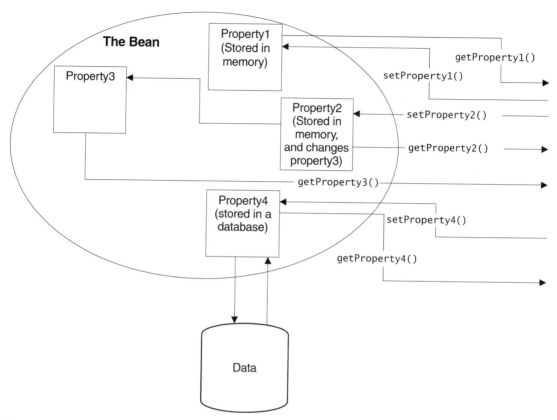

Figure 4.1 The "Black Box" View of a Bean

Here, "bean name" is the name that refers to the bean. There are only two restrictions on naming: It must be a valid Java identifier, meaning a combination of letters, numbers, and a few other characters, and it must be unique everywhere it is to be used, meaning that the ID cannot be the same for two different beans or the same as that of a variable or an intrinsic object.

The "bean class" is the name of a Java class that defines the bean. Chapter 5 will discuss classes in more detail, but for the moment a class can be thought of as the collection of code the bean comprises. The bean class must be available to the JSP Engine, so it must be somewhere in the CLASSPATH. Details on how to do this will vary between implementations, but most will provide some standard directory where new beans can be installed.

The trailing slash at the end of the tag is important—it signals that there is no corresponding `</jsp:useBean>` close tag and so an error will occur at translation time. In Chapter 6 we will see an instance where the close tag is used, but when it is not the JSP Engine must be told not to expect it.

There is another variation of the useBean tag that takes a type parameter as well as a class, which looks like this:

```
<jsp:useBean id="name" class="bean class"
type="another class">
```

In this version the bean will be cast into an object whose type is given by type. This is useful if a bean implements an interface and the JSP wishes to treat it as an instance of the interface instead of as an instance of the class. More information on interfaces and casts is available in the appendix, but this is not often likely to be an issue for page authors.

Getting a Property

Once a bean has been obtained with jsp:useBean, getting a property is as simple as using the getProperty tag, which looks like this:

```
<jsp:getProperty name="bean name" property="property name"/>
```

"Bean name" is the same name used in the *id* field, and "property name" is the name of the property to get. Listing 4.1 demonstrates the use of these tags.

Listing 4.1   A JSP That Gets Properties from a Bean

```
<jsp:useBean id="bean1" class="com.awl.jspbook.ch04.Bean1"/>
<HTML>
<HEAD><TITLE>Beans!</TITLE></HEAD>
<BODY BGCOLOR="#FFFFFF">
<P>Here is some data that came from bean1:</P>
<UL>
<LI>The name of this bean is:
<jsp:getProperty name="bean1" property="name"/>
<LI>The 7th prime number is:
<jsp:getProperty name="bean1" property="seventhPrimeNumber"/>
<LI>The current time is:
<jsp:getProperty name="bean1" property="currentTime"/>
</UL>
<CENTER>
<TABLE BORDER="0">
<TR>
<TD BGCOLOR="<jsp:getProperty name="bean1" property="color"/>">
<P>The information from a bean can be used
anywhere on the page!</P>
</TD>
```

```
</TR>
</TABLE>
</BODY>
</HTML>
```

The first thing this JSP does is get the bean. Here the ID has some relationship to the class name, but that need not be the case. It is also not necessary for the useBean tag to appear right at the top of the page, although it does need to appear before any getProperty tags.

Once the bean has been loaded, the getProperty tags get various properties from it. As promised, this hides a number of programming details from the page author. The method that gets the seventh prime number could just return it, or it could recompute it each time, or it could pull it out of a database. In fact, it does the easiest thing, merely returning the number 17. If 17 ever ceases to be the seventh prime number, please contact the author and a replacement bean will be cheerfully provided.

The method that gets the current date cannot rely on some similar trick, since it changes every time the page loads. This method must therefore have some code to it, which will be shown in Chapter 8.

By the way, the getProperty tag may seem similar to the expression tag, at least in that both cause values to be inserted on the page. In fact, a getProperty tag can be converted into an expression tag that calls the bean's GET method directly. For example, this tag from the previous example:

```
<jsp:getProperty name="bean1" property="seventhPrimeNumber"/>
```

could be rewritten as

```
<%= bean1.getSeventhPrimeNumber() %>
```

The latter form is a little shorter; however. the former is recommended because it makes it clear that the object is a bean. In addition, down the road the bean specification may be expanded so that a bean can comprise multiple classes, at which point this translation will not work any more.

Setting Properties

There are many ways to set a bean's properties, but the simplest looks almost exactly like getting a property:

```
<jsp:setProperty name="bean name" property="property name"
 value="property value">
```

Here name, as before, is the ID the bean was created with and "property name" is the name of the property to set. Value is the new value to assign to the property. The simplest type of value is a string enclosed in quotes such as "red" or "3." Listing 4.2 shows a JSP that uses a more advanced date bean that has two properties: format allows the JSP author to specify in what format the date should be presented; current time, as in Listing 4.1, provides access to the current date.

Listing 4.2   A JSP That Sets a Property

```
<jsp:useBean id="date" class="com.awl.jspbook.ch04.DateBean"/>
<HTML>
<HEAD><TITLE>The Date Bean</TITLE></HEAD>
<BODY BGCOLOR="#FFFFFF">
<P>Here is the current date, in a few different formats</P>
<UL>
<jsp:setProperty name="date" property="format"
 value="EEEE, MMMM dd yyyy 'at' hh:mm"/>
<LI><jsp:getProperty name="date" property="currentTime"/>
<jsp:setProperty name="date" property="format"
 value="hh:mm:ss MM/dd/yy"/>
<LI><jsp:getProperty name="date" property="currentTime"/>
<jsp:setProperty name="date" property="format"
 value="yyyyy.MMMMM.dd GGG hh:mm aaa"/>
<LI><jsp:getProperty name="date" property="currentTime"/>
</UL>
</BODY>
</HTML>
```

The format property is set numerous times in this example, which is perfectly valid. Each value of the property will be in effect until the next change unless something else in the bean changes it behind the scenes. The values used for format in this example are derived from the java.text.SimpleDateFormat class (see the documentation from Sun for more details).

Hard-coded values are fine for many purposes, but for beans to participate in dynamic pages they must be capable of interacting with other dynamic elements. One way of accomplishing this is to use an expression to set a property. The setProperty tag can accept as a value any expression that can be put in the <%= %> tag, including those from intrinsic classes, declared values, and so on. Listing 4.3 shows a JSP that reverses the name of the user's computer.

Listing 4.3   A JSP That Sets a Property from an Expression

```
<jsp:useBean id="rev" class="com.awl.jspbook.ch04.Reverser"/>
<HTML>
```

```
<HEAD><TITLE>Mirror image</TITLE></HEAD>
<BODY BGCOLOR="#FFFFFF">
<P>Here is the name of your computer,
and its mirror image</P>
<TABLE BORDER="0">
  <TR>
    <TH>Name</TH><TH>Mirror Image</TH>
  </TR>
  <TR>
    <TD><%= request.getRemoteHost() %></TD>
    <TD>
      <jsp:setProperty name="rev" property="hostName"
       value="<%= request.getRemoteHost() %>"/>
      <jsp:getProperty name="rev" property="reversedHostName"/>
    </TD>
  </TR>
</TABLE>
</BODY>
</HTML>
```

The syntax for setProperty used here may take some getting used to, since it appears to be two nested tags—an invalid syntax in regular HTML.

The Connection Between Forms and Properties

As discussed in previous chapters, most really interesting dynamic pages are driven at least partially by values that users provide through forms. Since most program logic resides in beans, it seems natural that many JSPs take input values from forms, pass these values into beans via setProperty tags, and then display other properties representing the result of some computation. Of course, form values could be passed to beans by a combination of techniques that have already been discussed, such as

```
<jsp:setProperty name="id" property="someproperty"
  value="<%= request.getParameter("formparam") %>">
```

This would work, but what a lot of effort! Happily, the JSP authors realized how common this situation would be and provided a shortcut. If the form is providing a value called formparam, and if the bean has a property that is also called formparam, the above code can be replaced by the single tag:

```
<jsp:setProperty name="id" property="formparam"/>
```

In this case the value is implied and assumed to come from the form. Sometimes the name of the form parameter and the name of the property will not match. They can be connected through another variation of the setProperty tag, as follows:

```
<jsp:setProperty name="id" property="propertyname"
 param="paramname"/>
```

Here the JSP uses the form parameter called `paramname` to set the property called `propertyname`.

There is one last version of the `setProperty` tag, which is the most powerful. This version looks through all the parameters provided by the form and all the methods provided by the bean, and links them together automatically. It looks like this:

```
<jsp:setProperty name="id" property="*">
```

If the form provides values called `param1`, `param2`, and so on, and the bean has methods called `setParam1()`, `setParam2()`, and so on, everything matches up perfectly. If the form provides some parameters for which there are no methods, these will be ignored and no error will occur. Of course, the JSP could do something else with those parameters, including pass them onto the bean manually. Likewise, if the bean provides methods for which the form does not supply values, these methods simply are not called. The JSP can call them manually if needed.

Listing 4.4 revisits the calculator from Listing 3.9, but now using beans.

Listing 4.4   A Bean Version of the Calculator

```
<jsp:useBean id="calc" class="com.awl.jspbook.ch04.CalcBean"/>
<jsp:setProperty name="calc" property="*"/>
<HTML>
<HEAD><TITLE>A simple calculator: results</TITLE></HEAD>
<BODY>
<P>
The sum of your two numbers is
<jsp:getProperty name="calc" property="sum"/>
</P>
</BODY>
</HTML>
```

This is much cleaner than the version in Chapter 3 because all the ugly code that had to deal with the inputs is hidden inside the bean along with the computation itself. Using a bean here has an extra bonus. It would be very easy to add a `getProduct()` method to the bean, so the same form could multiply as well as add.

There was a bug in Listing 3.9, and this bug is still present in Listing 4.4. If a user enters a value that is not a number, both programs return a cryptic error message. In Listing 4.4 the bean programmer could have chosen to simply ignore bad inputs, but this would have resulted in the page returning an incorrect answer instead of an error, which is potentially even worse. At least with the error message the user knows that something is amiss. What is really needed here is a way for the bean to tell the page whether the inputs were valid or not and for the page to display different text in either case. That this is possible will be shown in Chapter 6.

Hopefully, this has conveyed how well beans and forms work together. Now for a little fine print. This cooperation requires an echo of cooperation between the person writing the bean and the person writing the form. They must agree on the names of the form variables, which ones will be multivalued, and whether to return null or an empty array when there are no values in a multi-value form. This should not be any burden to either person since the bean interface makes both their jobs easier.

Bean Instances and Serialization

This chapter has talked a great deal about special properties of bean classes, but there is also something special about the instances of these classes. Most Java objects live only in memory, meaning that they cannot be passed between programs and that they live only as long as the Java Virtual Machine that created them lives. However, through a process called *serialization,* most bean instances can be saved into files and read back later.

Without serialization it would be difficult, although not impossible, for an object to make itself permanent. Consider how a hypothetical bean with a "color" property, would do this. It would have to include code to write the name or value of the color to a file and then read it back in the right way to recreate itself. If another bean contained a collection of color beans, it would need to worry about how to save all its own information as well as that of each of the color beans and so on. Serialization eliminates all this complexity by providing methods that will save any object to a file and later recreate the object from that file—no matter how complex the object is or how many other objects it contains. The only requirement is that every class to be saved in this way implement the *java.io.Serializable* interface.

Serialization is also useful to JSP authors because it allows beans to be tailored or customized before they are used. A software company might make a bean that computes how fast money in a bank account will grow, one property of which, obviously, would be the interest rate. Many banks could purchase this bean, use a program to create an instance of it, call `setInterestRate()` with the rate they offer, and save the instance to a file. Then, when the JSP authors at these banks created their web pages, they could use the standard bean tags to access the bean and none of the pages they created would need to worry about the interest rate. This also makes these sites easier to maintain. When the interest rate changes, the administrator just needs to replace the serialized file with one containing the new rate, and all the pages will automatically use the new value. In a sense, serialization can be used to "bake in" values that are appropriate to a site. JSPs can then use these values as if they were intrinsic to the bean.

Many bean editors can be used to create a new bean, examine or change its properties, and serialize it. Sun provides one called the Bean Box, although this is targeted primarily for people using beans to build graphic front ends and is overkill for the kinds of beans used in JSPs. A much simpler editor from Canetoad Software is included on the CD-ROM along with instructions for its use.

There is a slight variation in the way the useBean tag gets a serialized bean:

```
<jsp:useBean id="name" beanName="bean name"  type="bean class">
```

Here id is the name by which the JSP will use the bean, as always. BeanName should be the name of a file containing a serialized bean. By convention such files end with the *.ser* extension, but this extension should not be included in the name. Finally, type is the class or interface for which the bean is an instance.

Note that type is used instead of class, because the class is implicitly provided by the serialized file. An instance always knows what class it is an instance of, and this is true even when that instance has been stored in a file. Type is still necessary because the JSP still needs to assign a type to the variable that will hold the bean. Most of the time the type can be thought of simply as the bean's class.

Listing 4.5 shows a JSP that uses a serialized bean to get information about a record, in this case "Tinderbox" by Siouxsie and the Banshees.

Listing 4.5   A JSP That Uses a Serialized Bean

```
<jsp:useBean id="album" beanName="tinderbox"
 type="com.awl.jspbook.ch04.AlbumInfo"/>
<HTML>
<BODY
  BGCOLOR="<jsp:getProperty name="album" property="bgColor"/>"
  TEXT="<jsp:getProperty name="album" property="textColor"/>">
<H1><jsp:getProperty name="album" property="name"/></H1>
<P>Artist: <jsp:getProperty name="album" property="artist"/></P>
<P>Year: <jsp:getProperty name="album" property="year"/></P>
</UL>
</BODY>
</HTML>
```

BUG ALERT!   The current version of Tomcat does not provide support for serialized beans, but this should be fixed in upcoming releases of Jakarta.

Listing 4.5 looks much like the other examples in this chapter, except for the useBean tag and the fact that there is no obvious place where the properties have been set. In fact, they have not been set in the JSP, but have already been stored in the serialized file.

Notice that the background and text colors also come from the bean. This is a useful technique when creating online catalogs, since it allows each page to reflect the item.

This use of serialization makes beans behave a little like a database. Perhaps the "tinderbox" bean came as part of collection of beans for all of the Banshees' albums. To create pages for these others it would only be necessary to change beanName to say, "Hyaena" or "A Kiss in the Dreamhouse." There is a deep connection between beans and databases, which will be explored more fully in Chapter 9.

New Errors

Every new feature brings new errors to watch out for, and sadly this is true for beans. In fact, each new tag can generate a new error, although most of these can be found and fixed at translation time.

The most common problem is that the JSP Engine cannot find the bean's class, which is indicated by the JavaServer Pages Engine complaining about a java.lang.ClassNotFoundException followed by the name of the class. The fix is simple: Make sure that the class file, or the jar file containing the class, is in the JSP Engine's CLASSPATH. It may be necessary to stop and restart the engine to make this change take effect.

It is also possible to get a property that the bean does not provide. If a JSP tries to access a property named prop from a bean whose ID is "id," and this property does not exist, the following error will be generated:

```
com.sun.jsp.JspException:
    getProperty(id): can't find method to read prop
```

Most likely, the culprit is a typo in the property name, which can be easily corrected. If the JSP really does need a property that the bean does not have, the programmer will have to add it.

Likewise, someone might attempt to set a property that does not exist, causing an error very similar to the previous one, as in the following code.

```
com.sun.jsp.JspException:
    setProperty(id): Can't Find the method for setting prop
```

Again, simply correct the spelling of the property or request that it be added to the bean. Note that this error will not be generated when setting a bean's properties from a form. If the form names and properties do not match up, they are merely ignored.

Java News Today and Beans

Everyone at Java News Today loves beans, and they are planning to build the majority of their site around bean technologies. The question of the day is an obvious candidate for beans, since it is driven by a form, but there is a less obvious way that beans can help. Currently the text of the question is hard-coded into the JSP, which makes it difficult to update. Putting the question text into a serialized bean means that it can be updated daily via the Bean Box or another bean editor. Finally, the check that determines whether the user's answer is correct can also be moved into a bean. Listing 4.6 shows the new version of the JSP containing the quiz form.

Listing 4.6   The Bean Version of the Quiz

```
<jsp:useBean id="quiz1" beanName="todaysQuiz"
 type="com.awl.jspbook.ch04.QuizBean"/>
<P>
<jsp:getProperty name="quiz" property="question"/>
</P>
<FORM ACTION="quizresult.jsp" METHOD="POST">
<INPUT TYPE="radio" NAME="guess" VALUE="1">
<jsp:getProperty name="quiz" property="answer1"/><BR>
<INPUT TYPE="radio" NAME="guess" VALUE="2">
<jsp:getProperty name="quiz" property="answer2"/><BR>
<INPUT TYPE="radio" NAME="guess" VALUE="3">
<jsp:getProperty name="quiz" property="answer3"/><BR>
<INPUT TYPE="Submit" NAME="Go" VALUE="Go">
</FORM>
```

There are no surprises here. The serialized bean is obtained with the useBean tag, and properties are put on the page with getProperty. Unfortunately, the new version of the result page will have to wait for Chapter 6, since the page will want to display different text depending on whether or not the user guessed correctly.

The JNT designers are now ready to start thinking about personalization, at least at a very high abstract level. Even though it is not yet clear how personalization will work, it is safe to assume that every user will be modeled as a bean and that these beans will have various properties describing users' preferences. This is enough to start laying some groundwork. First, the designers will use this bean to better customize the header, as shown in Listing 4.7.

Listing 4.7 A Version of the Header That Gets `UserInfo` from a Bean

```
<jsp:useBean id="user" class="com.awl.jspbook.
                                 ch04.UserInfoBean"/>
<jsp:setProperty name="user" property="request"
 value="<%= request %>" />
<%-- Begin Header --%>
<H1>Welcome to Java News Today</H1>
<P>Your on-line home for up to the minute
Java news</P>
<CENTER>
  <FONT SIZE="-1">
    Welcome back,
      <jsp:getProperty name="user" property="name"/>!
  </FONT>
</CENTER>
<%-- End Header --%>
```

We still get `Hello user from <machine name>`, but this will be changed shortly. Notice that this example passes the whole request object to the bean, which will use various attributes within the request to determine the user's name.

Future Directions

As noted earlier, there are more to beans than just the names of SET and GET methods. Another feature beans provide is their ability to pass events to and from each other. For example, a bean used on one page could notify a bean used on another that a user had just visited that page, had provided some sort of input on a form, or had done any of a million other things. Currently JSPs have no built-in facility to connect beans in this way, so we will not go into this any further. However, it would not be surprising to see this as a feature in a future version of the JSP spec, so stay tuned. In the meantime, there is no reason interested programmers or page authors cannot use this ability manually, perhaps from scriptlet tags, which will be introduced in Chapter 6.

There are a number of products available that make beans even more powerful and useful. Sun provides a set of classes called the Infobus that extends the way beans can communicate. Another package, called the Java Activation Framework, allows beans to dynamically discover the type of pieces of data and the available methods related to that type.

Finally, the Java 2 Enterprise Edition makes extensive use of some additional types of beans, collectively known as *Enterprise JavaBeans,* or EJBs. EJBs provide a suite of methods for managing persistent data, ensuring that beans are kept in a consistent state, and using beans in distributed environments, where different beans may reside on different computers on a network. EJBs are beyond the scope of this book, but it is likely that the convergence between them and JSPs will grow.

Summary

Beans are Java's standard component model, and they integrate well with JSPs. Beans help separate Java code from HTML by providing standard tags that allow the JSP to get data to and from the bean via the bean's properties. They also facilitate writing dynamic pages that use forms by providing easy ways to send form data to beans and get results back. Beans also help pull changeable data out of pages by supporting serialization, which allows them to be customized and stored. This customization can tailor a bean to a site or a period of time.

Chapter 8 will discuss how to write beans in more detail, but in the meantime the source code for all the beans used in this chapter is included on the CD-ROM for interested readers to explore.

To complete the calculator and quiz examples from this chapter, a page must be able to customize itself based on certain criteria. For that it will need some embedded Java code. Before jumping into this code, the next chapter will introduce some important features of the Java Programming Language. Although by no means be a complete description, this will be enough to follow the remaining examples in this book and start writing JSPs. Readers already familiar with Java may wish to skip to Chapter 6.

CHAPTER 5

A Small Cup of Java

To those who have never programmed before, programming may seem like some eldritch art, beyond the ken of mortal man. OK, it may be a *bit* eldritch, but there is no reason that everyone cannot learn to do it.

This chapter will not teach programming, nor will it completely cover the Java language. There are many good books that do this, including *Introduction to Programming Using Java: An Object-Oriented Approach, Java 2 Update* by David Arnow and Gerald Weiss and *The Java™ Tutorial, Second Edition: Object-Oriented Programming for the Internet* by Mary Campione and Kathy Walrath. There are also a number of colleges and training centers that offer courses in Java for programmers and nonprogrammers. This chapter also will not explain how to use Tomcat or any other development environment. See the documentation for the relevant product for this information or the accompanying CD-ROM for information on setting up Tomcat.

What this chapter will do is introduce enough Java basics to follow the code that appears in the JSPs in this book. This should be as much Java as many JSP authors will ever need, although it is never a bad idea to know more. Learning to program in Java will enable JSP authors to create new beans and other utility classes, as well as write servlets instead of JSPs when appropriate.

Expressions

In Java an *expression* is simply a sequence of characters that expresses some value. Here is an incredibly simple expression:

    2

which, obviously, represents the number 2. Expressions can be more complex, such as

    ((8 / (2 * 4)) + 3) - (8/4)

which also represents the number 2. In this expression the +, -, *, and / are called *operators*, since they perform some operation on two expressions to produce a result. In a numeric context, these operators do the expected things.

Types

The numbers in the previous examples have been integers, that is, numbers with no fractional part. Division on integers works slightly differently than on numbers in the real world. In Java,

    7 / 2

evaluates to 3, since 3 is the largest integer that, when multiplied by 2, is less than 7. If a program wants this to evaluate to 3.5, the numbers should be Java *doubles*, or double precision floating-point numbers, instead of integers, expressed by decimal points:

    7.0 / 2.0

This illustrates an important and fundamental aspect of the Java programming language. Everything in Java has a *value*, such as 2 or 3.1415, and a *type*. If Java expects an expression of a certain type in some context, the possible values that can be used in that context are restricted.

Java supports a number of built-in, or *primitive*, types. We have already seen doubles and integers, which Java calls *ints*. Java can also manipulate text, using the String type. Strings are represented by surrounding quote marks, as in

    "This is a Java string!"

Keep in mind that "2" and 2 are very different things to Java, even though they may look the same. Do not be fooled—the types are different, which is what matters.

String expressions can also be more complex, such as

```
"This is a " + "Java string!"
```

Here the + operator denotes *concatenation,* which simply means two strings appended together. The result of this expression is the same as the previous one. This is the only important instance where an operator does two different things based on the type of the expression it is operating on. Technically + applied to two doubles does something different than + applied to two integers, but for the most part differences like this can be ignored.

Under some circumstances Java will automatically convert part of an expression from one type to another. For example, in

```
7.0 / 2
```

the 2 will be internally converted to 2.0, and the result of the expression will be a double. The full set of type conversion rules is available in any book on Java, but generally Java will never automatically go from one type to another type with less information. The double precision floating-point number 2.0 has more information than 2 has, so this conversion can happen automatically.

Java also will automatically convert most types to a string when the result of an expression should be one. The expression

```
"2" + 2
```

will evaluate to the string "22." The second 2 is first converted to a string yielding "2", which will then be appended to the first string.

It is also possible to explicitly convert a number of one type to one of another type by specifying the target type in parenthesis before the value. This might look like

```
(double) 3
```

which specifies a double number built from 3, which is equivalent to 3.0. It is also possible to do conversions that lose data in this way, such as

```
(int) 6.75
```

This yields the value 6, the simple result of chopping off the decimal part. Java would never perform such a conversion automatically, but it is perfectly valid for a programmer to do so.

This kind of moving from one type to another is called *casting.* It may help to think of an actor being "typecast," meaning that he is forced into a particular role. Casting will become very important when we look at objects and classes.

Variables

All the values we have seen so far have been *literals;* that is, they represent themselves. Java also supports *variables*. These can be thought of as boxes that can contain any value, which can be changed throughout the course of a program.

Before a variable can be used it must be *declared,* which will tell Java its name and type. A typical declaration might look like

```
int aNumber;
```

The semicolon designates the end of a Java *statement*, which is slightly different from an expression.

One way to picture this difference is that a statement *does* something, while an expression *has* something—a value. This statement creates a new "box" called aNumber, which can hold an integer. A value can be placed in this box with an *assignment,* which might look like

```
aNumber = 2 + 4 - 7;
```

and which sets aNumber to –1. Once a variable has a value, it can be used in expressions just like any other value, such as

```
2 - aNumber
```

which represents the number 2 – (–1), which equals 3. Variables can also be changed as many times as desired.

```
aNumber = 1;
aNumber = aNumber + 1;
```

Once these two lines are encountered in a program, aNumber will be 2. Note that this is starting to look like algebra, although the symbols have a subtly different meaning. In algebra, the second statement is meaningless, since a number can never be equal to itself plus 1. In Java, however, this statement means "compute aNumber + 1, which is 2; then put that value back in the box called aNumber."

If a statement or expression tries to mix types in a way that Java cannot automatically resolve, an error will be reported when the programmer tries to convert the program into runnable form. Either of these statements will cause an error:

```
aNumber = 2.0;
aNumber = "Hi there";
```

Method Calls

Java allows programmers to create *methods,* which can be thought of as black boxes with some number of inputs and one output. Values of particular types are dropped into the inputs, and a value of a possibly different type comes out as output. If a method has been defined called max, which takes two integers and returns the greater of the two, the expression

```
max(8,3)
```

will have the value 8. Method calls can be used in other expressions, as in

```
aNumber = max(8,3) + 2;
```

which will set aNumber to 10. The values given to a method, called its *arguments,* can also be arbitrary expressions. The following expressions are all valid:

```
max(3+2,12)
max(11,max(13,20))
```

However, the following is not valid, because max() can take only integer values:

```
max(2,"some string")
```

Some methods do not return a value and can be used as statements. One very common such method is System.out.println(). For now don't worry about the what seems to be a strange name; the important thing is what it does, which is print its argument to the user's terminal or window. Listing 5.1 shows some ways this method might be used.

Listing 5.1   Some Uses of a Method

```
System.out.println(2);
System.out.println( 7.3 / 2.1 );
System.out.println("Hello, world!");
System.out.println("The current value of aNumber is " + aNumber);
```

The last example converts aNumber to a string, appends this string to "The current value of aNumber is ", and prints the result.

Conditional Expressions

We have already seen a number of operators, such as + and /, most of which operate on numbers to produce other numbers. Another class of operators checks the truth of some expression, such as whether one value is less than another. They work in the way one might expect:

```
5 < 23
```

The type of this expression is *boolean,* meaning that it can have one of the two values: true and false. In this expression, the value is true.

Just like any other expression, any value can be replaced by a more complex expression, possibly including variables or method calls. For example,

```
max(aNumber,17) < anotherNumber
```

A boolean expression can also be combined with the "and" and "or" operators, expressed as && and || respectively. It might look like

```
(aNumber > 12) && (aNumber < 88)
```

This will be true if aNumber is greater than 12 and also less than 88.

It is possible to create boolean variables, assign the result of expressions to them, and so on. However, booleans are most often used in *conditionals,* which are Java statements that can do different things based on some expression. Conditionals consist of the word *if* and a boolean expression followed by a statement, possibly followed by the word *else* and another statement. If the boolean expression is true, the statement after the if will be executed; if not, the statement following the else will be executed. Listing 5.2 shows a simple conditional.

Listing 5.2   A Simple Conditional

```
if(aNumber < 0)
    System.out.println("aNumber is negative");
else
    System.out.println("aNumber is not negative");
```

By convention the statements are indented to make the code more readable. Moreover, they typically are enclosed in curly braces, which not only also aid readability but more important indicate that what they enclose is to be treated as a single statement. If a programmer not only wants to know if aNumber is negative but also wants to change it to positive if so, the code might look like Listing 5.3.

Listing 5.3   A Conditional with an Else Branch

```
if(aNumber < 0) {
    System.out.println("aNumber is negative");
    aNumber = -1 * aNumber;
} else {
    System.out.println("aNumber is not negative");
}
```

Loops

Conditional statements are the first of what is known as *control structures*, since they can control the flow through a program. The other control structures are *loops* which can perform the same action multiple times. The simplest loop is called a *while* loop, which performs some action while some boolean expression continues to be true. Listing 5.4 contains all the code needed for a program that counts from one to ten. The first line creates a variable and sets it to 1.

Listing 5.4   A While Loop

```
int count = 1;
while(count < 11) {
  System.out.println("Count is now " + count);
  count = count + 1;
}
```

Java is a very expressive language, so both creation and assignment of the variable can be done in one step. Then the while loop executes the statements within the curly braces until count reaches 11. Within the loop the value is printed and then incremented by 1.

The loop in Listing 5.4 displays a common pattern: A variable is created and initialized, a loop does some action until the variable reaches some value, and within the loop the value is changed. Because this combination of steps happens so frequently, another kind of loop makes it more convenient. This is called a *for* loop, so called because it does something for a certain number of times. The previous code can be rewritten as a for loop as shown in Listing 5.5.

Listing 5.5   A For Loop

```
for(int count=0;count<11;count++) {
  System.out.println("Count is now " + count);
}
```

This does exactly the same thing as the last example did, but it takes advantage of a number of shortcuts. First, all the code affecting the variable i has been moved into the for statement, including the creation and initialization, the boolean expression that checks whether i has reached 11, and the increment. Also, the increment i++ means exactly the same thing as i = i + 1—that is, i is set to one more than its current value. The body of the loop is now simply the print statement.

Defining Methods

A method definition looks something like a variable definition, the major difference being that a method must declare the types of its arguments as well as the type of the value it will generate. A method must also define the set of instructions it will perform to transform the inputs into the output. Listing 5.6 shows a simple method that takes two integers and adds them together.

Listing 5.6   A Method Definition

```
int add(int a, int b) {
   return a + b;
}
```

The declaration states that this method is called add, that it takes two integers, and that it returns another integer. The return line states that the two numbers should be added together and the resulting value should be given back to the code that called the method.

When this method is used in an expression, such as

```
add(12,8)
```

the variables in the method, a and b will be given the values 12 and 8, respectively. The method will then evaluate, add the two numbers together, and return 20.

Methods can contain loops, variable declarations, and anything else. Listing 5.7 shows a method that adds all the numbers between two other numbers and returns the sum.

Listing 5.7   A More Complex Method Definition

```
int total(int start, int end) {
   int total = 0;
```

```
        for(int i=start;i<=end;i++) {
          total = total + i;
        }
        return total;
    }
```

The `total` variable is created and initialized to zero. Then a for loop goes through all the values between `start` and `end`. Note that the test here is `<=`, meaning less than or equal to, which ensures that `i` will reach end. Each time through the loop the value of `i` is added to `total`. At the end, the value of `total` is returned.

Methods that do not return a value, like `System.out.println()`, have a special return type called `void`. What makes `void` special is that it has no values. An integer can be any whole number, a boolean can be "true" or "false," but nothing can be of type `void`.

Exceptions

An *exception* is generated when a Java statement or expression encounters a problem from which it cannot automatically recover—for example, an integer expression that tries to divide by zero. The result of such a computation cannot be stored in Java, so an exception is generated and, if nothing is done, the program terminates and reports the error.

Sometimes this behavior is perfectly fine, but more often a program will want to be able to detect exceptions and correct the problem. This can be done with a control structure called *try/catch*. Listing 5.8 shows a typical use. Here the computation is in the `try` clause. If `otherValue` happens to be zero, an *arithmetic exception* will be generated, causing the program to jump to the code in the `catch` clause, and then proceed to whatever follows.

Listing 5.8   Using Try to Catch Exceptions

```
try {
    result = value / otherValue;
    System.out.println("The result is " + result);
} catch (ArithmeticException e) {
    System.out.println("The computation could not be done");
}
```

If an exception is generated, the variable e that appears in Listing 5.8 will hold more information about the exception, including exactly where it happened. The use of this variable is beyond the scope of this chapter; suffice it to say that it can be very handy for figuring out why a program is not working the way a programmer expects it to.

Objects

Java is often described as an *object-oriented* language. To see what this term means, consider a "program" to play a CD, perhaps "Elyria" by Faith and the Muse. Traditional programming language would break this down into a set of steps that the computer would have to follow, such as those shown in Listing 5.9.

Listing 5.9   Pseudo Code Showing How to Play a CD

```
1. Search through the shelf for "Elyria"
2. Remove the CD in its case from the shelf
3. Open Jewel case
4. Remove CD
5. Place CD in CD player
6. Push 'play'
```

This is perfectly valid programming, but there is an alternative that treats the "things" in this example as more fundamental than the actions. The things here are the shelf, the CD case, the CD itself, and the CD player, and each contains a number of methods just like those we discussed previously. To put it another way, each object "knows" how to do certain things. The CD player can play a CD, the CD case can provide the CD, and the shelf can provide a CD in a case. With this approach, the program might look like Listing 5.10.

Listing 5.10   An Object-Oriented Approach to Playing a CD

```
1. CDInCase = shelf.findCD("Elyria");
2. CD = CDInCase.getCD();
3. CDplayer.insert(CD);
4. CDplayer.play()
```

In this version an expression like shelf.findCD("Elyria") means "ask the shelf object to find the CD," and CDplayer.play() means "ask the CD player to play whatever disk it currently contains."

Thinking in terms of objects can make a program much easier to write and maintain. One advantage is that it hides many cumbersome details. In

Listing 5.10 no code determines whether the CD case is a plastic jewel box or one of those cardboard cases with the CD in a sleeve. The object itself has the code to support the getCD() method, so the programmer who just needs to use a CD case never needs to think about it. Of course, the programmer who created the CD case object does need to know how this method should work, but once that code is written it becomes much easier for others to use.

Classes

Like everything else in Java, each object has an associated type, called its *class*. Classes are created by programmers and contain methods and variables. Listing 5.11 shows a very simple Java class.

Listing 5.11   A Complete Java Class

```
public class SimpleClass {
    private int value;
    public void setValue(int v) {
      value = v;
    }
    public int getValue() {
      return value;
    }
}
```

Here is the first example in this chapter that is completely valid Java. The code can be saved to a file, compiled, and then used in a JSP page.

This class contains two methods and one variable, although in class terms variables are more often called *fields*. The methods and fields look much like the examples we saw previously, with one addition. Everything in a class has a level of protection associated with it, which determines what other code is allowed to use it. If something is declared *private*, it may be used only in the class in which it is defined. In this example, the field *value* can only be accessed from within the methods that are also defined in this class. If a method or field is declared *public*, anyone may access that. Declaring the field private and the methods public, as Listing 5.11 does, ensures that other classes that use this class will go through the methods if they wish to access the field. This is called *information hiding*, and it is a very useful technique. If sometime in the future the *value* is stored in a database instead of in a simple variable, the implementations of getValue() and setValue will need to change but any programs that use this class will not. This is how the CD case class hides the details of what kind of case it is. As long as the methods stay the same, programmers can change the way they work without causing breakage of all the code that uses the class.

Once a class has been defined, it can be used like any other type. Two variables of type SimpleClass can be created by the statement:

```
SimpleClass a,b;
```

The variables a and b are in an interesting state after this statement is executed. Clearly they both have a type, but neither as yet has any value. Before they can be used, they must be given values, which are provided by the new operator.

Classes may be thought of as blueprints. Thus, new takes a blueprint and actually constructs an *instance* of that class, which is an object of the appropriate type. This is as simple as the following:

```
a = new SimpleClass();
b = new SimpleClass();
```

a and b will now have values and may be used in any number of ways, such as those shown in Listing 5.12.

Listing 5.12   Some Uses of the Simple Java Class

```
a.setValue(12);
b.setValue(14);
System.out.println(a.getValue() * b.getValue());
if(a.getValue() == b.getValue()) {
   System.out.println("The values are identical");
} else {
   System.out.println("The values are different");
}
```

The conditional at the end of the listing illustrates an important point, which is that each instance has its own copy of each of the fields that are defined in a class. If a blueprint contains the plans for a penthouse apartment, and several buildings are constructed from it, each will have its own penthouse.

Constructors

The lines that build new objects look like method calls, complete with parenthesis, is not a coincidence. Classes may contain methods called *constructors* that perform special actions when an object is built. If a programmer does not explicitly provide a constructor, a default constructor that takes no arguments is provided automatically.

Writing constructors is as easy as writing any other method. Listing 5.13 shows one that can be added to the `SimpleClass` class. This constructor is declared to be public, meaning that any other class or code can construct new instances. Now when new instances are constructed with `new`, `value` will start off at 12. Constructors can also take arguments, as shown in Listing 5.14.

Listing 5.13   A Constructor

```
public SimpleClass() {
    value = 12;
}
```

Listing 5.14   A Constructor That Takes a Value

```
public SimpleClass(int startValue) {
    value = startValue;
}
```

This version of the constructor takes an integer and initializes `value` to it. It can be called with a line of code like

```
SimpleClass a = new SimpleClass(20);
```

Constructors can do almost anything a regular method can, including contain loops and conditionals, construct other objects, and so on. The only thing they cannot do is return a value, since in a sense the object being constructed is the return value.

Null

Every object variable, regardless of its class, is allowed to have a special Java value called *null* that indicates "nothing at all." It is different from the *empty string*, which is a string with no characters, often represented as "". This is an important distinction, somewhat analogous to the difference between an empty box and no box at all. Null is a convenient value for an object that has not yet been initialized, as a special "flag" indicating a lack of data and in many other circumstances. It shows up often in almost all real Java programs.

Inheritance

Consider a class that represents an animal. Such a class might have fields representing the animal's gender, life expectancy, weight, preferred environment, and so on.

Now consider a class representing a fish. Since a fish is a particular kind of animal, it will share many of the characteristics of the general animal class. It will also have several fields of its own, such as speed at which it can swim and preferred water temperature. Likewise, a class representing mammals has several fields in common with the animal class but probably none of the fish fields.

A system to deal with all these animals would be severely inefficient if it recreated everything in the animal class for each species. Object-oriented languages get around this problem though *inheritance,* which allows one class to inherit the fields and methods of another. Java does this by allowing one class to extend another. The outline of the class definitions for the animal program is shown in Listing 5.15.

Listing 5.15   Some Animal-Related Classes

```
public class Animal {
    public boolean isFemale() {...}
    public double getWeight() {...}
    public void eat(Food someFood) {...}
}
public class Fish extends Animal {
    public double getSpeedInWater() {...}
    public double getWaterTemperature() {...}
}
public class Mammal extends Animal {
    public int getNumberOfLegs() {...}
}
Fish fishy = new Fish();
Mammal aMammal = new Mammal();
```

After this code executes, fishy will have all the methods that the Fish class has as well as the methods of the Animal class, so an expression like fishy.isFemale() will be valid. Likewise, aMammal will have all the Mammal methods as well as all the Animal methods. However, trying to call aMammal.getSpeedInWater() will result in an error. (No offense intended to any whales, dolphins, or other marine mammals who may be reading this.)

This idea may be extended further. It is possible to define a Cat class that extends Mammal, a Housecat class that extends Cat, and so on.

Objects may be cast to different types, just as integers can be cast to doubles, and vice versa. An object may always be cast to a class from which its class was extended, so the following would be legal:

```
Animal anAnimal = (Animal) fishy;
                   Animal anotherAnimal = (Animal) aMammal;
```

This operation is called *upcasting,* since it moves the object "up" into a larger class. *Downcasting,* where an object is cast into a more specific class, is called for if the thing being cast is of the more restrictive type. These two casts are legal:

```
(Fish) anAnimal
(Mammal) anotherAnimal
```

However, they cause an exception, specifically a class cast exception:

```
(Mammal) anAnimal
```

Interfaces

Animals kept as pets may require special fields or methods that untamed animals might not need such as a name. This would seem to call for a Pet class, but here we run into a problem. The Housecat class should extend the Cat class, but it should also extend the Pet class. Some languages do allow this sort of *multiple inheritance,* but not Java. However, Java does provide something almost as good, called an *interface.*

Interfaces are something like classes, except they contain no code. Instead, an interface states only what methods a class will provide. A class is said to *implement* the interface when it provides the methods specified in it. The definitions for the Pet interface and the Cat class are shown in Listing 5.16. The Pet interface specifies two methods, but provides no code. The Housecat class implements this interface, by providing code for these methods.

Listing 5.16 An Interface and a Class That Uses It

```
public Interface Pet {
    public String getName();
    public void setName(String name);
}
public class Housecat extends Cat implements Pet {
    ...
    public String getName() {...}
    public void setName(String name) {...}
}
```

Since interfaces provide no code, it may not be immediately obvious what they are for. The answer lies in the way Java treats types. A class that extends a class and implements an interface, such as Housecat has two types, Cat and Pet, which means it may be cast into either of these two types. This ensures that code makes sense. For example, there may be a method called buy that will purchase a pet. Obviously it would take an object of type Pet as an argument:

```
void buy(Pet aPet);
```

We could legally call this method on a Housecat, but not on some other kind of cat, such as a snow leopard, that does not implement the Pet interface. This ensures that only real pet animals can ever be purchased.

A class can extend only one other class, but it may implement any number of interfaces. This makes Java's type system much more powerful with interfaces than without them.

Packages

In a large program the sheer number of classes may become overwhelming, not to even mention the several hundred classes that are part of the Java language. To help manage these classes, Java includes packages, collections of classes and possibly, other packages. One such package is called java.util, and it contains a number of generally useful classes that programmers may use to make their lives easier. A commonly used class in this package, Vector, may be used to store an arbitrary number of objects of arbitrary types. To declare a variable of this type, it is just necessary to include the package name before the class name, as in

```
java.util.Vector v = new java.util.Vector();
```

This can be a little cumbersome when lots of classes are used from one or more packages. For simplicity, a program may *import* one, several, or all the classes from a package, after which it need only to specify the class name. Thus, the above example could be rewritten as

```
import java.util.Vector;
Vector v = new Vector();
```

All the import statements must appear at the top of a file containing a Java program. If a program wants to use several of the classes from the `java.util` class, it can have a separate import line for each or it can get them all with

```
import java.util.*;
```

The asterisk indicates that all classes in the `java.util` package should be imported.

Summary

This chapter is a long way from being a complete description of the Java language, but it should be enough for you to follow the Java code throughout this book. Although JSPs greatly reduce the need to program in Java, anyone with an interest can learn to program, and most will find it a very useful skill, not only for writing JSPs but for many other things. Readers are encouraged to pick up one of the books mentioned in the introduction or to look up a local class on Java programming.

In the next chapter, we will put Java to work in JSPs, allowing pages to show different text based on arbitrary conditions and loop over sets of data.

CHAPTER 6
More Advanced JSPs

Now that we have the full power of Java on our side, we can build pages that react to different situations. We have already seen the need for at least two kinds of reactions. First is the ability to check an expression and do different things based on its value; for example, a page might check which browser is being used and change its HTML appropriately. Second is the ability to handle expressions that may have zero or one or more values, such as user input on a multivalued menu in a form.

This chapter will lay some groundwork and then discuss some common *control structures* that allow pages to react in these ways and in many others. Control does not come from JSP tags but rather from capabilities built into Java. Therefore, readers who are not familiar with Java may want to read the preceding chapter.

Declarations and Explicit Objects

Most of the expressions presented in Chapter 3 came from the request object, which was identified as implicit, meaning that there is no need for a JSP to explicitly declare that it will use it. People seldom bother to have special names for one kind of thing unless there are other kinds, so it is not surprising that there are also explicit objects, those that a JSP creates before using. The tag that creates new objects is called a *declaration,* and it specifies the name and type of the object it is creating as well as an initial value for it. Here is a very simple one:

```
<%! int myInteger = 8; %>
```

This declares that the JSP will use a new integer called `myInteger` and that this integer will start life with a value of 8. In this case the name "explicit object" is somewhat misleading, since an integer is not an object. Just to keep the language clear, a better term for `myInteger` is *variable,* so named because its value can change.

Note the semicolon at the end of the declaration. A semicolon is necessary to signal the end of a Java statement, including declarations; without it, Java has no way of knowing whether the statement is over or more is coming. This declaration, which defines two integers, is also valid:

```
<%! int myInteger = 8, anotherInteger = 12; %>
```

Without the semicolon, there could potentially be another integer defined after `anotherInteger` and so on. Fortunately, a missing semicolon is one of those relatively easy errors that the JSP engine can identify and locate. If it were left out of the first example, the user would get one of those `Error 500` pages and the JSP Engine would print out something like

```
work/%3A8080%2Fjspbook/test_jsp_1.java:16: ';' expected.
        int i
          ^
```

which identifies the exact file and the exact problem.

Once a variable has been declared, it can be used just like an implicit object. In particular, it can be used in expressions. Listing 6.1 shows a number of variables declared and used.

Listing 6.1   A Page with Some Variables

```
<HTML>
<HEAD><TITLE>Some declared variables</TITLE></HEAD>
<BODY>
<%! int anInteger = 5; %>
<%! int anotherInt = 7; %>
<%! double pi = 3.1415926; %>
<P>The value of anInteger is now <%= anInteger %>.</P>
<P>The value of anotherInt is now <%= anotherInt %>.</P>
<P>The value of pi is now <%= pi %>.</P>
<P>The value of anInteger + 1 is <%= anInteger + 1 %>.</P>
<P>The area of a circle with a radius of 2 inches is
    <%= pi * 2 * 2 %> inches.</P>
```

```
<%! java.util.Date now = new java.util.Date(); %>
<P>Today's date is
    <%= now.getMonth() +1 %>/<%= now.getDate() %>
</P>
</BODY>
</HTML>
```

Most of this example is a logical extension of what has already been presented, but the date code at the bottom is worth noting. First, it shows that Java objects can be assigned to variables, just like integers or other simple types. Second, it shows that once such an object has been created it can be used just like an implicit object.

The Date class, like the Integer class in Chapter 3, is another useful tool. Indeed, it is worth looking over the other classes in the java.util package, since they were designed specifically to be useful. It is generally not necessary for JSP authors to know all the details of every class, but glancing over the documentation can only make things easier in the long run; see

http://java.sun.com/products/jdk/1.2/docs/api/index.html

By the way, the reason 1 is added to the result of getMonth() is that the Date class counts months from 0 to 11 instead of 1 to 12. Days of the month are counted from 1 to 30 (or 31) as usual. Someone probably has a very good reason for doing it this way, but it does not bear too much thinking about. This example will work as expected but when it is first accessed the JSP Engine will very likely print out a message something like this:

```
Note: work/%3A8080%2Fjspbook/example1_jsp_6.java uses a
      deprecated API.
Recompile with "-deprecation" for details.
1 warning
```

This is because the getMonth() and getDate() methods have been declared "obsolete" by Sun. There is a better way of getting the date information, using the Calendar class. However, it entails some additional complexity, so we will put it off for the time being.

Initial Values

Strictly speaking, it is not necessary to give a variable an initial value. The following two declarations, for example, are perfectly valid.

```
<%! int i; %>
<%! java.util.Date now; %>
```

That said, initial values are usually a good idea and are sometimes even required. If the variable i were used later in the page, it would just happen to have the value 0 because Java sets all integer variables to 0 if they do not have initial values. However, someone looking at the JSP might not know that, and it would be harder to determine what the page was supposed to do.

The problem is even more severe with the Date variable. Java initially sets all objects to null if they do not have a default value. This means that the first time the page tries to use "now," it will generate an error since null has no methods and cannot be called. In any case, this is just a roundabout way of saying that it is almost always best to give all declared variables an initial value.

A Few Words on Time and Space

Declared variables, like objects in the real world, have some constraints on where they must be placed and how long they can exist. First, variables must be declared before they are used. So the line declaring pi can come before the body tag or even at the top of the page before the HTML tag, but it must come before the line that shows its value.

Declared variables are also limited to the page in which they are defined, which means that the same variable cannot be accessed from multiple pages. However, this is not the case with the *names* of variables. A variable named anInteger can be on every page throughout a site, but it will be a different variable each time. It is the same as an office building where each office has a guy named Jim sitting in it. Each Jim is different; they just happen to have the same name.

Formally, the region or time during which a variable is valid is described by its *scope*. Declared variables become instance variables of the servlet that the JSP Engine generates, so they may be said to have a *servlet* or *instance scope*. In fact, there are ways to extend a variable to wider scopes, which allows for a lot of exciting applications. Scopes will be discussed in more depth in Chapter 7.

Going back to the office building analogy, even though there is a different Jim in each office, every time a visitor to the building goes to an office, she will find the same Jim who was there the last time she visited. The same is true of declared variables. Every time a user goes to a page generated by the JSP in Listing 6.1, he gets the same Date object. This can have an impact on dynamic behavior. If the page author also wants to display how many seconds have passed in the current minute, he can add this to the JSP:

```
<%= now.getSeconds() %> seconds have passed
in the current minute.
```

However, this number never changes. Actually, neither does the month or day, but it takes much longer for that to be obvious.

This is so because the Date class gets all its information when it is first created, not every time it is asked for something. Say Jim looks at how many doughnuts are in the coffee room on the way to his office. Every time someone asks him how many doughnuts are available, he gives the same answer because he does not check each time. Likewise, all declared variables get their initial values the first time the servlet class is loaded, and after that they do not change by themselves. Fortunately, there is a way to make a variable update its value.

Scriptlets

So far, all the variables we have seen—both the implicit objects and the declared variables—have been rather static things. Obviously, static variables will not make for good dynamic pages, so it should come as no surprise that there is a tag that allows them to be updated. In fact, this tag does a great deal more and is the gateway to all the dynamic behavior that was promised in Chapter 3. It is called the scriptlet tag, and it is written as <% %>. Any Java code can be placed within this tag, and it will be run each time the page is accessed. For that reason, it is the simplest way to unify HTML and Java.

One thing this tag can do is ensure that dates change as they should. The problem is that the Date object does not change after it is given an initial value. The solution is simply to give it a new value each time the page is requested. A JSP that does this is shown in Listing 6.2.

Listing 6.2   A JSP That Shows the Current Time

```
<%! java.util.Date now = new java.util.Date(); %>
<HTML>
<HEAD><TITLE>Current time</TITLE></HEAD>
<BODY>
<% now = new java.util.Date(); %>
Hello!  At the tone, the time will be exactly
<%= now.getHours() %>:<%= now.getMinutes() %>
and <%= now.getSeconds() %> seconds.
<P>
<B>BEEEP!</B>
</BODY>
</HTML>
```

The addition of <% now = new java.util.Date(); %> may not seem like much, but this line is executed every time the page is requested, which means that every time someone loads this page, now is given a new value containing the correct time. The expression tags consequently get their data from this new Date object and all is well. By the way, the declaration was moved to the top of the page to show that it is, in some sense, removed from the rest of the page.

The declaration happens only once and then gets out of the way; everything else happens whenever the page is accessed. In this case the initial value given to now when it is declared is superfluous, since every request will give it a new value. Still, it does little harm, so it may as well be left there.

This same approach can be used to build a counter that shows how many times a page has been accessed. Counters like this are in use all over the Web. JSPs make them especially easy to build, as Listing 6.3 shows.

Listing 6.3   A JSP with a Counter

```
<%! int count =0; %>
<HTML>
<HEAD><TITLE>A Counter</TITLE></HEAD>
<BODY>
<% count = count + 1; %>
<P>This page has been accessed <%= count %> times.</P>
</BODY>
</HTML>
```

A counter in three tags! This works because of the instance scope of the declared variables, which causes count to refer to the same variable every time the page is accessed. The scriptlet increments its value by 1, and the expression shows the current value. The next time someone accesses the page it will still be the same count, which will be incremented again and so on.

It is worth noting that count is stored in memory, so if the server is ever shut down, the value will be reset to zero. To avoid this the value could be stored in a file every time it is incremented, or it could be stored in a database, as we will discuss in Chapter 9.

Conditionals

Everything is now in place to start making pages even more dynamic by allowing them to customize themselves based on user input or other values. Although there is no JSP tag that can do this directly, Java has a mechanism called the if statement, which can do one of two things based on some condition. (The if statement is discussed in more detail in Chapter 5.) To get this same kind of dynamic behavior in a JSP, it is just necessary to include an if or two inside a scriptlet. Listing 6.4 shows a modification of the counter that displays a special message to the first person who visits the page.

Listing 6.4 A JSP with a Counter and a Special Message

```
<%! int count =0; %>
<HTML>
<HEAD><TITLE>A Counter</TITLE></HEAD>
<BODY>
<% count = count + 1; %>
<P>This page has been accessed <%= count %> times.</P>
<%
if (count == 1) {
    out.print("<P>Welcome, first visitor!</P>");
}
%>
</BODY>
</HTML>
```

Do not be alarmed by the fact that the scriptlet extends across multiple lines; it is just a more readable way of writing the code. As far as the JSP Engine is concerned, anything between the <% and %> tags is Java code, and the JSP does not care how it is formatted.

The new scriptlet simply checks whether count is currently equal to 1. If it is, it prints the message to the out object. Out is another implicit object—anything printed to it will be sent back to the user. In fact, everything on the page, even the plain old HTML, is sent through the out object, but most of the time this is hidden from the JSP author. Even so, just for the moment consider what the servlet generated from the JSP actually does. The page in Listing 6.4 might turn into something like Listing 6.5.

Listing 6.5 A Possible Translation from a JSP to Java

```
out.println("<HTML>");
out.println("<HEAD><TITLE>A Counter</TITLE></HEAD>");
out.println("<BODY>");
count = count + 1;
out.print("<P>This page has been accessed ");
out.print(count)
out.println(" times.</P>");
if (count == 1) {
    out.print("<P>Welcome, first visitor!</P>");
}
out.println("</BODY>");
out.println("</HTML>");
```

In reality, the generated code looks significantly different, but the principals are all there. Plain HTML turns into static strings, which get printed by out. Expressions are also printed by out. Scriptlets are unchanged and are inserted into the servlet exactly as the JSP author wrote them.

This works, but it is somewhat ugly. One of the points of JSPs is to pull HTML out of Java code to make both easier to maintain and read. Fortunately, a solution is at hand, and it derives from the way JSPs are turned into Java code. As Listing 6.5 showed, there are two ways to get something printed to out. The first is to explicitly write out.print() in the JSP. The second is to just write plain HTML and let the JSP Engine turn it into a print command. In all respects these two are equivalent. The only important thing to keep in mind is the *relation* of print statements to other Java code coming from scriptlets.

In particular, note that the statement that prints "Welcome, first visitor!" is surrounded by curly brackets. This associates this statement with the if statement and ensures that this line executes only if the statement is true. Given this fact, there is no reason that the message cannot be pulled out of the scriptlet as long as the curly braces stay in the same place. This translation turns the if statement into the following:

```
<% if (count == 1) { %>
  <P>Welcome, first visitor!</P>
<% } %>
```

which has split up the scriptlet into two pieces. Because the first one ends with a curly brace, anything up to the next closing curly brace will be connected to the if. And indeed the closing brace in the next scriptlet closes off the if. In between is some normal HTML, which, as always, the JSP Engine will turn into print statements.

In this particular example the code actually gets more complicated, since one scriptlet has turned into two, making the whole thing longer. However, if there are larger blocks of HTML that should be included only if some condition is true, writing the JSP this way will make things much easier.

The same pattern can be applied to if statements that have an else clause. Listing 6.6 shows the final version of the counter, which prints one message for the first visitor and a different message for everyone else.

Listing 6.6 A Counter with Different Messages

```
<%! int count =0; %>
<HTML>
<HEAD><TITLE>A Counter</TITLE></HEAD>
<BODY>
```

```
<% count = count + 1; %>
<% if (count == 1) { %>
    <P>Welcome, first visitor!</P>
<% } else { %>
    <P>You are not the first visitor. <%= count-1 %> other
    visitors have already been here,</P>
<% }%>
</BODY>
</HTML>
```

There are a few new things here. The first is the else clause, which divides
the conditional into three scriptlets: one for the if, one for the else, and one
for the closing brace. The second is the expression showing how many visitors have been to this page, which has been moved into the message for the
second and subsequent visitors. This illustrates an important point about the
way JSP tags can connect. It is illegal to put a tag inside another tag, such as
<% if (count == 1) <%= count %> %>, but apart from that restriction tags
can be combined any way that makes sense. There can even be another scriptlet in between the if and the else, as long as the code generated by the JSP
Engine is valid. Thus, expressions can be controlled by scriptlets, if statements can be nested inside other if statements, and so on.

Nesting allows for very sophisticated checks, such as determining the
exact make and version of the browser being used to access the site. For example, if Java News Today wanted to use features of HTML only available
in 4.0 and later browsers, they could do so with code such as that shown in
Listing 6.7.

Listing 6.7 Using Conditions to Do Browser Detection

```
<% String browser = request.getHeader("User-Agent"); %>
<% if (browser.indexOf("4.") != -1) { %>
<P>You have a recent browser, enjoy the site!</P>
<% } else { %>
    <% if (browser.index.of("MSIE") != -1) { %>
        <P>You do not have a recent enough version of IE
        to use all the features of this site. You can download
        one here...</P>
    <% } else if (browser.index.of("Mozilla") != -1) { %>
        <P>You do not have a recent enough version of Netscape
        Navigator to use all the features of this site. You can
        download one here...</P>
    <% } %>
<% } %>
```

More Solutions

Chapter 3 was filled with examples that wouldn't work under certain circumstances because there was no way to check a variable or expression and do different things based on its value. The scriptlet tag is the answer here, too.

One such problem was related to forms with multivalued menu items. If the user selected at least one value, the JSP was able to access it with the `getParameter()` method. However, if no values were provided, the user would see "null."

The solution is now clear—just use a conditional to check whether `getParameter()` returns null, and if not go ahead and use it. The revised version of the James Gosling questionnaire from Chapter 3 is given in Listing 6.8.

Listing 6.8   A JSP That Handles Empty Form Values

```
<HTML>
<BODY BGCOLOR="#FFFFFF">
<P>
You answered
"<%= request.getParameter("met") %>"
when asked if you've met Mr. Gosling.
</P>
<P>
Given the chance, you would ask the following question:
<%= request.getParameter("question") %>
</P>
<% if (request.getParameter("conferences") == null) { %>
   <P>You have never heard him speak at a conference.</P>
<% }else { %>
   <P>
   You heard him speak at a conference called
   <%= request.getParameter("conferences") %>
   </P>
<% } %>
</BODY>
</HTML>
```

This still does not completely solve the problem, since what this form really should do is print all the conferences the user selected. To do that, `getParameterValues()` instead of `getParameter()` should be used. When multiple values are submitted, `getParameterValues()` returns all of them as an array; when none are provided it returns null. It is now possible to look at how many values are returned by `getParameterValues()`. If there is only one, it will be safe to print the first element of the array. If there are two, it is safe to print two elements of the array and so on. Listing 6.9 shows how this is done.

Listing 6.9   A JSP That Handles 0, 1, or 2 Values

```
<%! String confs[] = null; %>
<HTML>
<BODY BGCOLOR="#FFFFFF">
<P>
You answered
"<%= request.getParameter("met") %>"
when asked if you've met Mr. Gosling.
</P>
<P>
Given the chance, you would ask the following question:
<%= request.getParameter("question") %>
</P>
<% confs = request.getParameterValues("conferences"); %>
<% if (confs == null) { %>
  <P>You have never heard him speak at a conference.</P>
<% } else { %>
  <% if (confs.length == 1) {%>
    <P>
    You heard him speak at a conference called
    <%= confs[0] %>.
    </P>
  <% } else if (confs.length == 2) { %>
    <P>
    You heard him speak at a conference called
    <%= confs[0] %>, and one called <%= confs[1] %>.
    </P>
  <% } else { %>
    <P>You have heard him speak at more than 2 conferences.</P>
  <% } %>
<% } %>
</BODY>
</HTML>
```

There is more Java code in this example than in any of the previous ones, as well as a couple of new features, which may make it look dauntingly complex to nonprogrammers. However, breaking it down into smaller pieces shows that it is really just the same few tags already discussed, just combined in new ways.

First, a variable called confs is declared. This is an array of strings, as opposed to something simpler like an integer, but there is no fundamental difference. It is given a value that comes from getParameterValues(), as always.

Next there is a conditional, which checks whether the array is null. If it is, no answers were provided and the appropriate message is sent to the user. If the array is not null, the JSP goes into another conditional. This is inside the else portion of the first conditional, which is fine since the JSP Engine will treat it the same as any other. This conditional checks to see how many elements are in the array. If there is one, the appropriate message is generated; if there are two, a different message is generated. The JSP could go on and check whether there were three, four, and so on, but this is enough to convey how this works.

Loops

Having to check an array for every possible length is clearly a major hassle. Even worse, it is impossible in the most general case since there may be no way to know how much data might be coming from a user or some other source. What is really needed is a way to go through all the elements in an array without knowing in advance how many there may be. Once again, the solution is a combination of the scriptlet tag and some Java code.

The code needed here is the for loop, presented in Chapter 5. In the simplest case, a for loop has a counter that starts at some value and repeats some action until that counter reaches another value. Each time it performs the action it can also add or subtract some quantity from the counter. For example, this for loop

```
for(int i=0;i<10;i++)
```

will do something ten times. First i will be 0. Then the i++ statement will set i to 1, and so on until it reaches 10. At that point the test i < 10 will no longer be true, and the loop will exit.

This is exactly what the doctor ordered for the conference problem. Instead of checking each possible length of the array, a for loop can go through as many values as actually provided. This changes the portion of the code in Listing 6.8 after the else to the code in Listing 6.10.

Listing 6.10   A For Loop in a JSP

```
<P>You heard him speak at the following conferences:</P>
<UL>
<% for (int i=0;i<confs.length;i++) { %>
  <LI><%= confs[i] %>
<% } %>
</UL>
```

Now the code will work with any number of conferences. After next year's Java One only the HTML input page will have to be updated for this JSP to continue to work. (It will also not run into any problems due to the fact that next year's conference will be Java One 2000—Java and JSPs are fully Y2K compliant, but that's another story.)

The scope of the variable i in this example is interesting. Since it appears in a declaration, it will not be the same each time the page is accessed. This can be referred to as *local scope*. In fact, a new variable will be created every time the servlet gets to the for line. Likewise, because it is created inside the for loop, it will last only as long as the loop does. It would be an error to add the following line after the closing </UL>:

```
I counted <%= i %> conferences.
```

because by that point the variable would have ceased to exist, or more formally, it would have "gone out of scope." The JSP Engine would catch this problem at translation time and alert the page author that she had used an undefined variable.

Although it might seem silly to create a short-lived variable like this, there is a very good reason for it. If i was declared and given an instance scope, very weird things could happen if two or more people tried to access the page at about the same time. Perhaps one person would access the page and the servlet would start the loop off with i equal to 0 and shortly after increment it to 1. If at that point another person accessed the page, the servlet would once again try to start i off at 0! If i had instance scope and was the same variable for both users, there would suddenly be a tug of war as each servlet tried to change the value of i. It is not clear what each user would see on the page, but it probably would not be what either of them was expecting.

This is an example of a more general problem called `threading`, which will be addressed in Chapter 14. Until then, a good rule of thumb is that loop variables should be locally declared, inside the loop. This will keep everything running smoothly.

By the way, it is common convention to use short names like i or j for loop variables. This is a holdover from the ancient days of FORTRAN and similar languages. Feel free to consider it either a quaint anachronism or a convenient excuse to save some typing time.

Other Kinds of Loops

Another problem discussed in Chapter 3 relates to the `getHeader()` method in the request object. It is a safe bet that every request will have information about the browser in the *User-Agent* field, as well as information about what types of information the browser will accept in the *Accept* field. However, there may be other headers of interest that are browser or request specific, and it would be useful to get a list of all the headers that are available.

Of course, JSPs allow this. There is a method in the request object called
getHeaderNames(), which as might be inferred returns the names of all the
headers that have been provided. We might expect that they would be returned
as an array of strings, as with getParameterValues(). However, for a number of reasons they are returned in an object called Enumeration from the
java.util packages. Here is another good reason to read over the documentation on that package!

An enumeration may be thought of as a collection of things, where each is
presented one at a time. In a sense, a recording artist is a kind of an enumeration. For example, if Happy Rhodes were written in Java, her fans could call a
method to get her next album that might be called getNextAlbum(). The first
time this method was called, Ms. Rhodes would hand over her first record,
"Rhodes I." The next time she would return "Rhodes II," and so on up to her
latest, "Many Worlds are Born Tonight." After that it could be determined
whether she had any more albums, perhaps by calling a method named
hasMoreAlbums(), which would return false since there are no others currently
available. Of course, in the real world she might go on to tell of plans for her
next release.

The enumeration object works pretty much the same way. It provides a
method called hasMoreElements(), which returns true if there are any more
available. It also has a method called getNextElement(), which returns, obviously enough, the next element available. getNextElement() will cause an error
if it is called and there are no more elements.

A for loop is not quite the right fit for this situation, so we will use a while
loop instead. Just as the for loop does something *for* a certain number of times,
a while loop does something *while* some condition continues to be true. Listing 6.11 shows Enumeration and a while loop being used to generate a page
with all the headers in a request.

Listing 6.11   A While Loop and an Enumeration

```
<HTML>
<BODY>
<% java.util.Enumeration e = request.getHeaderNames(); %>
<P>Here are the names of the headers that have been sent:</P>
<UL>
<% while (e.hasMoreElements()) { %>
<LI> <%= e.nextElement() %>
<% } %>
</UL>
</BODY>
</HTML>
```

As promised, the first thing this JSP does is get an `Enumeration` object from the request object. Once again, the variable e is defined in a scriptlet, not a declaration, which puts it in a local scope. Then a while loop starts up that checks whether `Enumeration` has any more elements. If it does, it shows the next one and continues. It stops when there are no more.

This is only half the problem solved, however, as it shows only the names of the headers, not their values. However, this is easily fixed. First, we will need a new variable to hold the name. This is because once `getNextElement()` is called and the name is printed, that element is lost and it cannot be used to then get the value. Thus, this new variable will hold the result of `getNextElement()` and can then be printed with an expression and used again to get the value. The value will be obtained with a call to `getHeader()`, same as before. Listing 6.12 shows the final version.

Listing 6.12   Using a Variable to Get Names and Values

```
<HTML>
<BODY>
<% java.util.Enumeration e = request.getHeaderNames(); %>
<P>Here are the names and values of all the headers that have
been sent:</P> <UL>
<TABLE BORDER="1">
<TR><TH>Name</TH><TH>Value</TH><TR>
<% while (e.hasMoreElements()) { %>
    <% String name = (String) e.nextElement(); %>
    <TR>
       <TD><%= name %></TD>
       <TD><%= request.getHeader(name) %></TD>
    </TR>
<% } %>
</TABLE>
</BODY>
</HTML>
```

The only other new thing in this example is the (`String`) that precedes the call to `getNextElement()`. By default, `Enumeration` returns general objects, so it can be used to enumerate any kind of data. However, `getHeader()` requires a string, so it is necessary to tell Java that the object being returned by `getNextElement()` really is a string and should be treated as one. This is called "casting," and it was discussed in detail in Chapter 5.

Try and Catch

We have now fixed most of the problems from Chapter 3, all with one little scriptlet tag, conditionals, and two kinds of loops. However, one last problem remains.

No matter how carefully constructed a JSP is, there will almost always be some kind of user input that the author did not expect, which will cause the JSP to break and generate an error instead of the proper page. One example of this is the calculator from Listing 3.9. If the user decides to put a non-numeric value in the form, the calculator will be unable to handle it.

In theory it is possible to check every input using some combination of conditionals and, if the input is bad, return some special message. In practice, however, this may be unrealistically difficult. A better solution is to let Java do what the page author wants and automatically detect if something went wrong. In the event something does go awry, the page should be able to recover and print an explanation to the user.

Java provides this capability through another type of control structure called the *try/catch* block. As its name suggests, this structure will "try" to do something, and if an error happens Java will "catch" it and proceed instead of giving up. In this context errors are called exceptions, perhaps because they are usually exceptionally bad news. There is a wide variety of exceptions, each of which is related to a particular kind of error. The one that occurs when a string cannot be converted to an integer is called NumberFormatException.

Listing 6.13 shows how the calculator JSP could be modified to catch a NumberFormatCondition. Rather than print the result out immediately, as in Listing 6.11, this JSP first saves the result to a temporary variable. It does so because everything inside a try block is executed up to the statement that causes the error. If an error does occur, we don't want the message "The sum of your number is" to be sent to the user, so we must ensure that this message comes after the statement that might have caused the problem.

Listing 6.13   Preventing an Error with Try/Catch

```
<HTML>
<HEAD><TITLE>A simple calculator: results</TITLE></HEAD>
<BODY>
<P>
<% try { %>
<% int result =
   Integer.parseInt(request.getParameter("value1")) +
   Integer.parseInt(request.getParameter("value2")); %>
<P>The sum of your two numbers is <%= result %></P>
<% } catch (NumberFormatException nfe) { %>
```

```
<P>
Sorry, I was unable to compute the result, because one of the
values provided was not an integer.
</P>
<% } %>
</BODY>
</HTML>
```

Now if something goes wrong, the user will get an error page that at least explains why there was a problem, which is infinitely preferable to a cryptic and unhelpful Error: 500.

Beans and Scriptlets

Beans and scriptlets complement each other quite nicely. First and foremost, most of the scriptlet code typically can be removed entirely from a page and placed in a bean. This will leave only the code that the page needs in order to react to different input or loop over a set of data obtained from the bean.

Listing 6.14 illustrates this cooperation by presenting yet another version of the calculator. This version is almost as clean as the one with no Java code from Chapter 4, but it will properly handle non-numeric input.

Listing 6.14   Beans and Scriptlets Together at Last

```
<jsp:useBean id="calc" class="com.awl.jspbook.ch06.CalcBean"/>
<jsp:setProperty name="calc" property="*"/>
<HTML>
<HEAD><TITLE>A simple calculator: results</TITLE></HEAD>
<BODY>
<% if (calc.isValid()) { %>
<P>
The sum of your two numbers is
<jsp:getProperty name="calc" property="sum"/>
</P>
<% } else { %>
<P>
Sorry, I could not compute the sum because
<jsp:getProperty name="calc" property="reason"/>
</P>
<% } %>
</BODY>
</HTML>
```

This is almost identical to Listing 5.6, except the output is enclosed in an if statement. This statement uses isValid(), a method in the bean, to determine if the input was valid. If so, it proceeds to show the result; if not, the bean makes another property, called `reason`, available, which contains a description of the problem.

Beans can also be enclosed in for loops, which can iterate over properties that are arrays. An example is shown in Listing 6.15, which revisits the album JSP from Listing 5.6 and adds a track listing.

Listing 6.15   A JSP with a While Loop and a Bean

```
<HTML>
<HEAD><TITLE>A simple calculator: results</TITLE></HEAD>
<BODY>
<P>
<% try { %>
<% int result =
   Integer.parseInt(request.getParameter("value1")) +
   Integer.parseInt(request.getParameter("value2")); %>
<P>The sum of your two numbers is <%= result %></P>
<% } catch (NumberFormatException nfe) { %>
<P>
Sorry, I was unable to compute the result, because one of the
values provided was not an integer.
</P>
<% } %>
</BODY>
</HTML>
```

This page loops through the tracks by first obtaining the full array. It is also possible for the bean to provide a `hasMore()` method and for the page to use a while loop to get tracks until no more are available.

Java News Today

The folks at Java News Today are well on their way to making their site dynamic. First, they have decided to add a counter to their home page. Everyone else has one, and since JSPs make them so easy, why not? Listing 6.16 shows the new home page.

Listing 6.16   The JNT Home Page with a Counter

```
<%! int count = 0; %>
<HTML>
<HEAD><TITLE>Java News Today!</TITLE>
<BODY BGCOLOR="#FFFFFF">
```

```
<TABLE BORDER="0" WIDTH="100%">
  <TR>
    <TD BGCOLOR="#0000FF" ALIGN="CENTER" COLSPAN="2">
      <%@include file="global/header.jsp"%>
    </TD>
  </TR>
  <TR>
    <TD ALIGN="LEFT" WIDTH="20%" BGCOLOR="#000077">
      <%@include file="global/navigation.jsp"%>
    </TD>
    <TD>
      <FONT SIZE="-1">
        <% count = count + 1; %>
        <P>This page has had <%= count %> visitors</P>
      </FONT>
      <!-- Content goes here -->
    </TD>
  </TR>
</TABLE>
</BODY>
</HTML>
```

Note that the counter code has been put in the home page and not in the header. Since the header will appear on all pages, the counter located there would be the same throughout the whole site. Placing it on the home page allows it to be different on each page if desired.

Next, JNT's designers return their attention to the quiz that was started in Chapter 3 and placed in a bean in Chapter 4. They can now make the quiz determine whether or not the answer is correct using a conditional statement. In addition, they have decided to keep a running count of how many people have answered correctly and incorrectly. The new quiz result page is shown in Listing 6.17.

Listing 6.17   The New JNT Quiz Result Page

```
<jsp:useBean id="quiz1" beanName="todaysQuiz"
  type="com.awl.jspbook.ch06.QuizBean"/>
<jsp:setProperty name="quiz1" property="*"/>
<%! int rightCount = 0; %>
<%! int wrongCount = 0; %>
<HTML>
<HEAD><TITLE>Java News Today: Quiz Result</TITLE>
<BODY BGCOLOR="#FFFFFF">
<TABLE BORDER="0" WIDTH="100%">
  <TR>
    <TD BGCOLOR="#0000FF" ALIGN="CENTER" COLSPAN="2">
      <%@include file="global/header.jsp"%>
```

```
      </TD>
    </TR>
    <TR>
      <TD ALIGN="LEFT" WIDTH="20%" BGCOLOR="#000077">
        <%@include file="global/navigation.jsp"%>
      </TD>
      <TD VALIGN="TOP">
        <%-- Content starts here --%>
        <P>
        The question was:
        <jsp:getProperty name="quiz1" property="question"/>
        </P>
        <P>
        You responded
        "<jsp:getProperty name="quiz1" property="guess"/>"
        </P>
        <% if (quiz1.isRight()) { %>
          <% rightCount++; %>
          <P>That's exactly right!</P>
        <% } else { %>
          <% wrongCount++; %>
          <P>
          Sorry, that's wrong. You might want to read more
          on this topic,
          <A HREF="<jsp:getProperty name="quiz1" property="url"/>">
          here</A>.
          </P>
        <% } %>
        <P><%= rightCount %> people have answered this
            question currently, and <%= wrongCount %>
            people have answered incorrectly.</P>
        <%-- End of content area --%>
      </TD>
    </TR>
  </TABLE>
  </BODY>
</HTML>
```

When the authors at Java News Today first wrote this page, they called the
bean quiz instead of quiz1 and were surprised when the JSP Engine generated
an error at translation time—com.sun.jsp.JspException: Duplicate bean
name: quiz. After a little thought, though, they realized that this was because
the result page includes the navigation bar, which includes the quiz. The quiz
also loads the quiz bean and calls it quiz. The JSP Engine cannot guarantee that
it is the same bean being loaded from each useBean tag, so to be on the safe side
it stops processing and reports the error. The lesson here is that, even when
bean names look unique, they may not be. The obvious fix is to use a different
ID for the bean. The less obvious but more powerful fix is to use a request-time

instead of a translation-time include. This solution will be further explored in Chapter 7.

The counters here work almost exactly like the page counter on the index page. The only difference is that there are two separate variables and the increment happens inside the conditional. This is yet another example of how JSP tags can combine to provide lots of flexibility.

Summary

This was a big chapter, and it introduced many new things: declarations and how new variables are created; the conditional statement and how to check values; for and while loops, which can iterate over arbitrarily large amounts of data; and try/catch blocks, which let JSPs catch errors before they reach the user.

The chapter had more Java code than any of the previous ones. This may seem a bit frustrating, since one of the motivations behind JSPs was separating code from HTML and allowing for nonprogrammers to write dynamic pages without needing to program.

The good news is that most of the code can be placed in beans, leaving only a few loops and conditionals to format the page or to present multiple pieces of data. This greatly simplifies the Java that a JSP author needs to know, and 90 percent of the time the logic in a JSP will actually be simpler than what was in these examples.

So far beans have been fairly transient entities, appearing when the useBean tag is called and vanishing as soon as the page is built. The next chapter will look at how to extend a bean's life and allow it to live across multiple pages or tie itself to a particular user. This ability will take beans, which are already extremely useful, to the next level.

CHAPTER 7

Bean Scopes

Chapter 4 talked extensively about beans and what they can do for page authors. Chapter 6 combined beans with scriptlets, making them even more powerful. As useful as beans are, so far they have had one major limitation, which is that they were available only on the page from which they were created. This does not prevent the same bean from being used on multiple pages, nor does it prevent values stored in serialized beans from being available whenever the bean is obtained. However, it does make it impossible to use beans to build a page counter, such as the one from Chapter 6, or for one page to change a property and have that change show up on some other page.

This chapter will show how to extend the range and lifespan of a bean or variable, permitting a wide variety of new dynamic behavior.

Local and Instance Scopes

Chapter 6 made use of two kinds of scope. Variables created with the declaration tag have a *instance* scope, meaning that they are associated within an instance of the servlet built by the JSP Engine. That is, these variables are the same every time the servlet runs. Variables created in scriptlet tags have a *local* scope, meaning that they are recreated each time scriptlet is executed.

Class variables are useful whenever some data needs to be shared across all occasions a page is used and especially when the data is likely to change. We have already seen how this scope makes it very easy to build counters, but there are also more complex uses for it, such as message boards.

Message boards allow users to add their comments to a page and read all the comments others have left. They are a very popular feature on the Web, since they let users participate in the site and thus build a sense of community. A site might have many such boards, each associated with a different page. This might be implemented in the JSP by giving each page a declared variable containing some sort of MessageBoard object. Because these objects will have instance scope, any messages one user adds to it will be available to the next user.

Java News Today wants to use message boards on their site, and there is an easy way to build them using beans. The JNT board pages will be presented later in this chapter.

On the opposite end of the spectrum from class variables are local variables, which are recreated for every page request. This is useful when data should be kept private—obvious examples include credit card numbers or other personal information. Variables used in loops, such as integers used in for loops or enumerations, should also be kept local to eliminate the possibility of two or more users who are going through the same loop at the same time interfering with each other.

Class and local variables and their corresponding scopes are an intrinsic part of the Java language. The JSP standard defines four other scopes that objects or beans can occupy.

The Page Scope

The page scope is the simplest of the JSP scopes. Any object whose scope is the page will disappear as soon as the current page finishes generating. As far as behavior is concerned, this is equivalent to local scope but it is implemented differently. An object with page scope may be modified as often as desired within the page, but all these changes will be lost when the page exits. Thus, if a serialized bean is loaded into the page scope and then several of its properties are altered, the next person to access the page will still see the original values.

The terminology used here is a little counterintuitive. It might seem that a page is always the same no matter how many times it is accessed and thus anything in "page scope" should remain available for every request. In other words, it might seem that something called "page scope" should behave like "instance scope." This notion of what constitutes a page is a holdover from static HTML files, where the same URL always gives the same page. With JSPs, whenever a URL is accessed an entirely new page is generated at request time and sent to the user. This concept of a page, as something generated each time, gives the page scope its name.

By default, all beans have a page scope. If a page author wishes to make this explicit, `scope="page"` can be added to the `jsp:useBean` tag, as in

```
<jsp:useBean id="id" class="beanclass" scope="page"/>
```

The Request Scope

The second kind of scope is associated with the request object, as discussed in Chapter 3. Any objects created in the request scope will be available as long as the request object is.

This may seem no different from the page scope, since presumably the request object lasts exactly as long as the page it requested. However, there are a couple of mechanisms by which requests can be separated from pages.

Consider a JSP as an assembly line that starts with a request at one end and produces HTML at the other. Now imagine the web server or Tomcat as a big factory with lots of such assembly lines. Normally the web server will put the request on the right line in response to a user's request for a page. However, there is no reason that one of the workers on one assembly line cannot pass his request to someone on a different assembly line. At the end of the second assembly line either the resulting HTML can be sent to the user or the HTML and the original request can be passed back to the original worker, who then continues the request processing.

The JSP specification supports both these models. The first, where the original JSP does not get the request back, is called a JSP *forward*, and it works much like forwarding a phone call. There may be many reasons why one JSP would want to forward its request to another, such as security. If a user tries to access a page she is not authorized for, the page may wish to send her to another page that explains why she has been denied and perhaps gives her the option to join some premium service. This might look like the following code fragment:

```
...
<% if user.isNotAuthorized() { %>
    <jsp:forward page="register.jsp">
<% } else { %>
... show the user the page ...
<% } %>
```

This is not absolutely necessary, since whatever is on the register page could be included on this one, between the if and the else. It is likely that there would be many such protected pages, in which case having to replicate the entire register page would soon become a maintenance burden. The register page could also be included with the include directive, but forwarding the request is a better model for what is happening here.

It would also be possible for a protected JSP to issue a *redirect* to the register page. Using a redirect, the web server would tell the browser that the information it wants is really at some other URL, which the browser would then ask the server for.

Redirects have two problems. The first is that they are slower than includes because more communication has to go back and forth between the browser and server. The second is that a redirect restricts the kind of information that the first page can send to the second. The second page will not know that the user is going there because of a redirect, what the URL of the first page was, or anything else. There are some ways around this problem that involve passing lots of information around in the query string, but this is ugly and problematic for other reasons.

Using a forward, however, any kind of information can be passed from the first page to the second. Since the only thing the two pages have in common is the request object, it makes sense to tie the data being transferred to the request, and this is exactly what the request scope is for. The first page can place any information into the request scope, and the second page can look for that information and act on it.

One way to put data into the request scope is to do it manually, in a scriptlet. The request class has two methods that support this. The first is called setAttribute(), and it allows a JSP to add a new attribute representing the data to the request. The second is called getAttribute(), and it allows a JSP to retrieve a value from the request scope.

Listing 7.1 shows a simple form that allows the user to select a destination page as well as provide some additional information. This form will call a JSP that will use the forward tag to send the request to the appropriate page.

Listing 7.1   A Form That Requests One of Three Pages from a JSP

```
<HTML>
<BODY>
<P>Which page would you like?</P>
<FORM ACTION="dispatcher.jsp">
<INPUT TYPE="radio" NAME="which" VALUE="red" CHECKED>red<BR>
<INPUT TYPE="radio" NAME="which" VALUE="green">green<BR>
<INPUT TYPE="radio" NAME="which" VALUE="blue">blue<BR>
What is your favorite number?
<INPUT TYPE="TEXT" NAME="favorite"><BR>
<INPUT TYPE="SUBMIT" NAME="Go" VALUE="Go">
</FORM>
</BODY>
</HTML>
```

Listing 7.2 shows the JSP. It stores the user's favorite number in the page scope using a scriptlet that saves the value directly in the request object. It then looks at the request page and forwards the request to it.

Listing 7.2   A JSP That Uses the Forward Tag and the Request Scope

```
<%-- Put the favorite number in the request scope,
        by placing it in the 'favorite' attribute
        of the request --%>
<% request.setAttribute("favorite",
                    request.getParameter("favorite")); %>
<%-- now dispatch to the user's requested page --%>
<% String which = request.getParameter("which"); %>
<% if (which.equals("red")) { %>
    <jsp:forward page="/ch06/red.jsp"/>
<% } else if (which.equals("green")) { %>
    <jsp:forward page="/ch06/green.jsp"/>
<% } else if (which.equals("blue")) { %>
    <jsp:forward page="/ch06/blue.jsp"/>
<% } %>
<HTML>
<BODY>
You asked for a page which does not exist!
</BODY>
</HTML>
```

If the requested page matches any of the pages that this JSP knows about, the user will see the results of that page exactly as if he had gone there directly. If the user requests some unknown page, he will see the HTML included in this JSP. If all goes well, the forward tag will never return to this page, and so under normal circumstances the user will not see the error message.

Finally, Listing 7.3 shows the red page. As expected, this JSP gets the number from the request using the `getAttribute()` method. It also uses another method of the request object, `getAttributeNames()`, to show all of the currently available attributes. In most cases this will contain only the favorite number, but it is possible that some implementations will automatically add other attributes. Compare this with the `getHeaderNames()` method, as shown in Listing 4.10. *Green.jsp* and *blue.jsp* are pretty much the same thing, so they will not be presented here, although they are on the CD-ROM.

Listing 7.3   A JSP That Pulls Data from the Request Scope

```
<HTML>
<BODY BGCOLOR="#FF0000">
<H1>Welcome to the red page</H1>
```

```
Your favorite number is
<%= request.getAttribute("favorite") %>
Here is the full list of attributes:
<TABLE BORDER="1">
  <TR><TH>Name</TH><TH>Value</TH></TR>
  <% java.util.Enumeration e = request.getAttributeNames(); %>
  <% while(e.hasMoreElements()) { %>
    <% String name = (String) e.nextElement(); %>
    <TR>
      <TD><%= name %></TD>
      <TD><%= request.getAttribute(name) %></TD>
    </TR>
  <% } %>
</TABLE>
</BODY>
</HTML>
```

If for some reason *red.jsp* had forwarded this request to another page, the favorite number would still have been available. In general, any number of pages can play "hot potato" with a request and pass it around; however, if a page tries to forward a request to itself, the JSP Engine may go into an infinite loop and get stuck.

It is always possible to put variables directly into the request object, as Listing 7.2 does, although it takes some extra programming to do so. Just as beans were able to simplify JSPs in previous chapters, they can make JSPs that use the request scope much simpler as well. In fact, all that is needed to place a bean in the request scope is a change of scope="page" in the useBean tag, to scope="request". Listing 7.4 shows a rewritten version of the page dispatcher that uses beans.

Listing 7.4   A Bean in the Request Scope

```
<jsp:useBean id="which"
             class="com.awl.jspbook.ch07.WhichPageBean"
             scope="request"/>
<jsp:setProperty name="which" property="*"/>
<% if (which.getWhich().equals("red")) { %>
  <jsp:forward page="/ch06/red1.jsp"/>
<% } else if (which.getWhich().equals("green")) { %>
  <jsp:forward page="/ch06/green1.jsp"/>
<% } else if (which.getWhich().equals("blue")) { %>
  <jsp:forward page="/ch06/blue1.jsp"/>
<% } %>
<HTML>
<BODY>
You asked for a page which does not exist!
</BODY>
</HTML>
```

The bean version can get the form variables automatically, just as before. In addition, the whole bean, form values and all, is placed in the session scope. This means that the JSP that receives the forwarded request will be able to access the same bean and get modified properties from it, as illustrated in Listing 7.5.

Listing 7.5 Retrieving Data from the Request Scope with a Bean

```
<jsp:useBean id="which"
             class="com.awl.jspbook.ch07.WhichPageBean"
             scope="request"/>
<HTML>
<BODY BGCOLOR="#00FF00">
<H1>Welcome to the green page</H1>
Your favorite number is
<jsp:getProperty name="which" property="favorite"/>
</BODY>
</HTML>
```

Obviously, the bean version is much cleaner, and whenever possible beans should be used instead of the request methods being called directly. However, it never hurts to be able to store things in the request manually if needed.

Includes Revisited

When we compared JSPs to assembly lines, we mentioned that there were two things that could happen to a request after one line had passed it off to another. The second line could send the resulting HTML to the user and close the request, which is what the forward tag does. Alternately, the second line could return the request to the first. This is what the jsp:include tag does.

Chapter 3 spent a good deal of time discussing the include directive, which tells the JSP Engine to include some additional text as it builds the servlet. We noted that, because this happens at translation time, the resulting servlet has no way to determine if the included file has changed.

The include tag, as opposed to the include directive, is a request-time include. Request-time includes are in many ways better than the translation-time version. Their primary advantage is that they allow JSP authors to treat every file as a stand-alone page without worrying about whether one page will be included in another. Recall that in Listing 6.17 a bean name had to be changed because the same name was being used by both the Java News Today navigation bar and the quiz result page. This happened because a translation-time include is equivalent to copying the entire included file into the main one, which caused the JSP Engine to see two useBean tags for the same bean.

This would not have been the case had the include tag been used, because the include tag works by including the output from one page in another page, instead of including the source text.

The other advantage of request-time includes is that they ensure that changes to an included file will become available immediately. When the JSP Engine notices that a *.jsp* file has changed, it rebuilds the servlet. However, if a file included from a *.jsp* file changes, the JSP Engine does not rebuild the servlet because it has no way to know that it needs rebuilding. This means that when Java News Today updates its navigation bar, all the servlets that depend on the navigation must be forcibly rebuilt. The easiest way to do this is to shut down Tomcat and rebuild it, but that means that the whole site will be unavailable for a few moments. Using the include tag, the servlet for *navigation.jsp* will be rebuilt when the navigation changes, and all included requests will immediately start using the new version. This makes site maintenance much easier.

Listing 7.6 shows the new version of the JNT home page, now using request-time includes. As this example shows, the jsp:include tag takes two attributes, the page to include and a parameter called "flush." In current implementations flush must be set to true, which indicates that the page that has been built up to that point should be sent to the user before the included page starts processing.

Listing 7.6   The JNT Home Page, Using the Include Tag

```
<%! int count = 0; %>
<HTML>
<HEAD><TITLE>Java News Today!</TITLE>
<BODY BGCOLOR="#FFFFFF">
<TABLE BORDER="0" WIDTH="100%">
  <TR>
    <TD BGCOLOR="#0000FF" ALIGN="CENTER" COLSPAN="2">
      <jsp:include page="/ch06/global/header.jsp"
        flush="true"/>
    </TD>
  </TR>
  <TR>
    <TD ALIGN="LEFT" WIDTH="20%" BGCOLOR="#000077">
      <jsp:include page="/ch06/global/navigation.jsp"
        flush="true"/>
    </TD>
    <TD>
      <FONT SIZE="-1">
      <P>This page has had <%= count %> visitors</P>
      </FONT>
      <!-- Content goes here -->
    </TD>
```

```
    </TR>
   </TABLE>
  </BODY>
</HTML>
```

The *header.jsp* file does not need to change at all, since it does not care how it is being included. The navigation does not need to change either, but since includes tags are better than the include directive, it makes sense to change the way the quiz is included as well.

The request object for this page is now going on quite a tour. It starts with the index page, is passed to the header, then to the navigation, and then to the quiz. This order is significant because it dictates which of these components can communicate through the request scope. If the index page sets some attribute of the request at the top of the file, all the included files will have access to it. Likewise, if the header sets or changes an attribute, that change will be visible to the navigation since it receives the request after the header does.

This mechanism enables the navigation to adjust itself based on what file is including it. It could be implemented by having each page set an attribute in the request indicating which page it is, and then having the navigation check the value of this attribute to decide which page contains it. There is an interesting fact about the request that makes this a little easier. One of the methods in the request object returns the URI requested. When one JSP includes or forwards to another, this method continues to return the URI of the original page, which is all the information the navigation bar needs. Listing 7.7 shows the new *navigation.jsp* that alters itself to reflect the current page. Specifically, it changes the section symbol next to the current page to a right angle bracket.

Listing 7.7   A Self-Modifying Version of Navigation

```
<% String indexTag      = "&sect;"; %>
<% String industryTag   = "&sect;"; %>
<% String enterpriseTag = "&sect;"; %>
<% String standardTag   = "&sect;"; %>
<% String microTag      = "&sect;"; %>
<% String beanTag       = "&sect;"; %>
<% String editorialTag  = "&sect;"; %>
<% if (request.getRequestURI().indexOf("index") != -1)
     indexTag = "&raquo;"; %>
<% if (request.getRequestURI().indexOf("industry") != -1)
     industryTag = "&raquo;"; %>
<% if (request.getRequestURI().indexOf("enterprise") != -1)
     enterpriseTag = "&raquo;"; %>
<% if (request.getRequestURI().indexOf("standard") != -1)
     standardTag = "&raquo;"; %>
```

```
<% if (request.getRequestURI().indexOf("micro") != -1)
    microTag = "&raquo;"; %>
<% if (request.getRequestURI().indexOf("bean") != -1)
    beanTag = "&raquo;"; %>
<% if (request.getRequestURI().indexOf("editorial") != -1)
    editorialTag = "&raquo;"; %>
<%-- Begin Navigation --%>
<FONT COLOR="FFFFFF">
<FONT COLOR="#FF0000"><%= indexTag %></FONT>
Home Page<BR>
<FONT COLOR="#FF0000"><%= industryTag %></FONT>
Industry news<BR>
<FONT COLOR="#FF0000"><%= enterpriseTag %></FONT>
Enterprise Java<BR>
<FONT COLOR="#FF0000"><%= standardTag %></FONT>
Standard Edition Java<BR>
<FONT COLOR="#FF0000"><%= microTag %></FONT>
Micro edition &amp; devices<BR>
<FONT COLOR="#FF0000"><%= beanTag %></FONT>
Beans<BR>
<FONT COLOR="#FF0000"><%= editorialTag %></FONT>
Editorials<BR>
<HR>
Today's quiz:<BR>
<jsp:include page="/ch06/global/quiz.jsp"
 flush="true"/>
<%-- End Navigation --%>
```

At the top this JSP sets all the "position indicators" to the section symbol. Note that it does this though a number of local variables. A bean could have been used here, but it would not have made the code significantly simpler. The JSP will alter one of these variables based on the URI and display each tag through an expression next to the appropriate section name.

The Session Scope

So far, all the scopes associate data with pages, which is certainly useful. Since users, not pages, are really the focus of the site, there should be some way to tie data to a particular user so that whatever page he visits, the data will be available and adjustable. An obvious example of this is a shopping cart. Multiple users can see the same "checkout" page of a shopping site, but each user will see his own selections. Likewise, many users may view a particular item, but when one elects to buy it, the item goes into his shopping cart and no one else's.

In JSP terms, data associated with a user is in the *session scope*. A session does not correspond directly to a user; rather, it corresponds with a particular period of time the user spends at a site. Typically this period is defined as all visits a user makes to a site between starting and exiting her browser, but various JSP implementations may define it somewhat differently. A possible alternate definition could end the session if the user takes more than an hour between visiting pages on the site.

Data from a session can be made more permanent so that every time a user visits a site the data will be available. This can be useful for storing users' preferences or customization settings, a key part of many modern sites. This will be discussed in more detail in Chapter 11.

Using the Session Scope Manually

As with the request scope, it is possible to enter and access data from the session scope either manually using scriptlets or automatically using beans. We will first look at the manual process.

The heart of the session scope is the `javax.servlet.http.HttpSession` class, which provides the methods for storing, listing, accessing, and changing session data. Properties in a session work much like headers and attributes in the request object. There are methods to put a named piece of data into a session, to get the data out by name, and to get an enumeration of names.

A JSP can get the current session object through the request object. The session is not technically part of the request, but the request has access to all the necessary system information to find and return it. Listing 7.8 shows the session scope in use. It keeps track of two counters—the first is at the class level and counts the total number of times the page has been accessed (the same as the counters in Chapter 6); the second is associated with the session and counts the number of times the current user has accessed the page.

Listing 7.8   A Counter in the Session Scope

```
<%! int count = 0; %>
<HTML>
<BODY>
<P>
This page has been accessed <%= count %> times.
</P>
<% HttpSession theSession = request.getSession(true); %>
<% Integer scount =
   (Integer) theSession.getValue("scount"); %>
<% if (scount == null) { %>
<P>
This is your first visit to this page!
```

```
</P>
<% theSession.putValue("scount",new Integer(1)); %>
<% } else { %>
<P>
You have accessed this page
<%= scount %> times.
</P>
<% theSession.putValue("scount",
        new Integer(scount.intValue() + 1)); %>
<% } %>
<% count++; %>
</BODY>
</HTML>
```

This JSP gets the session object from the request object and looks in it for an integer named scount. If this integer is null, scount was not found, so the user must be new. In that case the program sends a welcoming message and the bean's counter is set to zero and placed in the session. If scount was found, the JSP sends its value and increments it. Simultaneously, the JSP keeps track of the total number of visits in the count variable.

This page is best demonstrated by having two or more people sit at separate computers, load the page, and then repeatedly hit their browsers' reload button. Each person will see the same total number for count but a different value for his own scount. If either closes down his browser and starts it up again, his scount will start over again at 0.

Using the Session Scope Automatically

If Listing 7.8 seems unnecessarily complicated, that is only because it is. Once again, the use of beans can simplify matters and remove most of the programming involved in using the session scope. As might be expected, this is done by just adding scope="session" to the useBean tag.

There is another option to the useBean tag that we have not covered yet. In all the examples until now this tag has ended with a trailing slash and has had no corresponding </jsp:useBean> tag. If there is a closing tag, anything between the open and close tags will be executed only when the bean is first created. This is not very useful in the page or request scopes, because the bean usually is recreated every time a user visits the page. In the session scope, however, this option can be used to print some welcoming message or to set up the bean.

All the standard JSP tags are valid between <jsp:useBean> and </jsp:useBean>, including setProperty, getProperty, scriptlets, and so on. Arbitrary HTML can also be used.

Listing 7.9 shows a version of the counter program from Listing 6.3, rewritten to use a bean. Note the use of the text inside the useBean tag.

Listing 7.9   A Bean in the Session Scope

```
<%! int count = 1; %>
<jsp:useBean id="scounter"
 class="com.awl.jspbook.ch07.Counter"
 scope="session">
<P>
This is your first visit to this page!
</P>
<jsp:setProperty name="scounter" property="count" value="0"/>
</jsp:useBean>
<HTML>
<BODY>
<P>
This page has been accessed <%= count %> times.
</P>
<P>
You have accessed this page
<jsp:getProperty name="scounter" property="count"/>
times.
</P>
<% count++; %>
</BODY>
</HTML>
```

When a user first visits this page, a new scounter bean is created for her. When this happens the This is your first visit message will be included on the page and the bean's counter will be set to 1. On subsequent visits, this will not happen.

Incidentally, there is no need to tell this bean to increment its counter after each visit, because that functionality has been built into the bean's getCount method. This is just one more example of how beans can make life easier.

A More Complex Session Example

The session scope enables a wide variety of user-driven applications. Single-user games are a prime example, since they typically involve maintaining some sort of game state that will be different for each user playing at any given time. A solitaire game might need to keep track of the state of the deck and each stack, but it will need to track a different deck for each user.

Listing 7.10 shows a JSP implementation of the classic Hangman game, where a user guesses letters in a word. The user will lose a turn for every letter

he guesses that is not in the word, and when he is out of turns the game is over.
This version adds a new feature, where the user can ask for up to two clues
about the word, although asking for a clue counts as a turn.

This is by far the most complex example in this book yet, but it is still fairly
straightforward. This is because all the hard work of keeping track of the game
is in the bean and all the hard work of keeping track of the session is handled
automatically.

Listing 7.10   The Hangman Game, Using Beans in the Session Scope

```
<HTML>
<HEAD><TITLE>Hangman</TITLE></HEAD>
<BODY>
<jsp:useBean id="game"
 class="com.awl.jspbook.ch07.HangmanBean"
 scope="session">
  <%-- this is done when the bean is first created --%>
  <P>Welcome to hangman, JSP edition!</P>
  <P>
  At each turn, you may either guess a letter
  or ask for a clue.  Getting a clue or guessing
  a letter that is not in the word costs you
  one turn.  Good luck!
  </P>
  <jsp:setProperty name="game"
   property="word"
   value="disintegration"/>
  <% String tmp ="One of the kids on South Park once " +
      "called this 'The greatest album ever.'"; %>
  <jsp:setProperty name="game"
   property="clue1"
   value="<%= tmp %>"/>
  <jsp:setProperty
   name="game"
   property="clue2"
   value="The Cure's 1989 release."/>
  <jsp:setProperty
   name="game"
   property="numGuessesLeft"
   value="7"/>
</jsp:useBean>
<%-- everything else is outside the useBean tag,
     so it will happen for every request --%>
<%-- Load the form variables --%>
<jsp:setProperty name="game" property="*"/>
<% if(game.hasLost()) { %>
    <%-- Do this if the user has lost --%>
    <P>
    Sorry, you're out of turns!  The word was
    "<jsp:getProperty name="game" property="word"/>"
```

```
          </P>
          <P>
          Better luck next time!
          </P>
<% } else if(game.hasWon()) { %>
          <%-- Do this if the user has won --%>
          <P>
          You've won!  You guessed the word
          <jsp:getProperty name="game" property="word"/>
          with
          <jsp:getProperty name="game" property="numGuessesLeft"/>
          guesses left!
          </P>
<% } else { %>
          <%-- The JSP comes here if the game
            has neither been won nor lost --%>
          <P>
          Word so far:
          <jsp:getProperty name="game" property="wordSoFar"/>
          </P>
          <P>
          Letters used:
          <jsp:getProperty name="game" property="lettersUsed"/>
          </P>
          <P>Clues:</P>
          <UL>
          <% if(game.getNumClues() == 1) { %>
            <LI><jsp:getProperty name="game" property="clue1"/>
          <% } %>
          <% if(game.getNumClues() == 2) { %>
            <LI><jsp:getProperty name="game" property="clue1"/>
            <LI><jsp:getProperty name="game" property="clue2"/>
          <% } %>
          </UL>
          <FORM ACTION="hangman.jsp" METHOD="POST">
            <P>
            What would you like to do:<BR>
            <INPUT TYPE="radio" NAME="type" VALUE="guess">
            Guess the letter:
            <INPUT TYPE="TEXT" NAME="guess" SIZE="1"><BR>
            <INPUT TYPE="radio" NAME="type" VALUE="clue">
            Get a clue
            </P>
            <INPUT TYPE="SUBMIT" NAME="Ok" VALUE="Ok">
          </FORM>
          <P>
          You have
          <jsp:getProperty name="game" property="numGuessesLeft"/>
          guesses remaining.
<% } %>
</BODY>
</HTML>
```

The first time the bean is created, the instructions are sent and the bean is initialized with the word, the clues, and the number of guesses remaining. This information could also have come out of a serialized instance of the bean, but in this case it is better to put it on the page itself.

By the way, the variable tmp that holds the first clue is not really necessary. It is used only because the clue is too long to fit on a single line of this book and there is no way to cut it into two lines and still make it a valid Java expression. In a real site, the clue would have been in the value parameter of the tag.

The bulk of the game is outside the useBean tag. The values the user provided last time, if any, are placed in the bean through the usual form of the setProperty tag. Then a conditional checks if the user has won or lost by asking the bean. If the game is still in progress, the JSP reports on the current status and provides a form. The form points back to the same JSP, and the whole process repeats.

The Application Scope

Although both of the session examples we looked at consisted of single pages, a session can be retained across multiple pages as long as the same bean ID is used. In some sense this makes the session scope "larger" than the page or request scope, which are both shorter-lived and more limited in space. There is one scope that is even bigger than sessions, the *application scope,* which extends across all users and all pages.

The application scope is useful for keeping data that multiple users will see and that appears on multiple pages. Consider again the question of message boards. If all the messages on a given topic are to be contained on one page, then each board can have its own bean in the instance scope of that page. This greatly limits what can be done with boards. Java News Today would like to be able to put a summary of several boards' content on one page while still having each full board on another, but this clearly cannot be done in a class scope, since it will span several pages. It cannot be in the request or page scope because the data will need to persist across multiple requests. It also cannot be put in a session, since more than one user will need access to it. The application scope is the only alternative.

The need to use multiple boards from multiple pages presents some interesting implementation dilemmas. Each board will need to be in the application scope, so we need some way to identify which board is wanted in any given context. The ideal solution would be to use useBean's *id* field and give each bean it's own ID. Unfortunately, the *id* field has to be a constant string; it cannot be a request-time expression, which means that all the IDs would have to be hard-coded into pages, and this may be a limitation.

To get around this problem, the JNT message boards will be implemented as two beans. The first, a single AllBoards bean, will hold all the messages for all the boards in the application scope. The second, BoardProxyBean, will accept an ID as a property and gateway all other property requests to AllBoards, passing it the ID.

For example, imagine the that AllBoards bean contains two boards, called JavaEnterprise and JavaMicro. On a page that reads the JavaEnterprise board, we will create BoardProxyBean and set its property to JavaEnterprise. When we then ask BoardProxyBean for a property such as numMessages, it will in turn ask AllBoards for the number of messages in the JavaEnterprise board. Likewise, when BoardProxyBean is asked for the actual messages, it will get them by asking AllBoards for all messages in the JavaEnterprise board and so on. In this way, BoardProxyBean acts as a *view* into a subset of the data in AllBoards. This is somewhat similar to the way beans talk to databases, which is the topic of Chapter 9, so consider this a preview.

Listing 7.11 shows a form that can be used to jump into any currently active message board or to create a new one. Once a board has been created, the JSP in Listing 7.12 can be used to read it and add new messages.

Listing 7.11   A JSP with a Bean in the Application Scope

```
<jsp:useBean
 id="allBoards"
 class="com.awl.jspbook.ch07.AllBoardsBean"
 scope="application"/>
<%-- If the user requested a new board be created,
     this line will handle the creation.  --%>
<jsp:setProperty name="allBoards" property="*"/>
<HTML>
<HEAD><TITLE>Board chooser</TITLE></HEAD>
<BODY>
<FORM ACTION="readboard.jsp" METHOD="POST">
  <% String boardNames[] = allBoards.getBoardNames(); %>
  <P>Select a board to read:</P>
  <SELECT NAME="boardId">
    <% for (int i=0;i<boardNames.length;i++) { %>
      <OPTION VALUE="<%= boardNames[i] %>"><%= boardNames[i] %>
    <% } %>
  </SELECT>
  <INPUT TYPE="SUBMIT" NAME="Read" VALUE="Read">
</FORM>
<FORM ACTION="chooseboard.jsp" METHOD="POST">
  <P>
```

```
        Or, create a new board named:
        <INPUT TYPE="TEXT" name="newBoardName">
        </P>
        <INPUT TYPE="SUBMIT" NAME="Create" VALUE="Create">
</FORM>
</BODY>
</HTML>
```

Listing 7.12   The Board JSP, Which Uses Two Beans in Different Scopes

```
<jsp:useBean
 id="allBoards"
 class="com.awl.jspbook.ch07.AllBoardsBean"
 scope="application"/>
<jsp:useBean
 id="board"
 class="com.awl.jspbook.ch06.BoardProxyBean"
 scope="page"/>
<%-- This connects the proxy bean to the all boards bean --%>
<jsp:setProperty
 name="board"
 property="allBoards"
 value="<%= allBoards %>"/>
<%-- This sets the board bean to the specific board we're
     interested in --%>
<jsp:setProperty
 name="board"
 property="boardId"/>
<%-- This creates a new message, if requested --%>
<jsp:setProperty name="board" property="*"/>
<HTML>
<HEAD>
  <TITLE>
    Boards:
    <jsp:getProperty name="board" property="boardId"/>
  </TITLE>
</HEAD>
<BODY>
<% while(board.hasMoreMessages()) { %>
  <P>
  From: <jsp:getProperty name="board" property="from"/><BR>
  Subject: <jsp:getProperty name="board" property="subject"/><BR>
  <BLOCKQUOTE>
  <jsp:getProperty name="board" property="text"/>
  </BLOCKQUOTE>
  </P>
  <HR>
<% } %>
<P>Leave a message:</P>
<FORM ACTION="readboard.jsp" METHOD="POST">
```

```
    <INPUT TYPE="HIDDEN" NAME="boardId"
     VALUE="<jsp:getProperty name="board"
             property="boardId"/>">
    <P>
    Your name: <INPUT TYPE="TEXT" NAME="from"><BR>
    Subject: <INPUT TYPE="TEXT" NAME="subject"><BR>
    Text: <TEXTAREA NAME="text"></TEXTAREA>
    </P>
    <INPUT TYPE="SUBMIT" NAME="Submit" VALUE="Submit">
</FORM>
</BODY>
</HTML>
```

This first page accesses AllBoards, creates BoardProxyBean, and then sets the id property to connect the two. From then on, all calls to board access the specific data related to id within BoardProxyBean. Note that this is separate from setting all the properties from the form, even though id is one of these properties. This is because id must be set first so that all subsequent operations will operate on the correct data. When setting multiple properties with the setProperty tag, there is no guarantee regarding the order they will be set in. If the text, subject, and from properties were set before id, they would have nowhere to go.

The rest of this JSP is pretty standard by now. A while loop goes through all the messages in the bean and displays them, and then a form allows a new message to be entered by calling back to the same JSP. When this is done, the appropriate properties will be set and the bean will add the message. The only element worth noticing here is the use of the hidden field, which causes the JSP to send the ID back to itself. This is a common trick to carry data across pages when there is no bean in a scope that extends across the pages in question.

Java News Today

It is possible to construct nearly arbitrary kinds of message boards from the basic recipe in Listing 7.12. All that is needed is some way of identifying which board to display. Listing 7.12 took that information as a form variable, but Java News Today will get it from an ID associated with each story they publish. This will allow them to create one board per story.

Unfortunately, the ability to enter content will have to wait until Chapter 10, but in the meantime JNT can use some of the information on scopes from this chapter to further build their site.

One obvious thing they can do is move UserInfoBean, introduced in the last chapter, into a session scope. This will make the site much faster, since now this bean doesn't need to be recreated every time it is used, which is every page. The change to the text is minor so it will not be included here, but the implications are vast, as will be seen in Chapter 11 when we discuss personalization.

The other change JNT can make is a further enhancement to the daily quiz. Finally, after planning this since Chapter 3, they are ready to keep a running tally of users with the most correct answers. The problem up to now has been where to store this data. It could have been kept in an instance scope, but remember that the class changes every time the page is altered, so each time they modified the poll all the data would be lost. This data clearly does not belong in the session scope, since multiple users need to see it. Likewise, the page or request scopes are too shortlived to be useful. Here then, is another candidate for the application scope.

Listing 7.13 shows the new version of the quiz results page that uses a new bean called winners to keep track of everyone's score and present it. JNT will also include UserInfoBean on this page, which will supply the users' names.

Listing 7.13 The Quiz Result Page, with the Top Ten Players

```
<jsp:useBean
  id="winners"
  type="com.awl.jspbook.ch07.WinnerBean"
  scope="application"/>
<jsp:useBean
  id="user"
  type="com.awl.jspbook.ch06.UserInfoBean"
  scope="session"/>
<jsp:useBean id="quiz1" beanName="todaysQuiz"
  type="com.awl.jspbook.ch06.QuizBean"/>
<jsp:setProperty name="quiz1" property="*"/>
<%! int rightCount = 0; %>
<%! int wrongCount = 0; %>
<HTML>
<HEAD><TITLE>Java News Today: Quiz Result</TITLE>
<BODY BGCOLOR="#FFFFFF">
<TABLE BORDER="0" WIDTH="100%">
  <TR>
    <TD BGCOLOR="#0000FF" ALIGN="CENTER" COLSPAN="2">
      <jsp:include page="/ch06/global/header.jsp" flush="true"/>
    </TD>
  </TR>
  <TR>
    <TD ALIGN="LEFT" WIDTH="20%" BGCOLOR="#000077">
      <jsp:include page="/ch06/global/navigation.jsp"
        flush="true"/>
    </TD>
```

```
<TD VALIGN="TOP">
  <%-- Content starts here --%>
  <P>
  The question was:
  <jsp:getProperty name="quiz1" property="question"/>
  </P>
  <P>
  You responded
  "<jsp:getProperty name="quiz1" property="guess"/>"
  </P>
  <% if (quiz1.isRight()) { %>
    <% rightCount++; %>
    <P>That's exactly right!</P>
    <%-- Add a point to this user's score! --%>
    <jsp:setProperty
     name="winners"
     property="name"
     value="<%= user.getName() =>"/>
  <% } else { %>
    <% wrongCount++; %>
    <P>
    Sorry, that's wrong.  You might want to read more
    on this topic,
  <A HREF="<jsp:getProperty name="quiz1" property="url"/>">
  here</A>.
   </P>
  <% } %>
  <P><%= rightCount %> people have answered this
      question currently, and <%= wrongCount %>
      people have answered incorrectly.</P>
  <%-- Show the top 10 guessers, and their scores --%>
  <% String names[] = winners.getNames(); %>
  <% int scores[]    = winners.getScores(); %>
  <P>Top ten quizmasters:</P>
  <OL>
  <% for (int i=0;i<10;i++) { %>
    <LI><%= names[i] %> (<%= scores[i] right %>)
  <% } %>
  </OL>
  <%-- End of content area --%>
    </TD>
  </TR>
</TABLE>
</BODY>
</HTML>
```

This is not substantially different from the last version; there are just a few additions. When the user guesses correctly, the winner bean is given his name, and at the bottom the winner bean generates a top-ten list.

Summary

The five scopes that JSPs provide give a rich set of methods of organizing data. Briefly, they are the following:

- *Class:* for data that should always be available from a given page. There is one class scope for each unique JSP, and it will last until the JSP is changed.

- *Page:* for data that should be available only within the current JSP. There is one page scope for each request, and it will last until the request completes or is handed off to another JSP.

- *Request:* for data associated with the request even if the request is forwarded or another JSP is included. There is one request scope per request, and it will last until a complete page has been delivered to the user.

- *Session:* for data connected to a particular user during a particular visit. There is one session scope for each user, and each will last until the corresponding user leaves the site.

- *Application:* for data that may be needed on any page at any time. There is exactly one application scope, and it lives from the time the JSP Engine starts up to the time it shuts down.

In any given situation, it will usually be obvious which scope is appropriate. The good thing about this architecture is that if there is ever any need to change a bean's scope it is necessary only to change the tag—neither the page nor the bean code need to be altered.

Now that we have seen all the things that beans can do and the ways in which they can share data between users, pages, or a whole application, it is time to uncover some of the magic. This next chapter will present a programmer's-eye view of beans and will focus on how to write new ones.

CHAPTER 8

Writing Beans

The last few chapters covered a JSP author's view of beans—what they do and the tags that use them, as well as different scopes that can make the same bean available from different pages or to different users. This chapter will go into beans from a programmer's perspective and describe how to create beans and make their properties available to JSPs. The material is not required for an understanding of the rest of the book, so page builders who are new to programming may wish to skip it for the time being.

How Beans Are Implemented

Internally, a bean is just an instance of a Java class, although in common terminology the class itself may also be referred to as a bean. The most basic kind of bean simply exposes a number of properties by following a few simple rules regarding method names. In general, a bean provides two methods for each property: one to *get* the property and one to *set* the property, corresponding directly to the JSP getProperty and setProperty tags. Together, these methods are known as *accessors*. Listing 8.1 shows a very simple bean with two properties.

Listing 8.1 A Simple Bean

```
package com.awl.jspbook.ch08;
public class SimpleBean {
```

```
        private int age;
        private String name;
        public int getAge() {return age;}
        public void setAge(int age) {this.age = age;}
        public String getName() {return name;}
        public void setName(String name) {this.name = name;}
    }
```

In general, for a property named "foo," which is of type type, the GET method returns an element of type and is called getFoo; the SET method accepts an argument of type and is called setFoo. There is no restriction on the type; it may be something simple like an integer or a string, or it may be a class or interface type. The type may also be an array of some other type, in which case the property is referred to as *indexed*. In this case the accessor methods operate on the whole array, and the bean may wish to provide methods to operate on the individual elements, as in Listing 8.2.

Listing 8.2   A Bean with an Array Property

```
package com.awl.jspbook.ch08;
public class ArrayBean {
    private String things[];
    public String[] getThings() {return things;}
    public void setThings(String things[]) {this.things = things;}
    public String getThings(int i) {return things[i];}
    public void setThings(int i, String thing) {
        things[i] = thing;
    }
}
```

If an attempt is made to set or get an element with an index larger than the size of the array, the method will throw an ArrayOutOfBounds exception. This could, and probably should, be made explicit by declaring it in the throws clause of the method signature. In either case, any calling class should be prepared for this exception and catch and recover appropriately.

Technically there is no reason that an element set outside the array could not be trapped and handled by the bean, perhaps by creating a larger array and copying all the existing elements to it. The JavaBean specification states that the only way to change the size of an array is to use the array version of the SET method, passing in a larger array. Programmers can weigh the value of strict adherance to the standards against the need to catch exceptions elsewhere in their programs.

Currently there is no JSP tag that allows an indexed property to be obtained or set, although, of course, a scriptlet can call these methods directly. Although a JSP can get an entire array through a getProperty tag, doing so probably will not be useful. This is because printing an array does not print each element but only a sort of internal representation of the array as a whole. The JSP tags thus are not useful when dealing with indexed properties, and page authors will have to resort to scriptlets. Perhaps a future version of the JSP specification will allow an "index" argument in the getProperty and setProperty tags.

Although it is customary to provide both a SET and a GET method, this is not required. A property that cannot be set is called *read-only,* and one with no GET method is called *write-only.* Read-only properties are fairly common; write-only ones are less so.

Nothing we have said so far places any restrictions on what these accessor methods actually do. The preceding examples simply held their properties in private variables, but any other Java class, including a servlet or JSP, will be able discover and access the properties as long as the naming conventions are adhered to.

Listing 8.3 shows DateBean, which was used in Listing 4.2. We see that this code is more complicated because it uses a formatting class. As mentioned in Chapter 4, getting date fields directly from the Date object has been deprecated. On the other hand, using this code is much simpler than getting the date was in Chapter 4 because the bean hides all the implementation details from the page author.

Listing 8.3   More Complex Accessor Methods

```
package com.awl.jspbook.ch04;
import java.text.*;
import java.util.*;
public class DateBean implements java.io.Serializable {
  SimpleDateFormat sdf;
  public void setFormat(String format) {
    sdf = new SimpleDateFormat(format);
  }
  public String getCurrentTime() {
    return sdf.format(new Date());
  }
}
```

This example has both a read-only and a write-only property, although there is no fundamental reason that a GET method cannot be provided for the format string. However, the SET method for the date will presumably need to change time, which will not be possible until Sun comes out with a "Java 2 Time Traveler Edition."

One thing this example does not have is an explicit constructor. A bean is allowed to provide as many different constructors as the programmer wants, but in this case it must provide one that takes no arguments.

Automatic Conversion

Bean properties can be of any type, yet for the most part JSPs deal with strings. This is certainly true of form parameters, the entities most often passed to beans' SET methods. If a bean's SET method is expecting an integer and is passed a string, a runtime exception will occur. In most common cases this problem is transparently resolved by the setProperty tag, which tries to convert the string to an appropriate type. If the method is expecting an integer, the JSP system calls Integer.parseInt() to obtain an integer value. If this conversion fails, perhaps because the user has entered a string that cannot be turned into an integer, the SET method simply will not be called.

This can be a problem if some later code expects that all the parameters have been set successfully. There are a few ways to handle it. The first and most obvious is for all SET methods to accept strings and do the conversion themselves. However, a more elegant approach is to use some auxiliary boolean values to reflect whether the property has been set. The calculator bean used in Listing 6.14 took this approach, and its code is shown in Listing 8.4.

Listing 8.4   Detecting Data Conversion Errors

```
package com.awl.jspbook.ch06;
public class CalcBean implements java.io.Serializable {
  private int value1;
  private int value2;
  private String valueS1;
  private String valueS2;
  private boolean value1_OK = false;
  private boolean value2_OK = false;
  public void setValue1(String value1) {
    valueS1 = value1;
    try {
      this.value1 = Integer.parseInt(value1);
      value1_OK  = true;
    } catch (NumberFormatException nfe) {}
  }
```

```
public void setValue2(String value2) {
  valueS2 = value2;
  try {
    this.value2 = Integer.parseInt(value2);
    value2_OK   = true;
  } catch (NumberFormatException nfe) {}
}
public int getSum() {
  return value1 + value2;
}
public String getReason() {
  if (value1_OK) {
    if(value2_OK) return "";
    else return """ + valueS2 + "" is not an integer";
  } else {
    if(value2_OK) return """ + valueS1 + "" is not an integer";
    else return "neither value is an integer";
  }
}
public boolean isValid() {
  return value1_OK && value2_OK;
}
}
```

Using this approach, the SET methods take the appropriate type and set the property, and then set the corresponding boolean flag to true. Later processing checks all the flags, enabling the bean to both report whether the data is valid and determine why it failed if not.

How Beans Work

All of the JSP/bean functionality is built on the ability of one Java class to discover and invoke methods on another class at runtime. The mechanism that supports this is called *introspection,* which has been built into Java since version 1.1. Introspection is an extremely powerful capability and one that is missing from many other object-oriented languages. In those languages everything must be known in advance, and once a program is built it may have to be changed significantly to extend it with new functionality.

Introspection is possible because a lot of information about method names and signatures is stored in *.class* files, and there are methods that can access and organize it. An easy way to see the kinds of information that introspection provides is via the *javap* utility included in the JDK. Javap is run from the command line and is invoked with the name of a class. If it is given SimpleBean from Listing 8.1, it will generate the output shown in Listing 8.5.

Listing 8.5   The Output of Javap

```
Compiled from SimpleBean.java
public synchronized class SimpleBean extends java.lang.Object
    /* ACC_SUPER bit set */
{
    public int getAge();
    public void setAge(int);
    public java.lang.String getName();
    public void setName(java.lang.String);
    public SimpleBean();
}
```

Although javap may not use introspection to generate this output, the principle is the same. It is able to pull out the names of all the methods and the type of their arguments and return values. From this a person or program can infer that there is a property called name that is a string and so on.

Introspection also provides a mechanism to create a new instance of an object once its class has been loaded. It constructs this instance by looking for a constructor that takes no arguments. Notice that, although our original code did not contain a constructor, one shows up in Listing 8.4 and, in accordance with the bean requirements, it takes no arguments. That is because all classes, whether used as beans or not, have a default no-argument constructor that provides the minimal functionality to build an instance of the object. If any constructor is provided, whether or not it takes arguments, this default constructor is not placed in the class, which is why beans that need a constructor must provide one without arguments.

The classes related to introspection are all in the java.beans and java.lang.reflect packages, and the whole process starts with the java.beans.Introspector class. The use of these classes is beyond our scope, but we encourage you to read through the JDK documentation to see how all this is accomplished.

Serialization

One of the remarkable features of beans discussed in Chapter 4 is the ability to store a bean instance, perhaps containing some local configuration data, in a file. As mentioned, this requires no special code in the bean; the class simply must implement the java.io.Serializable interface. Listing 8.6 shows a bean with a main() method that allows instances to be created, saved, and loaded. There is no reason that the code that does the saving and loading must be in the main() method of this class, since any class can read or write saved in-

stances of any other class. This is what makes general bean editors, as well as
JSPs, possible.

Listing 8.6 A Bean That Uses Serialization

```
package com.awl.jspbook.ch08;
import java.io.*;
import java.util.*;
import java.text.*;
public class SaveableBean implements Serializable {
  private Date createTime;
  private String message;
  public SaveableBean() {
    setDate(new Date());
  }
  public void setDate(Date createTime) {
    this.createTime = createTime;
  }
  public Date getDate() {return createTime;}
  public void setMessage(String message) {
    this.message = message;
  }
  public String getMessage() {return message;}
  public static void main(String argv[])
    throws Exception
  {
    if (argv[0].equals("-create")) {
      SaveableBean sb = new SaveableBean();
      sb.setMessage(argv[2]);
      ObjectOutputStream out = new ObjectOutputStream(
                              new FileOutputStream(argv[1]));
      out.writeObject(sb);
      out.close();
      System.out.println("Bean created and saved!");
    } else if (argv[0].equals("-load")) {
      ObjectInputStream in = new ObjectInputStream(
                            new FileInputStream(argv[1]));
      SaveableBean sb = (SaveableBean) in.readObject();
      in.close();
      SimpleDateFormat sdf =  new SimpleDateFormat("hh:mm:ss
                              dd/MM/yy");
      System.out.println("This bean was created at: " +
                  sdf.format(sb.getDate()));
      System.out.println("This bean says: " +
                  sb.getMessage());
    }
  }
}
```

The `Serializable` interface does not have any methods; it is enough for a class to declare itself serializable. However, there is one restriction on such classes: All their members must themselves be serializable, as must the members' members, and so on. Most of the classes from the core Java libraries that a bean would contain are serializable, so this is not often a concern.

When a bean does need a nonserializable member, this member can be declared *transient,* and the serialization methods will simply ignore it when saving or loading. This may be desirable even when it is not necessary. For example, if a bean will be used to show the current date, saving its `Date` object in a file may not make sense.

The obvious downside of transient members is that they will be in some uninitialized state, probably null, after the bean loads. The serialization mechanism allows a bean to "know" when it is being unserialized, so that it can put its transient members into some consistent state. To do this it is necessary only for the bean to have a `readObject` method, which might look like Listing 8.7.

Listing 8.7   A Stub readObject Method

```
private void readObject(java.io.ObjectInputStream stream)
    throws java.io.IOException, ClassNotFoundException
{
    stream.defaultReadObject();
    ... initialize transient members here ...
}
```

Likewise, a bean can know when it is being serialized, in case it needs to do some special processing before it is written, by being provided a `writeObject` method. See the page for `java.io.Serializable` in the JDK documentation for more details.

Events

So far beans have been fairly self-contained. When a property is obtained or changed, or when an instance is saved or loaded, the only objects that know about it are the one that performed the action and the bean itself. Frequently it may be desirable for beans to communicate with each other. For example, a JSP might have a bean that is used as a shopping cart and there might be another bean in the system that handles inventory. When a product is placed in the cart, the inventory bean should be told that there is one less of this product available for other shoppers. The JSP could handle this manually, by calling the appropriate methods on both beans, but besides being inconvenient, this would risk programmers forgetting to call the right methods in the right order. Instead, beans have numerous ways to communicate directly with each other.

Beans were originally designed as graphic components, like buttons or menus, and thus were driven by *events,* such as a button click. Some beans would need to *listen* for a set of events and react appropriately. This led to the incorporation of an event-based communication mechanism in the bean specification, which has turned out to be useful for server-side programs as well. The shopping cart might generate, or *fire,* an event when an item is placed in it, and the inventory bean might listen for this event and react by decrementing its supply.

Event programming is almost as easy as property programming, and once again it is mostly expressed as a set of naming conventions. First, it is necessary to define a class to represent the event. Listing 8.8 shows an event that represents an item being placed in a shopping cart.

Listing 8.8   An Event

```
package com.awl.jspbook.ch08;
public class PurchaseEvent extends java.util.EventObject {
   private String itemName;
   public PurchaseEvent(Object source,String itemName)
   {
     super(source);
     this.itemName = itemName;
   }
   public String getItemName() {return itemName;}
}
```

Once the event has been defined, it is necessary to define an interface that will listen for other events of that type, such as the one in Listing 8.9. Listeners are defined as interfaces to enable any class to declare that it will listen for any events.

Listing 8.9   A Listener Interface

```
package com.awl.jspbook.ch08;
public interface PurchaseListener
   extends java.util.EventListener
{
   public void purchaseMade(PurchaseEvent e);
}
```

Listing 8.9 shows only one method, but it is allowable for a listener interface to have an arbitrary number. In a real e-commerce system, the listener might need a second method to handle removal of an item from a shopping cart. This could go in the same `PurchaseListener` interface or in a separate one. In the latter case, the inventory bean would need to implement both interfaces.

Once the event and the listener have been defined, one or more beans can set themselves up as event sources. Two methods accomplish this: one adds a listener and the other removes it. The method names include the type of event, which allows introspection to automatically figure out what kinds of events a bean may generate.

Listing 8.10 shows a shopping cart bean that generates purchase events. The names `addPurchaseListener` and `removePurchaseListener` are enough for the system to figure out that there must be a `PurchaseEvent` class and a `PurchaseListener` interface. This information can be used in a graphic bean builder to hook two or more beans together.

Listing 8.10   A Bean Representing a Shopping Cart

```
package com.awl.jspbook.ch08;
import java.io.*;
import java.util.*;
public class ShoppingCartBean implements Serializable {
  public String items[];
  public int numItems;
  public Vector purchaseListeners;
  public ShoppingCartBean() {
    purchaseListeners = new Vector();
    items           = new String[50];
    numItems        = 0;
  }
  public void setItem(String item) {
    items[numItems++] = item;
    firePurchaseEvent(item);
  }
  private void firePurchaseEvent(String item) {
    PurchaseEvent pe = new PurchaseEvent(this,item);
    Enumeration e = purchaseListeners.elements();
    while(e.hasMoreElements()) {
      ((PurchaseListener) e.nextElement()).purchaseMade(pe);
    }
  }
  public void addPurchaseListener(PurchaseListener p) {
    purchaseListeners.addElement(p);
  }
  public void removePurchaseListener(PurchaseListener p) {
    purchaseListeners.removeElement(p);
  }
}
```

Finally, Listing 8.11 shows the inventory bean, which can handle purchase events. As expected, this class implements the `PurchaseListener` interface and does the obvious thing when a purchase event is received.

Listing 8.11   A Bean Representing an Inventory That Handles Purchase Events

```
package com.awl.jspbook.ch08;
import java.io.*;
import java.util.*;
public class InventoryBean
  implements Serializable,PurchaseListener
{
  private static final Integer ONE = new Integer(1);
  private Hashtable inventory      = new Hashtable();
  public void addInventory(String name) {
    Integer count = (Integer) inventory.get(name);
    if(count == null) {
      inventory.put(name,ONE);
    } else {
      inventory.put(name, new Integer(count.intValue() + 1));
    }
  }
  public void removeInventory(String name)
  {
    Integer count = (Integer) inventory.get(name);
    if(count == null) {
      return;
    } else if(count.equals(ONE)) {
      inventory.remove(name);
    } else {
      inventory.put(name, new Integer(count.intValue() - 1));
    }
  }
  public void purchaseMade(PurchaseEvent pe) {
    removeInventory(pe.getItemName());
  }
}
```

There is still more that needs to be done to hook the shopping cart to the inventory. In particular, the shopping cart will presumably live in one or more session scopes and the inventory will reside in the application scope. Thus, there must be some way for these beans to "discover" each other. And there are numerous other details that remain to be filled in, such as how the inventory should respond if it receives a request for an item that is out of stock.

Special Events

"Special Events" does not refer to the recent Halloween-night concert to launch the Crüxshadows' latest release, although that *was* pretty special. In the bean sense this term refers to a couple of event types that are of particular interest to bean authors working with JSPs.

The first type is PropertyChangeEvent, and a bean may fire one of these any time one of its properties changes to alert other beans to the change. A property that generates PropertyChangeEvent when it is modified is referred to as a *bound*.

A bean can also refuse to set a property to a new value by generating VetoEvent, typically when another object tries to set a property to an unacceptable value. The inventory bean might throw this exception if someone tried to change the number of items it is holding to –1. A property that can generate a VetoEvent is referred to as *constrained*.

These two events are defined in the bean specification. The JSP specification defines an additional event, HttpSessionBindingEvent, which can be used to notify a bean that it has been added to or removed from a session scope. Recall that a session will end if a user does not come back to the site after a certain length of time. When this happens, the session will be deleted to make room in memory for other sessions and any data in it will be lost. However, before the session is killed all data objects connected to it are sent HttpSessionBindingEvent, which gives them a chance to save data to a database or file or to do any other cleanup. Listing 8.12 shows a bean that saves itself when the session shuts down.

Listing 8.12   A Bean That Listens for Session Binding Events

```
package com.awl.jspbook.ch08;
import java.io.*;
import java.util.*;
import javax.servlet.http.*;
public class SessionBean
   implements Serializable, HttpSessionBindingListener
{
  private String fileName;
  private String message;
  public void setFileName(String fileName) {
    this.fileName = fileName;
  }
  public String getFileName() {return fileName;}
  public void setMessage(String message) {
    this.message = message;
  }
```

```
public String getMessage() {return message;}
public void valueBound(HttpSessionBindingEvent b) {
}
public void valueUnbound(HttpSessionBindingEvent b) {
  save();
}
public void save() {
  try {
    ObjectOutputStream out = new ObjectOutputStream(
      new FileOutputStream(fileName));
    out.writeObject(this);
    out.close();
  } catch (Exception e) {}
}
public static void main(String argv[]) {
  SessionBean sb = new SessionBean();
  sb.setFileName(argv[0]);
  sb.setMessage(argv[1]);
  sb.save();
}
}
```

An instance of this bean may be created and saved in a file with its `main()` method. A JSP may then use this serialized bean and change its message property. Some time later, when the session is expired, the bean saves itself, including the current message string, back into the file. Note that there is no guarantee of when this will happen. The JSP Engine may expire the session after some fixed timeout period, or it may do so when it needs more memory or when the web server is shut down.

Bean Errors

The most common drawback to using a bean within a JSP is that introspection tends to mask programmer exceptions, making it difficult to see where the problem lies. If a SET method throws an exception, the JSP Engine will likely print out something cryptic like

```
java.lang.reflect.InvocationTargetException
  at com.sun.jsp.runtime.JspRuntimeLibrary.introspecthelper
  at com.sun.jsp.runtime.JspRuntimeLibrary.introspect
  ... etc ...
```

The easiest way to discover the real problem is to put the bodies of all the SET and GET methods in try/catch blocks and have the catch clause dump the exception to `System.err`. However, although this generates useful debugging information, it leaves the bean in an inconsistent state. There is no hard and fast rule about what to do in such a situation. The SET method could leave the property in its last known state, or it could be reset to some sensible default. Another possibility is to throw the original exception. The user will get an error page, but this might be preferable to getting weird results. Perhaps in a future version of the JSP specification the JSP Engine will listen for VetoEvent, which a method will fire on receiving an exception.

Consider what would happen if a class contained a member of type int, a serialized instance of this class was created, and then the programmer rewrote the class to make the member a string. Even if the deserialization process was able to build something from this, the result would probably not be meaningful. To prevent this problem, all classes and serialized instances have an ID called serialVersionUID. When an object is deserialized the ID of the instance is checked against that of the class; if the two do not match an exception is thrown. The output from the JSP Engine in that case looks something like this:

```
java.io.InvalidClassException: SaveableBean;
Local class not compatible:
stream classdesc serialVersionUID=8221280906864288240
local class serialVersionUID=-8806858158408665433
```

If a field really has changed types, there is not much that can be done about such an error, and the only option is to recreate all the serialized instances with the new class. However, some changes are more benign. For example, adding a new field or method should not affect the ability to load old data, as long as it is acceptable to leave the new fields in an uninitialized state after loading.

In most classes the UID value is not implicit; rather, it is computed on the basis of properties. When the class structure changes, so does this value. However, if old serialized instances must still work with a new class, an explicit form of the ID can be provided to make sure the IDs match. In the above case, it would just be necessary to tell the class to use the same ID as the stream found, which could be done by adding the following line to the class:

```
private static final long
    serialVersionUID=8221280906864288240L;
```

If an ID changed because new members were added to the class, the new version of the bean can be given a readObject method to initialize the new fields after loading.

Summary

Beans are really nothing more than Java classes that adhere to certain naming conventions. They make properties available by providing GET and SET methods, which obtain and modify the property, respectively. Beans may also be serializable, meaning that they can write their data out to disk and restore it later. Finally, they may generate or listen to events, and such events can be used to tie beans together. Of particular interest is the `HttpSessionBindingListener` interface, which a bean can use to be notified when another bean in a session scope is about to be retired.

Anyone who can write a Java class can write beans for use in JSPs. Correspondingly, we can turn almost any Java class into a bean by thinking about what it does in terms of properties and by exporting those properties with appropriately named methods.

Many of the beans in the last few chapters have been used to store data, and they have done so admirably. Nonetheless, beans are not well suited for storing or organizing large quantities of data. That task is better handled by a database, the subject of the next chapter.

CHAPTER 9

Databases

At one level all web sites are about information, or data, which is really the same thing. The stories on a news site are data, as are the items in a catalog. There is also a great deal of data behind the scenes, such as information about each user or the types of data he or she is interested in.

The problem of organizing large amounts of data is not a new one. Many companies had to organize inventory or customer data long before the Web, giving rise to an application called a *database*—a repository of structured information optimized to store and retrieve data quickly. Databases also allow multiple users to access or even change the same data simultaneously without corrupting it.

Here we present a brief overview of database technology, including built-in features of Java that make working with databases easier. We then discuss a low-level approach JavaServer Pages use to access databases, and we move from there to a much simpler approach using beans.

A Quick Introduction to Databases

There are many kinds of databases. The most common type of commercial database is referred to as *relational*.

Relational ndatabases store information in conceptually simple structures called *tables*. A table in a database is something like an HTML table or, for that matter, a table in book. Here, for example, is a table containing some information about a CD collection. The table data is organized into *rows* where each row describes a single CD. The rows have *columns* or *fields*, each of which contains a simple attribute. Each column also has a name, specified in the table header.

Artist	Album Name
Sunshine Blind	Love the Sky to Death
Sunshine Blind	Liquid

A table in a database also has rows containing named columns. The only additional feature is that each column also has a specified type. Most databases handle types that are very familiar to Java developers, such as integers, characters, strings, dates, floats, and so on. Some fields can have a null value, which, much like Java's null, is an indicator that no data is available.

Suppose we wanted to store track information in the CD table. We could simply add fields such as track title and track length to the preceding table, but that would mean that every entry would need to contain the album and artist name as well, which would waste space on the page, or, in the case of a real database, on disk. It would be much more efficient to use two tables, one for tracks and one for CDs. The two could be linked by giving each CD a unique integer ID and referencing that ID to each track. This would lead to the following tables.

Artist	Album Name	ID
Sunshine Blind	Love the Sky to Death	1
Sunshine Blind	Liquid	2

Album ID	Name	Length
1	Chimera	202
1	Neon	267
2	Is There	248
2	Keyeslough	227

Using integers to link tables is very common, especially when mapping what are called *one-to-many* relationships, where one element in a given table may link to many elements in another table. Integers are small and so do not take up much space in the database. Also, because integers are easy to sort and manipulate, looking up information based on an ID is typically very fast. Similarly, since artists usually have many albums, another possible efficiency is to move them into their own tables and use an artist ID to map them to their albums.

There are many, many databases available. A number of business sites use products from Oracle or Sybase, but there are also several high-quality free databases available that are perfectly suitable for small to midsized sites or development and are very attractive to people who cannot afford the large commercial variety. MySQL and PostgreSQL are prime examples. MySQL is available from *http://www.mysql.org*, and PostgreSQL is available from *http://www.postgresql.org*. All the examples in this book use PostgreSQL, although for the most part converting them to another database should not be difficult. More information on PostgreSQL is available on the accompanying CD-ROM.

SQL, a Database Language

For humans and databases to work together, they must speak a common language. Although in principle every database manufacturer could define its own such language, this would cause problems for both users and database vendors. Instead, a standard called *Structured Query Language,* or SQL, has been defined, which all database vendors support, though frequently with some enhancements specific to their products.

Most databases provide a utility program that allows users to interactively enter SQL commands and get results back. PostgreSQL's version is called *psql,* and one such command might be instructions to create a new table by specifying the names and types.

The SQL commands to create the CD and track tables we just saw are shown in Listing 9.1. They define the columns in the tables by giving each one a name and a type. The semicolons here indicate the end of each SQL command, much as they signal the end of a Java statement. This is a common convention, but it is not universal—some SQL interpreters require the word "go" after each command.

Listing 9.1 SQL Commands to Create Tables

```
CREATE TABLE artist (
     artistid int,
     name     text
);
CREATE TABLE cd (
     albumid  int,
     artistid text,
     name     text
);
CREATE TABLE track (
     albumid  int,
     name     text,
     length   int
);
```

SQL has no exact match for Java's String type. Most database implementations support fixed-size arrays of characters, which are described in a CREATE command as something like char(30). Fixed-length arrays are typically very efficient, but if the data being stored is less than the allocated space, the extra will be wasted. If an attempt is made to store too much data for the space allocated, either an error will be reported or the excess will be discarded. The text type has no fixed length and can store arbitrarily long strings, but there may be some internal overhead and the strings may be slower to use. A general rule of thumb is that fixed-size data is good when it is known that all the data will be about the same size or will always be small; text is better otherwise.

Once the tables have been created, data can be stored in them with SQL's INSERT command, as shown in Listing 9.2. These commands build rows in the database by specifying the value for each column in a row.

Listing 9.2 SQL Commands to Put Data into Tables

```
INSERT INTO artist VALUES(1,'Sunshine Blind');
INSERT INTO cd VALUES(1,1,'Liquid');
INSERT INTO cd VALUES(2,1,'Love the Sky to Death');
INSERT INTO track VALUES(1,'Chimera',202);
INSERT INTO track VALUES(1,'Neon',267);
INSERT INTO track VALUES(1,'Release',295);
INSERT INTO track VALUES(2,'Is there',248);
INSERT INTO track VALUES(2,'Keyeslough,',227);
INSERT INTO track VALUES(2,'Crescent and the star',226);
```

Of course, data is only useful if it can be retrieved, and SELECT is the SQL command that does this. SELECT has a number of variations, but the simplest just lists all data from the database. For example, this command lists all tracks for all albums:

```
SELECT * FROM track;
```

The asterisk indicates that all fields should be retrieved. If only the track name and duration are desired, the asterisk is replaced by `name,length`.

Generally, pulling all the rows from a table is not that interesting. The code in the preceding snippet retrieves the tracks from both albums, which is unlikely to be particularly useful. For that reason, a select statement can be modified by a where clause, which imposes one or more conditions that must be true in order for the row to be retrieved. To pull only the names of the tracks on "Liquid," the SQL command is:

```
SELECT name from track WHERE albumid = 1;
```

This obtains the desired data, but to construct this query it is necessary to know the album ID, which can be found in the CD table with this query:

```
SELECT albumid from cd WHERE name='Liquid';
```

This is cumbersome. Fortunately, it is also unnecessary as the two queries can be combined into a single command by selecting from the two tables simultaneously and imposing a condition that connects them. Such a query is called a *join* because it joins two or more tables together. The SQL looks like this:

```
SELECT track.name FROM cd, track
WHERE cd.albumid = track.albumid
AND    cd.name   = 'Liquid';
```

The field to select is specified as the table name, a dot, and the column name. This is necessary because both the CD and the track tables have a *name* field and adding the table name *disambiguates* it. The select is done on both the CD and the track tables, and they are joined by the condition that the `albumid`s must match. An additional requirement on the album name limits the tracks returned to those from that album.

The select statement has many more options, but this is enough to follow the examples throughout the book.

There are also SQL statements to delete and update rows. Delete, like select, takes a where clause and deletes all rows where the condition in the where clause is satisfied. Update also takes a where clause as well as a set of new values. For example, to change one of the track names an SQL statement like this can be used:

```
UPDATE track
SET name='Is there?'
WHERE name='Is there';
```

This will find all rows where the title track is named "Is there" and replace the name with the version containing a question mark.

Database Access from Java

Although it is possible to do many useful things by manually entering SQL commands into an interpreter, the power of a database increases a thousand-fold if its features can be accessed from a programming language. Traditionally a language- and database-specific set of functions called an *Application Programming Interface,* or API, did the job. The API consisted of a set of functions or classes that exposed the basic database functionality. For example a select function could be passed some data structures representing the fields and the where clause; it would return another data structure representing the returned rows.

One of the fundamental goals of Java was to make programming independent of hardware, operating system, and other external aspects of the environment. This approach was extended to databases with the introduction of the *Java DataBase Connectivity,* or JDBC, classes. These classes protect programmers from specific details about the database being used by allowing queries and commands to be written in standard SQL and data to be retrieved through a standard, unified API. More information about JDBC, as well as databases in general, is available in *JDBC™ API Tutorial and Reference, Second Edition: Universal Data Access for the Java™ 2 Platform* by Seth White, Maydene Fisher, R.G.G. Cattell, Graham Hamilton, and Mark Hapner.

The first step in using JDBC is to obtain a JDBC *driver* for the specific database. This is a collection of classes that acts as the intermediary between the JDBC classes and the database itself. There are many kinds of drivers, but it is usually preferable to use one written completely in Java. In any case, before it can be used the driver must be loaded into the program. Some JSP implementations have a property file where drivers can be specified, but it always safe to manually load the driver by explicitly loading its class with a call to `Class.forName()`.

Once a driver has been loaded a connection to a database can be made. Databases in JDBC are specified by URLs, which look something like web page URLs. The one for PostgreSQL is *jdbc:postgresql:* followed by the name of the database. Since all the examples in this book use a database called *jspbook,* the URL is *jdbc:postgresql:jspbook.*

Many drivers for different databases can be loaded and made available at the same time, which allows a JSP or other Java program to use more than one database simultaneously. This is possible because each driver is configured to handle a particular type of database URL.

The connection makes available a `Statement` object, which actually issues queries. Queries come in two basic flavors: those that return results, such as the select statement, and those that change the state of the database, such as create, insert, and delete. Corresponding to this are two methods in the `Statement` class: `executeUpdate()`, which returns an integer indicating how many rows were affected, and `executeQuery()`, which returns a `ResultSet` object describing a returned set of rows and columns.

The `ResultSet` class contains methods to iterate through the rows and get the data in each column. However, because Java types do not exactly correspond to SQL types, the methods that get column data must specify the type of data expected. For example, to get the track length after doing a select on the track table, a program calls `getInt("length")`. Or it can use `getObject()`, which returns the data as an object that the program can then cast to an integer or string or other appropriate type. `ResultSet` can also be used to obtain a `ResultSetMetaData` object, which contains information about field names, types, and the like.

Listing 9.3 displays these ideas in action. By default this JSP shows the names of all CDs in the database. When a user clicks on one, its track listing is presented. This example very closely follows the pattern described in the preceding paragraphs. First the driver class is loaded, which happens only the first time the page is requested. After that the Java Virtual Machine will already have the class and subsequent requests to load it will be ignored. The driver is then used to get a connection, and the connection is used to create a statement.

Listing 9.3   A JSP That Uses JDBC

```
<%-- Load the JDBC driver class --%>
<% Class.forName("postgresql.Driver"); %>
<%-- Get a connection --%>
<% java.sql.Connection db =
   java.sql.DriverManager.getConnection (
                         "jdbc:postgresql:jspbook",
                         "dbuser","dbuser"); %>
<%-- Get a statement --%>
<% java.sql.Statement st = db.createStatement(); %>
<%-- Prepare a result set --%>
<% java.sql.ResultSet rs; %>
<HTML>
<HEAD>
  <TITLE>CD info</TITLE>
</HEAD>
<%-- if the user has asked for detail on an album,
     provide it --%>
```

```
<% String albumname = request.getParameter("albumname"); %>
<% String albumid   = request.getParameter("albumid"); %>
<% if(albumname != null) { %>
  <%-- Ensure the input is valid --%>
  <% int aId = 0; %>
  <% try {aId = Integer.parseInt(albumid);}
     catch (NumberFormatException e) { %>
  <P>Your input was invalid</P>
  <% } %>
   <H1>Tracks on "<%= albumname %>"</H1>
   <TABLE BORDER="1">
     <TR><TH>Name</TH><TH>Length</TH></TR>
     <%-- Do the search --%>
     <% rs = st.executeQuery(
         "SELECT name,length from track " +
         "WHERE albumid = " + aId + ";"); %>
     <%-- go through the results --%>
     <% while (rs.next()) { %>
        <TR>
          <TD><%= rs.getString("name") %></TD>
          <TD><%= rs.getInt("length") %></TD>
        </TR>
     <% } %>
   </TABLE>
<% } else { %>
  <%-- No album requested, give a list -- %>
  <H1>Select an album:</H1>
  <UL>
    <%-- Do the search --%>
    <% rs = st.executeQuery("SELECT name,albumid from cd; "); %>
    <%-- go through the results --%>
    <% while (rs.next()) { %>
        <% String name = rs.getString("name"); %>
        <% String name2 = name.replace(' ','+'); %>
        <LI><A HREF="cdinfo.jsp?albumname=<%=
            name2 %>&albumid=<%= rs.getInt("albumid") %>">
            <%= name %></A>
    <% } %>
  </UL>
<% } %>
</BODY>
</HTML>
<%-- Clean up after ourselves --%>
<% rs.close(); %>
<% st.close(); %>
<% db.close(); %>
```

Next the JSP checks to see if details on a specific album have been requested and if so whether the request is a valid integer. This is an important security consideration—without it there is nothing to stop a malicious user from manually specifying a URL such as

```
cdinfo?albumid=1;+delete+*+from+tracks;
```

causing the query sent to the database to be

```
SELECT name,length from track
WHERE albumid = 1; delete * from tracks;
```

In this case, some databases stop processing after the first complete statement, but others proceed to the second, wiping out all data from the table. Generally, it is a bad idea to pass input from users directly to the database. The input should always be verified first.

Assuming that the parameters look valid, a query is constructed to retrieve the track listing. This is submitted to the `Statement`, and a `ResultSet` is returned. A `while` loop then goes through each row and gets the data from each column.

If the user does not request information on an album, a different query is used to obtain a list of all currently available albums. Again the results are returned as `ResultSet` and a while loop goes through them. Each time through the loop a new URL is constructed that calls back to the same JSP, passing the name in the query string. Since some album names may have spaces, a second version of the name is constructed that replaces the spaces with + symbols because a space is not a valid character in a URL.

Although the driver class is loaded only once and so does not present any performance problems, the connection is reopened each time the page generates. This can seriously affect the page speed and is not necessary. Statements and the `ResultSet` class should be in a local scope so that multiple pages do not step over each other requesting data. It would be disastrous if one page made a request and while getting data another page restarted the query or issued a different one.

Multiple pages can share a connection, however; this means that the example can be rewritten so that the connection is in an instance scope or even be in the application scope and shared across all pages. All that is required is a small modification following the `Get a connection` comment. This modification is shown in Listing 9.4.

Listing 9.4 Storing the Connection in the Application Scope

```
<%-- Get a connection from the application scope --%>
<% javax.servlet.ServletContext sc =
    getServletConfig().getServletContext(); %>
```

```
<% java.sql.Connection db =
   (java.sql.Connection) sc.getAttribute("connection"); %>
<% if (db == null)
      db = java.sql.DriverManager.getConnection (url);
   sc.setAttribute("connection",db); %>
```

In a more realistic example there would also be checks in place to ensure that the connection was still valid and to re-establish it if not. In a high-traffic web site a pool of connections might even be created in advance. Each page would request a connection from the pool when needed and release it back into the pool when it was finished. Most application servers provide built-in support for pools.

JDBC and Beans

Yet again Java code is threatening to overwhelm a JSP page, and yet again beans come to our rescue. The key is how much beans and database tables have in common. It is especially easy to think of database columns as bean properties and the various GET methods in the `ResultSet` class as specialized `getProperty` tags.

We can also translate the notion of setting a property into database terms. The obvious corresponding concept is a database UPDATE command, but there is an even more useful equivalent, which Listing 9.3 hints at. In that example data from a form is used to construct a where clause. Since form parameters are also the most common way to set properties, this suggests that it may be useful to make settable bean properties into where clause restrictions. In other words, if properties are going to map to columns, setting a property can be thought of as restricting the possible value of that column, which is exactly what the where clause does.

Tools are available that automatically build a class or bean that reflects a table. One such product from Sun, called Java Blend, can do all manner of sophisticated translations from Java to databases and vice versa. More information is available at *http://www.sun.com/software/javablend/index.html*. A much simpler tool, Table2Bean from Canetoad Software (included on the accompanying CD-ROM), takes an SQL table and builds a bean that supports auto-setting of fields, selects, and updates. See the documentation on the CD for more details.

Listing 9.5 shows a somewhat modified version of the kind of bean Table2Bean generates based on the CD table. As expected, each column maps to a property, which maps to a field in the class. In addition, there are

members that indicate whether the properties have been set. When the
select() method is called it constructs a where clause based on which
properties have been set. The next() method may then be used to walk
through the result set, and the usual property accessors can be used to access
the column data within each row.

Listing 9.5   A Bean That Simplifies Working with the CD Table

```
package com.awl.jspbook.ch09;
import java.sql.*;
import java.net.URLEncoder;
public class CDBean {
  private String name;
  private int artistid;
  private int albumId;
  private boolean nameSet    = false;
  private boolean artistSet   = false;
  private boolean albumIdSet = false;
  private String orderBy     = "";
  private Statement st = null;
  private ResultSet rs;
  /**
   * Sets the orderBy field, which changes the
   * order in which the results are returned
   */
  public void setOrderBy(String orderBy) {
    this.orderBy = orderBy;
  }
  /**
   * Sets the name field, and indicates that it changed
   */
  public void setName(String name) {
    this.name = name;
    nameSet   = true;
  }
  /**
   * Sets the artist field, and indicates that it changed
   */
  public void setArtistId(int artistid) {
    this.artistid = artistid;
    artistSet     = true;
  }
  /**
   * Sets the albumId field, and indicates that it changed
   */
  public void setAlbumId(int albumId) {
    this.albumId = albumId;
    albumIdSet   = true;
  }
  /**
```

```
 * Do a select, based on which fields have been set
 * then reset all the change indicators
 */
public void select() {
  try {
    if (rs != null) rs.close();
    if (st != null) st.close();
    Connection tmp = PersistentConnection.getConnection();
    st = tmp.createStatement();
    String query = "SELECT * FROM cd ";
    String where = buildWhere();

    rs = st.executeQuery(query + where + " " + orderBy);
    albumIdSet = false;
    nameSet    = false;
    artistSet  = false;
  } catch (Exception e) {
    e.printStackTrace(System.err);
  }
}
/**
 * Does an insert, creating a new row from all
 * current values.
 */
public void insert() {
  try {
    if (rs != null) rs.close();
    if (st != null) st.close();
    Connection tmp = PersistentConnection.getConnection();
    st = tmp.createStatement();
    StringBuffer query = new StringBuffer(100);
    query.append("INSERT INTO cd VALUES(");
    query.append(albumId);
    query.append(",");
    query.append(artistid);
    query.append(",\"");
    query.append(name);
    query.append("\")");
    st.executeUpdate(query.toString());
  } catch\ (Exception e) {
    e.printStackTrace(System.err);
  }
}
/**
 * Does an update, changing all fields, using the
 * albumId as primary key
 */
public void update() {
  try {
    if (rs != null) rs.close();
    if (st != null) st.close();
    Connection tmp = PersistentConnection.getConnection();
```

```
            st = tmp.createStatement();
            StringBuffer query = new StringBuffer(100);
            query.append("UPDATE cd ");

            if(nameSet) {
             query.append(" SET name = \"");
             query.append(name);
             query.append("\" ");
            }
            if(artistSet) {
             query.append(" SET artistid = ");
             query.append(artistid);
             query.append(" ");
            }
             query.append("WHERE albumid=");
             query.append(albumId);
             st.executeUpdate(query.toString());
          } catch (Exception e) {
            e.printStackTrace(System.err);
          }
        }
        /**
         * Constructs a where clause from the currently
         * set fields
         */
        private String buildWhere() {
          StringBuffer where   = new StringBuffer(20);
          boolean nonEmpty     = false;
          if(nameSet) {
            where.append("name = \"");
            where.append(name);
            where.append("\" ");
            nonEmpty = true;
          }

          if(artistSet) {
            if(nonEmpty) where.append(" AND");
            where.append(" artistid = ");
            where.append(artistid);
            where.append(" ");
            nonEmpty = true;
          }
          if(albumIdSet) {
            if(nonEmpty) where.append(" AND");
            where.append(" albumId = ");
            where.append(albumId);
            nonEmpty = true;
          }
          String res = where.toString();
          if(nonEmpty) res = " WHERE " + res;
          return res;
        }
```

```
/**
 * Goes to the next row
 */
public boolean next() {
  if(rs == null) return false;
  try {
    return rs.next();
  } catch (Exception e) {
    e.printStackTrace(System.err);
    return false;
  }
}
/**
 * Gets the name field from the current row
 */
public String getName() {
  if(rs == null) return null;
  try {
    return rs.getString("name");
  } catch (Exception e) {
    e.printStackTrace(System.err);
    return null;
  }
}
/**
 * Gets the artist field from the current row
 */
public int getArtistId() {
  if(rs == null) return null;
  try {
    return rs.getInt("artistid");
  } catch(Exception e) {
    e.printStackTrace(System.err);
    return null;
  }
}
/**
 * Gets a URL-encoded version of the name field.
 */
public String getNameURLEncoded() {
  if(rs == null) return null;
  try {
    return URLEncoder.encode(rs.getString("name"));
  } catch (Exception e) {
    e.printStackTrace(System.err);
    return null;
  }
}
/**
 * Gets the albumId field from the current row
 */
public int getAlbumId() {
  if(rs == null) return 0;
```

```
        try {
          return rs.getInt("albumId");
        } catch(Exception e) {
          e.printStackTrace(System.err);
          return 0;
        }
      }
      /**
       * Cleans up by closing all open
       * objects.
       */
      public void cleanup() {
        try {
          if (rs != null) rs.close();
          if (st != null) st.close();
        } catch (Exception e) {
        }
      }
    }
```

After a select is performed, all the flags are reset. If any of the properties are subsequently altered, the update() method can be used to change the corresponding row in the database. Finally, this bean can be used to create new rows in the database with the insert() method.

To perform any of these actions, the bean needs access to a connection, which it gets from a static method in the PersistentConnection class. We will see shortly how this class obtains the connection.

There is an additional property in this bean, orderBy, that is not used in any of the examples. SQL allows a query to specify in what order the results should be returned. For example, to get the album names in reverse order, orderBy can be set to names desc. This will become important when we get to the Java News Today section, since the most recent articles will need to be presented first.

There are two implications of using one bean per table. First, it makes it slightly more difficult to do joins, but these can still be done manually or custom beans can be written for more complex database access. Some databases also support the idea of a *view,* which is a sort of "virtual table" comprising of multiple real tables and some relation between them.

Second, it makes it harder to combine multiple database references on one page, since each bean needs the full set of form parameters. In the CD example, if a form passes a name to a page that accesses both the CD and the track tables, it is unclear which bean should get the name parameter. However, this problem is also not insurmountable, since it is always possible to manually set the properties of interest when the setProperty tag's automatic features are not appropriate.

Listings 9.6 and 9.7 show bean versions of the CD information pages from
Listing 9.3. The previous version included both the CD and the track pages in
one listing, but because it is easier to separate them in the bean model these
have been split up. Listing 9.6 gets the list of available albums, and Listing 9.7
shows the tracks on a selected album.

Listing 9.6   A JSP That Uses a Bean to Get CD Data

```
<%@ include file="dbconnect.jsp" %>
<jsp:useBean id="cd" class="com.awl.jspbook.ch09.CDBean"/>
<% cd.select(); %>
<HTML>
<HEAD><TITLE>CD List</TITLE></HEAD>
<BODY>
<P>Please select a CD for more info:</P>
<UL>
<% while (cd.next()) { %>
    <LI><A HREF="trackinfo3.jsp?albumId=<jsp:getProperty
         name="cd"
         property="albumId"/>&albumName=<jsp:getProperty
         name="cd"
         property="nameURLEncoded"/>">
       <jsp:getProperty name="cd" property="name"/></A>
<% } %>
</UL>
</BODY>
</HTML>
<% cd.cleanup(); %>
```

Listing 9.7   A JSP That Uses a Bean to Get Track Data

```
<%@ include file="dbconnect.jsp" %>
<jsp:useBean id="track" class="com.awl.jspbook.ch09.TrackBean"/>
<jsp:setProperty name="track" property="*"/>
<% track.select(); %>
<HTML>
<HEAD><TITLE>Track List</TITLE></HEAD>
<BODY>
<P>
Tracks on "<%= request.getParameter("albumName") %>"
</P>
<TABLE BORDER="1">
  <TR><TH>Name</TH><TH>Length</TH></TR>
  <% while (track.next()) { %>
    <TR>
     <TD><jsp:getProperty name="track" property="name"/></TD>
     <TD><jsp:getProperty name="track" property="length"/></TD>
    </TR>
  <% } %>
```

```
</TABLE>
</BODY>
</HTML>
<% track.cleanup(); %>
```

These listings are structurally very similar. They both start by including another JSP that handles building the connection. This will be shown shortly. Both then create a bean that interfaces to the table of interest and call its `select()` method, which retrieves the data from the database. Next they each run through a while loop, iterating over all the rows and using bean properties to present the information.

Listing 9.7 sets properties from form parameters before calling `select()`. Although there is no form in Listing 9.6, the values passed in the query string are essentially the same thing. The upshot of this is that `TrackBean`'s `setAlbumId()` method is called, which adds a condition to the where clause when the select is done.

These examples also introduced a new bean that holds the connection in the application scope. Because the connection is always obtained in the same way, and because it is somewhat cumbersome, it has been hidden in *dbconnect.jsp*, which is shown in Listing 9.8. This code retrieves the `PersistentConnection` bean from the application scope; and if the bean has not yet been created, it will be initialized with the database classname and URL. When `PersistentConnection` is created and its properties are set, it creates a connection object and places it in a static member. The other beans can then access this connection through the static `getConnection()` method, as was shown in Listing 9.5.

Listing 9.8 A JSP That Obtains and Initializes the DB Connection

```
<%-- Create the connection, if it does not yet exist --%>
<jsp:useBean
     id="dbConnection"
     class="com.awl.jspbook.ch09.PersistentConnection"
     scope="application">
  <%-- If we are creating this bean now, initialize it --%>
  <jsp:setProperty
      name="dbConnection"
      property="dbClass"
      value="postgresql.Driver"/>
  <jsp:setProperty
      name="dbConnection"
      property="dbUserName"
      value="dbuser"/>
```

```
<jsp:setProperty
      name="dbConnection"
      property="dbPassword"
      value="dbuser"/>
<jsp:setProperty
      name="dbConnection"
      property="url"
      value="jdbc:postgresql:jspbook"/>
</jsp:useBean>
```

Summary

A database is a collection of tables. These tables contain rows of data organized into columns, each of which contains one attribute of the row. SQL is a common language that allows humans to communicate with databases. JDBC frees Java programs from having to know the details of which database they are using, by providing database-independent methods to send SQL to the database and get results back. Similarly, beans can free JSP from worrying about the details of JDBC.

Up to this point Java News Today has been a pretty uninteresting site. However, armed with a knowledge of databases, its developers are ready to actually start building pages with content. How they will do this is the subject of the next chapter.

CHAPTER 10

Java News Today

Finally, after all the preliminaries, tweaks to the header and navigation, and variations of the quiz, Java News Today is ready for some actual content. This was not been possible before now because there was no place to store the content, and it would not have made sense to write a brand new JavaServer Page for each article or to manually modify the index page each time a new story was published. What was needed was a way of programmatically storing and retrieving data so a single JSP could handle any story. Databases, as we saw in the preceding chapter, provide this functionality.

Designing the Tables

The first and most important issue when designing a databases-driven site is to specify the set of tables and their relationships to each other. Tables and their relationships are collectively known as the database *schema*. It is worth thinking about the kinds of data that need to be stored and how they interrelate so that tables can be built correctly the first time. There is nothing worse than getting halfway through building a site and then realizing that the database has some serious deficiency. Some database products make it relatively painless to modify tables, but it is likely that some previously built pages will need to be revisited, which can affect yet other pages and so on.

JNT knows that the primary focus of their site will be the articles, so it makes sense for them to start by considering what the article table will contain.

First and foremost, each article will have the actual text as well as a headline, and each will have a summary, which will be presented on the index and section pages. Each article will also be associated with a particular section and will have a timestamp indicating when it was published. Users might want to search for articles by particular authors, so an author field will also be needed. Finally, an article may be tagged with one or more keywords that describe the broad topics it covers. This will be useful for searches and also for customization, as will be discussed in the next chapter.

At this point a table could be constructed with a text field for each of these elements, but it makes sense to consider first what one-to-many relationships may exist. One approach is to see which of these fields will have additional information associated with them and pull them into separate tables. Sections are one natural candidate, since each section might have a small description. Likewise, each author will have a first and last name, an email address so users can send feedback, and perhaps a short biography. Authors will also have a password, which they will use to log on to the site and enter new stories. This suggests separate author and section tables, with integer IDs to join them to the article table.

Listing 10.1 shows the SQL commands that create these tables. Each column has an ID field that uniquely identifies each element in the table. In PostgreSQL, this is done by creating a `sequence` and tying one of the fields in the table to it, thereby ensuring that the database will automatically assign a new value for the ID to each row inserted. The only time this feature is not desirable is when creating an entry for the index page in the section table. As we will see, the index page needs special treatment in some cases, and to make this easier it helps for its ID to have a known value in advance. Explicitly giving it a value accomplishes this.

Listing 10.1   The Table Definitions for Articles and Related Elements

```
CREATE SEQUENCE articleid_seq;
CREATE SEQUENCE authorid_seq;
CREATE SEQUENCE sectionid_seq;
CREATE TABLE articles (
    articleid      integer
                   default
                   nextval('articleid_seq')
                   primary key,
        sectionid  int,
        authorid   int,
        pubtime    datetime,
        headline   text,
```

```
        summary      text,
        body         text
);
CREATE TABLE authors (
        authorid        integer
                        default
                        nextval('authorid_seq')
                        primary key,
        firstname       char(10),
        lastname        char(10),
        email           char(30),
        password        char(15),
        bio             text
);
CREATE TABLE sections (
        sectionid       integer
                        default
                        nextval('sectionid_seq')
                        primary key,
        name            text,
        description     text
);
```

The section table can be initialized by the SQL code shown in Listing 10.2. The only question left is how the keywords will be represented. Because there may be any number of keywords associated with a story, we will need a separate table joining keywords and articles. Other compelling reasons to make keywords a separate table are to allow the JNT editors to create a defined set of keywords, which will encourage consistency across the articles, and to make it easier for authors to tag their stories, as we will see shortly when we discuss the editing screens. Listing 10.3 shows the table definitions for the keyword and related tables.

Listing 10.2   SQL to Initialize the Sections Table

```
insert into sections values(0,
 'Home Page',
 'Your on-line home for up to the minute Java news');
insert into sections(name,description)
 values('Industry News','Business happenings');
insert into sections(name,description)
 values('Enterprise Java',
 'The latest on the Enterprise Edition APIs and implementations');
insert into sections(name,description)
 values('Standard Edition','What's new in the standard JDK');
insert into sections(name,description)
     values('Micro Edition &amp; devices',
            'Java in the palm of your hand');
```

```
insert into sections(name,description)
    values('Beans','New APIs and product announcements');
insert into sections(name,description)
    values('Editorials','Our staff mouths off');
```

Listing 10.3   The Keyword Table Definitions

```
CREATE SEQUENCE keyid_seq;
CREATE TABLE keywords (
    keywordid      integer
                   default
                   nextval('keyid_seq')
                   primary key,
    keyword        char(10),
    description  text
);
CREATE TABLE articlekeywords (
    articleid      int,
    keywordid      int
);
```

Designing the Beans

Once the tables have been designed, it is possible to consider what pages will be needed, which in turn informs the set of beans that need to be written. For example, there could be a different JSP for each section, or there could be a single section page that customizes itself to the section being viewed. Likewise, there could be a different page for each article or for each article within a given section or for only one article page. It is preferable to reduce the number of pages when possible to reduce the work of building and maintaining them. Thus since all the section pages will be similar it makes sense to combine them, and the same with the article pages. However, it does not make sense to combine section and article pages into one "everything" page, since there will likely be large differences between them that will result in complex nested conditionals.

The next step is to specify what beans will be needed. JNT has decided on a page structure that closely mirrors the table structure. For the most part, therefore, the tables can be converted directly into beans using a tool such as Canetoad's Table2Bean, which will build the beans' SectionBean, ArticleBean, AuthorBean, and KeywordBean. It is also possible to build KeywordBean and ArticleKeywordBean, but as these will always be associated with the articles, it makes more sense to put the relevant methods into ArticleBean. These beans will follow the pattern of Listing 9.5 and so will not be shown here. For the sake of efficiency, JNT will also use PersistentConnection from Chapter 9.

In addition to the database-related beans, several others will be needed. Even at this early stage, it is obvious that the new navigation will need to access the section table in order to present all the available sections. The alternative would be to hard-code the sections into *navigation.jsp*, but that would not be taking full advantage of the database.

The downside of putting a database access in the navigation is the performance overhead. Thus, since this data will not change very often, it makes sense to hold onto, or *cache*, it locally. Caching can be done by modifying SectionBean, but for clarity the JNT programmers have decided to make a separate bean called SectionHolder that will live in the application scope and provide a constructor which will load all the data from the section table. Only one SectionHolder will be constructed because it will be in the application scope, and after that the data will be available to any page that needs it. This means that the web server will need to be shut down in order to force the bean to reread the section data, but since new sections will be added very infrequently this is acceptable.

The section page will need to know what section has been requested, and the article page will need to know what section and article to access. The easiest way to do this is to pass this information in form-like variables in the query string or as post data. To make this information easily accessible to the pages, a pageInfo bean will also be created that can take its values directly from the parameters.

The message boards associated with each article will be provided by AllBoardsBean and BoardProxyBean from Chapter 7. Likewise, QuizBean from Chapter 4 will be used to store the question of the day. In principle there is no reason that both boards and questions cannot be stored in the database as well. However, JNT expects the boards to be pretty active, which means that lots of information will need to be read continually from the database, and this is another performance problem. Even worse, it is likely that lots of users will post new comments, which means lots of writes to the database, which in most systems are even slower than reads.

For these reasons, the decision has been made to keep boards in memory. Thus, when the web server is shut down all messages will be lost, which is clearly less than desirable. What is really needed is some way of caching boards in memory, and writing the boards out to the database when it will have the least impact. This solution will be presented in Chapter 14, when we discuss advanced coding techniques.

Finally, UserInfoBean will be used to encapsulate information about the current user. It will not be used for anything new in this chapter and so will act mostly as a placeholder for personalization, to be discussed in the next chapter.

The Header and the Navigation

Everything is now in place to start writing JSPs. The navigation and header will appear on every page, so it makes sense to start with these. Since the header is the simplest it will have the distinction of being written first and is shown in Listing 10.4.

Listing 10.4   The Header with Database Elements

```
<jsp:useBean
 id="user"
 class="com.awl.jspbook.ch10.UserInfoBean"
 scope="session"/>
<jsp:useBean id="pageInfo"
    class="com.awl.jspbook.ch10.PageInfo"
    scope="request"/>
<%-- Begin Header --%>
<H1>Welcome to Java News Today</H1>
<H2>
<jsp:getProperty name="pageInfo" property="sectionName"/>
</H2>
<P>
<jsp:getProperty name="pageInfo" property="sectionDescription"/>
</P>
<CENTER>
  <FONT SIZE="-1">
    Welcome back,
    <jsp:getProperty name="user" property="name"/>!
  </FONT>
</CENTER>
<%-- End Header --%>
```

This JSP starts by accessing two beans, `UserInfo` from the session scope and `PageInfo` from the application scope, which it uses in fairly straightforward ways to present the section name and description and a customized greeting to the user. The only point that requires special notice is what this will do on the index page. That page will have no `SectionId` in the query string, so the `PageInfo` bean will not be given a value. If this bean is designed to return 0 by default, it will match the definition for the index page given in the section table and so will produce the standard JNT greeting "Your home for up to the minute Java news" on the index page.

The new navigation page is up next and is presented in Listing 10.5. This JSP also starts by getting the same `PageInfo` and `SectionHolder` beans that the header used. Then the navigation gets the list of section names and IDs from `SectionHolder` and iterates through all sections, displaying each. When it encounters the current section it presents it slightly differently, with a different character and no link.

Listing 10.5 The Navigation with Database Elements

```
<%@include file="dbconnect.jsp" %>
<jsp:useBean id="pageInfo"
    class="com.awl.jspbook.ch10.PageInfo"
    scope="request"/>
<jsp:useBean id="sections"
     class="com.awl.jspbook.ch10.SectionHolder"
     scope="application"/>
<% String sectionNames[] = sections.getNames(); %>
<% int sectionIds[] = sections.getIds(); %>
<%-- Begin Navigation --%>
<FONT COLOR="FFFFFF">
<% for (int i=0;i<sectionNames.length;i++) { %>
    <% if (sectionIds[i] == pageInfo.getSectionId()) { %>
        <FONT COLOR="#FF0000"><B>&raquo;<B></FONT>
        <%= sectionNames[i] %><BR>
    <% } else { %>
        <FONT COLOR="#FF0000"><B>&sect;<B></FONT>
        <A HREF="../section.jsp?sectionId=<%= sectionIds[i] %>">
        <%= sectionNames[i] %></A><BR>
    <% } %>
<% } %>
<HR>
Today's quiz:<BR>
<jsp:include page="/ch10/global/quiz.jsp"
 flush="true"/>
<%-- End Navigation --%>
```

Once again, there is no special treatment for the index page, and again this is resolved by having `PageInfo` return a `SectionId` of 0 by default.

The Article Page

Now that the included components have been completed, the actual content pages are next. The article page is a pretty straightforward matter of retrieving the content from the database and presenting it. It is shown in Listing 10.6 and illustrated in Figure 10.1.

Listing 10.6 The Article Page

```
<%@include file="global/dbconnect.jsp" %>
<jsp:useBean id="sections"
     class="com.awl.jspbook.ch10.SectionHolder"
     scope="application"/>
<jsp:useBean id="pageInfo"
    class="com.awl.jspbook.ch10.PageInfo"
    scope="request">
```

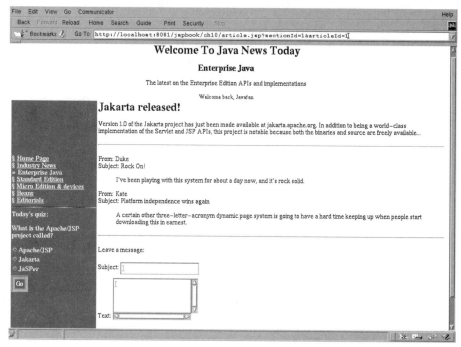

Figure 10.1   The JNT Article Page

```
<jsp:setProperty name="pageInfo" property="*"/>
</jsp:useBean>
<jsp:useBean
 id="user"
 class="com.awl.jspbook.ch10.UserInfoBean"
 scope="session">
<jsp:setProperty name="user" property="request"
 value="<%= request %>" />
</jsp:useBean>
<HTML>
<HEAD>
  <TITLE>
    Java News Today:
    <jsp:getProperty name="pageInfo" property="sectionName"/>
  </TITLE>
</HEAD>
<BODY BGCOLOR="#FFFFFF">
<TABLE BORDER="0" WIDTH="100%">
  <TR>
    <TD BGCOLOR="#0000FF" ALIGN="CENTER" COLSPAN="2">
      <jsp:include page="/ch10/global/header.jsp"
       flush="true"/>
    </TD>
```

```
  </TR>
  <TR>
    <TD ALIGN="LEFT" WIDTH="20%" BGCOLOR="#000077">
      <jsp:include page="/ch10/global/navigation.jsp"
       flush="true"/>
    </TD>
    <TD>
      <%-- Content goes here --%>
      <%-- get the article --%>
      <jsp:useBean
            id="articles"
            class="com.awl.jspbook.ch10.ArticleBean"/>
      <%-- restrict the search to this section and article --%>
      <jsp:setProperty
            name="articles"
            property="*"/>
      <% articles.select(); %>
      <% articles.next(); %>
      <H1>
      <jsp:getProperty
            name="articles"
            property="headline"/>
      </H1>
      <P>
      <jsp:getProperty
            name="articles"
            property="body"/>
      </P>
      <HR>
      <jsp:include page="/ch10/board.jsp" flush="true"/>
    </TD>
  </TR>
</TABLE>
</BODY>
</HTML>
```

True to form, the article page starts by initializing a number of beans. It first sets up the `PersistentConnection` bean, as in Chapter 9, which ensures a minimum of overhead to contact the database. Next, it builds the `SectionHolder` bean in the application scope. It may not look as though `SectionHolder` is ever initialized—useBean here is the version without the closing tag and so there is no special code executed when it is first constructed. However, all the special setup is handled in the bean's constructor. The first time this JSP is called, the servlet notices that there is no `SectionHolder` in the application scope and constructs one. At this point the database will be accessed and the section list will be built.

The JSP then builds the `PageInfo` bean for the current request. If this is the first time the bean is created, which should be the case, it is initialized with the `SectionId` and `ArticleId` parameters, which in turn become available to the header and navigation. Next the `UserInfo` bean is built so that it can be used by the header.

The body of the page includes the header and navigation. It uses `ArticleBean` to retrieve the article and present the headline and body to the user. Finally, this page includes another JSP to handle the board, which is shown in Listing 10.7.

Listing 10.7   The JSP That Handles Message Boards

```
<jsp:useBean id="pageInfo"
    class="com.awl.jspbook.ch10.PageInfo"
    scope="request"/>

<jsp:useBean
 id="allBoards"
 class="com.awl.jspbook.ch10.AllBoardsBean"
 scope="application"/>

<jsp:useBean
 id="user"
 class="com.awl.jspbook.ch10.UserInfoBean"
 scope="session"/>

<jsp:useBean
 id="board"
 class="com.awl.jspbook.ch10.BoardProxyBean"
 scope="page"/>

<%-- This will create the board if it
     doesn't exist yet --%>
<jsp:setProperty name="allBoards"
    property="newBoardName"
    value="<%= pageInfo.getArticleIdString() %>"/>

<%-- This connects the proxy bean to the AllBoardsBean --%>
<jsp:setProperty
 name="board"
 property="allBoards"
 value="<%= allBoards %>"/>

<%-- This sets the board bean to the specific board we're
     interested in --%>
<jsp:setProperty
 name="board"
 property="boardId"
 value="<%= pageInfo.getArticleIdString() %>"/>

<%-- This creates a new message, if requested --%>
<jsp:setProperty name="board" property="*"/>
<% while(board.hasMoreMessages()) { %>
  <P>
  From: <jsp:getProperty name="board" property="from"/><BR>
  Subject: <jsp:getProperty name="board" property="subject"/><BR>
```

```
<BLOCKQUOTE>
<jsp:getProperty name="board" property="text"/>
</BLOCKQUOTE>
</P>
<HR>
<% } %>
<P>Leave a message:</P>
<FORM ACTION="<%= request.getRequestURI() %>" METHOD="POST">
  <INPUT TYPE="HIDDEN" NAME="articleId"
   VALUE="<jsp:getProperty name="pageInfo"
          property="articleid"/>">
  <INPUT TYPE="HIDDEN" NAME="sectionId"
   VALUE="<jsp:getProperty name="pageInfo"
          property="sectionid"/>">
  <INPUT TYPE="HIDDEN" NAME="boardId"
   VALUE="<jsp:getProperty name="pageInfo"
          property="articleid"/>">
  <INPUT TYPE="HIDDEN" NAME="from"
   VALUE="<jsp:getProperty name="user"
          property="name"/>">
  <P>
  Subject: <INPUT TYPE="TEXT" NAME="subject"><BR>
  Text: <TEXTAREA ROWS="5" COLUMNS="20" NAME="text"></TEXTAREA>
  </P>
  <INPUT TYPE="SUBMIT" NAME="Submit" VALUE="Submit">
</FORM>
```

This JSP uses the `PageInfo` and `UserInfo` beans as well as the board beans. It gets `ArticleID` from `PageInfo` and uses it to create the board if it does not exist and to access it once it does. It uses `UserInfo` to automatically provide a name for the new post.

New messages are posted by sending the form data back to the article page that contains the board, which is obtained by the call to `request.getRequestURI()`. The article and section IDs are passed in as hidden fields to ensure that the same article is retrieved. In addition, the form provides the new message parameters, which will be captured when the article page again includes the board JSP.

The Section Page

The section page looks very similar to the article page, which should not be surprising since they are meant to produce similar HTML. The section page's major difference is in the content included in the main table cell and in some additional elements at the beginning. The code for the section page is shown in Listing 10.8, and a typical rendering is shown in Figure 10.2. This page loads all the beans that the article page loads and, in addition, the board beans. This is done so that each listed article can also show a sample of the related conversation.

Listing 10.8   The Section Page

```
<%@include file="global/dbconnect.jsp" %>
<%-- Set up the section holder --%>
<jsp:useBean id="sections"
     class="com.awl.jspbook.ch10.SectionHolder"
      scope="application"/>

<jsp:useBean id="pageInfo"
     class="com.awl.jspbook.ch10.PageInfo"
     scope="request">

<jsp:setProperty name="pageInfo" property="*"/>
</jsp:useBean>

<jsp:useBean
 id="user"
 class="com.awl.jspbook.ch10.UserInfoBean"
 scope="session">

<jsp:setProperty name="user" property="request"
 value="<%= request %>" />
</jsp:useBean>

<jsp:useBean
 id="allBoards"
 class="com.awl.jspbook.ch10.AllBoardsBean"
 scope="application"/>

<jsp:useBean
 id="board"
 class="com.awl.jspbook.ch10.BoardProxyBean"
 scope="page"/>

<%-- This connects the proxy bean to the AllBoardsBean --%>
<jsp:setProperty
 name="board"
 property="allBoards"
 value="<%= allBoards %>"/>
<HTML>
<HEAD>
   <TITLE>
     Java News Today:
     <jsp:getProperty name="pageInfo" property="sectionName"/>
   </TITLE>
</HEAD>
<BODY BGCOLOR="#FFFFFF">
<TABLE BORDER="0" WIDTH="100%">
   <TR>
     <TD BGCOLOR="#0000FF" ALIGN="CENTER" COLSPAN="2">
```

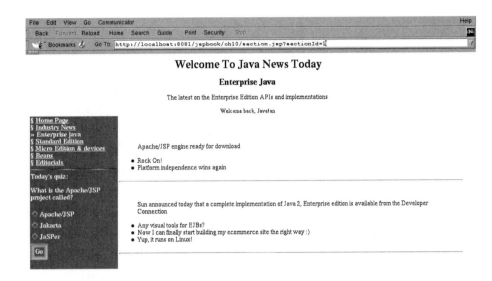

Figure 10.2 The JNT Section Page

```jsp
      <jsp:include page="/ch10/global/header.jsp"
        flush="true"/>
    </TD>
  </TR>
  <TR>
    <TD ALIGN="LEFT" WIDTH="20%" BGCOLOR="#000077">
      <jsp:include page="/ch10/global/navigation.jsp"
        flush="true"/>
    </TD>
    <TD>
      <%-- Content goes here --%>
      <%-- get the last ten articles --%>
      <jsp:useBean
          id="articles"
          class="com.awl.jspbook.ch10.ArticleBean"/>
      <%-- restrict the search to this section --%>
      <jsp:setProperty
          name="articles"
          property="*"/>
      <%-- Search in reverse order, to get latest
          stories first --%>
      <% articles.setOrderBy("articleId desc"); %>
      <% articles.select(); %>
```

```
<%-- Get a maximum of ten stories --%>
<% int count = 0; %>
<% while (articles.next() && count < 10) { %>
  <% count++; %>
  <% String URL="article.jsp?sectionId=" +
                   pageInfo.getSectionId() +
                   "&articleId=" +
             articles.getArticleId(); %>
  <FONT SIZE="+1">
    <A HREF="<%= URL %>"><jsp:getProperty
                           name="articles"
                           property="headline"/></A>
  </FONT>
  <BLOCKQUOTE>
    <jsp:getProperty name="articles" property="summary"/>
  </BLOCKQUOTE>
  <!-- top three comments from board go here. -->
  <%-- This will create the board if it
   doesn't exist yet --%>
  <jsp:setProperty name="allBoards"
   property="newBoardName"
   value="<%= articles.getArticleIdString() %>"/>
  <%-- This sets the board bean to the specific board
       we're interested in --%>
  <jsp:setProperty
   name="board"
   property="boardId"
   value="<%= articles.getArticleIdString() %>"/>
  <%-- Get up to three messages --%>
  <UL>
  <% while(board.hasMoreMessages()) { %>
    <LI>
    <jsp:getProperty name="board" property="subject"/>
  <% } %>
  </UL>
  <HR>
<% } %>
      </TD>
    </TR>
  </TABLE>
  </BODY>
</HTML>
```

The heart of the section page is `ArticleBean`. First its `SectionId` property is set from the form parameter, which in turn is used to build a where clause. Then an SQL select accesses all articles in that section, which are iterated through. A variable called `count` counts how many articles have been presented, and once ten have been shown the loop exists. If this check were not included, this page would quickly become to long to be useful.

Inside the loop, `ArticleBean` builds the URL to the page containing the article, as well as presents the headline and a summary. `ArticleId` is also given to `BoardProxyBean` and the top three messages are accessed. Unlike the way it is used on the article page, the board here cannot be easily separated into a different JSP. This is because `articleId` is not included in the request, so the only way for this page to pass that information to another is by creating an auxiliary bean in the request scope, which is possible but more trouble than it is worth.

The Index Page

The last page of the JNT site to be built is the index page. In most respects this page acts like a section page, so it is not surprising that it will be almost identical. It is shown in Listing 10.9.

Listing 10.9　The Index Page

```
<%@include file="global/dbconnect.jsp" %>
<%-- Set up the section holder --%>
<jsp:useBean id="sections"
      class="com.awl.jspbook.ch10.SectionHolder"
      scope="application"/>

<jsp:useBean id="pageInfo"
     class="com.awl.jspbook.ch10.PageInfo"
     scope="request">
<jsp:setProperty name="pageInfo" property="*"/>
</jsp:useBean>

<jsp:useBean
 id="user"
 class="com.awl.jspbook.ch10.UserInfoBean"
 scope="session">
<jsp:setProperty name="user" property="request"
 value="<%= request %>" />
</jsp:useBean>

<jsp:useBean
 id="allBoards"
 class="com.awl.jspbook.ch10.AllBoardsBean"
 scope="application"/>

<jsp:useBean
 id="board"
 class="com.awl.jspbook.ch10.BoardProxyBean"
 scope="page"/>
<%-- This connects the proxy bean to the AllBoardsBean --%>
```

```
<jsp:setProperty
 name="board"
 property="allBoards"
 value="<%= allBoards %>"/>
<HTML>
<HEAD>
  <TITLE>
    Java News Today:
    <jsp:getProperty name="pageInfo" property="sectionName"/>
  </TITLE>
</HEAD>
<BODY BGCOLOR="#FFFFFF">
<TABLE BORDER="0" WIDTH="100%">
  <TR>
    <TD BGCOLOR="#0000FF" ALIGN="CENTER" COLSPAN="2">
      <jsp:include page="/ch10/global/header.jsp"
       flush="true"/>
    </TD>
  </TR>
  <TR>
    <TD ALIGN="LEFT" WIDTH="20%" BGCOLOR="#000077">
      <jsp:include page="/ch10/global/navigation.jsp"
       flush="true"/>
    </TD>
    <TD>
      <%-- Content goes here --%>
      <%-- get the last ten articles --%>
      <jsp:useBean
          id="articles"
          class="com.awl.jspbook.ch10.ArticleBean"/>
      <%-- Search in reverse order, to get latest
           stories first --%>
      <% articles.setOrderBy("articleId desc"); %>
      <% articles.select(); %>
      <%-- Get a maximum of ten stories --%>
      <% int count = 0; %>
      <% while (articles.next() && count < 10) { %>
          <% String URL="article.jsp?sectionId=" +
                      articles.getSectionId() +
                      "&articleId=" +
                      articles.getArticleId(); %>
          <FONT SIZE="+1">
            <A HREF="<%= URL %>"><jsp:getProperty
                                    name="articles"
                                    property="headline"/></A>
          </FONT>
          <BLOCKQUOTE>
            <jsp:getProperty name="articles" property="summary"/>
          </BLOCKQUOTE>
          <!-- top three comments from board go here. -->
          <%-- This will create the board if it
               doesn't exist yet --%>
```

```
                    <jsp:setProperty name="allBoards"
                     property="newBoardName"
                     value="<%= articles.getArticleIdString() %>"/>
                    <%-- This sets the board bean to the specific board
                         we're interested in --%>
                    <jsp:setProperty
                     name="board"
                     property="boardId"
                     value="<%= articles.getArticleIdString() %>"/>
                    <%-- Get up to three messages --%>
                    <UL>
                    <% while(board.hasMoreMessages()) { %>
                      <LI>
                      <jsp:getProperty name="board" property="subject"/>
                    <% } %>
                    </UL>
                    <HR>
                <% } %>
            </TD>
          </TR>
        </TABLE>
      </BODY>
    </HTML>
```

The only major difference between the index page and the section page is that no properties are set in `ArticleBean`. Thus when its `select()` method is called, there will be no restriction in the where clause and consequently stories from all sections will be retrieved. The other differences with this page concern how it is called, and these differences are already accounted for in the navigation and header JSPs.

Creating New Stories

Displaying content is only half the challenge of building a web site; the other half is adding new content. Right now this could be accomplished by having the reporters write SQL statements to insert new rows into the articles table, but that would be unacceptable for many reasons. Fortunately, it is just as easy to write a JSP that puts content into a database as it is to write one that gets content out.

The first piece needed is a means for reporters to log in to the system. This can be done at the web server level, using the normal mechanisms for protecting pages, but it is also possible to have a JSP handle it. The login page is shown in Listing 10.10.

Listing 10.10   The Reporters' Login Screen

```
<%@ include file="global/dbconnect.jsp" %>
<jsp:useBean
      id="authors"
      class="com.awl.jspbook.ch10.AuthorBean"/>
<HTML>
<HEAD>
<TITLE>Newsdesk: Login</TITLE>
</HEAD>
<BODY>
<FORM ACTION="newsdesk.jsp" METHOD="POST">
<P>
Who are you:
<SELECT NAME="authorId">
<% authors.select(); %>
<% while (authors.next()) { %>
<OPTION  VALUE="<%= authors.getAuthorId() %>"><jsp:getProperty
                      name="authors"
                      property="firstName"/> <jsp:getProperty
                      name="authors"
                      property="lastName"/>
<% } %>
</SELECT>
</P>
<P>
Password:
<INPUT TYPE="PASSWORD" NAME="password">
</P>
<P>
<INPUT TYPE="SUBMIT" NAME="Login" Value="Login">
</FORM>
</HTML>
```

By now this kind of page should be quite familiar. It uses AuthorInfo to get the list of authors, which is presented as a menu whose values are the author IDs; in addition, the form requests a password. These values are then sent to the newsdesk, where new stories can be entered.

The Newsdesk Page

The newsdesk is another simple page, which serves primarily as a form where all story information can be entered. The code is given in Listing 10.11, and the resulting page is shown in Figure 10.3. This page uses SectionHolder to present the list of possible sections and KeywordBean to get the list of possible keywords. Because keywords are unlikely to change frequently, the keyword list can be cached in another bean. However, this optimization is less pressing here, since new stories are added much less often than the sections are listed.

Listing 10.11   The New Story Entry Page

```
<%@ include file="global/dbconnect.jsp" %>
<%@ include file="global/authorvalid.jsp" %>
<jsp:useBean id="sections"
    class="com.awl.jspbook.ch10.SectionHolder"
    scope="application"/>
<% String sectionNames[] = sections.getNames(); %>
<% int sectionIds[] = sections.getIds(); %>
<HTML>
<HEAD><TITLE>Newsdesk</TITLE></HEAD>
<BODY>
  <H1>Story Creation Page</H1>
  <P>Create a new story:</P>
  <FORM ACTION="storycreate.jsp" METHOD="POST">
  <TABLE>
  <TR>
    <TD>Choose a section:</TD>
    <TD>
      <SELECT NAME="sectionId">
      <% for(int i=0;i<sectionNames.length; i++) { %>
        <OPTION VALUE="<%= sectionIds[i] %>"><%=
                          sectionNames[i] %>
      <% } %>
      </SELECT>
    </TD>
  </TR>
  </TR>
    <TD>Subject:</TD>
    <TD><INPUT TYPE="TEXT" NAME="headline"></TD>
  </TR>
  <TR>
    <TD>Summary:</TD>
    <TD><TEXTAREA ROWS="5" COLS="25"
        NAME="summary"></TEXTAREA></TD>
  </TR>
  <TR>
    <TD>Body:</TD>
    <TD><TEXTAREA ROWS="5" COLS="25"
        NAME="body"></TEXTAREA></TD>
  </TR>
  <TR>
    <TD>Select all applicable keywords:</TD>
    <TD>
      <SELECT NAME="keywords" MULTIPLE="yes">
      <jsp:useBean
          id="keyword"
          class="com.awl.jspbook.ch10.KeywordBean"/>
      <% keyword.select(); %>
      <% while (keyword.next()) { %>
```

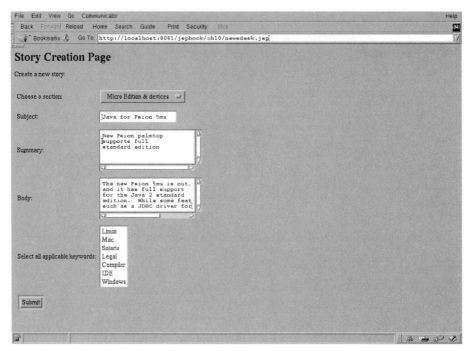

Figure 10.3   The Newsdesk Page

```
          <OPTION VALUE="<jsp:getProperty name="keyword"
                    property="keywordid"/>">
                              <jsp:getProperty
                                name="keyword"
                                property="keyword"/>
      <% } %>
      </SELECT>
    </TD>
  </TR>
  <TR>
    <TD COLSPAN="2">
      <INPUT TYPE="SUBMIT" NAME="Submit" Value="Submit">
    </TD>
  </TR>
</TABLE>
</BODY>
</HTML>
```

The most interesting thing about this page is the *authorvalid.jsp* page
included at the top, which will ensure that the user has logged in and is au-

thorized to access this page. Shown in Listing 10.12, this JSP will attempt to create `AuthorValidBean` in the session scope. The bean itself contains only a boolean that indicates whether the user has been validated. If not, the page will check whether a user ID and password have been provided as form parameters. If not, the request will be forwarded to the login page.

Listing 10.12   A JSP That Ensures That a User Is Valid

```
<jsp:useBean
     id="authorvalid"
     class="com.awl.jspbook.ch10.AuthorValidBean"
     scope="session">
<% if (!authorvalid.isValid()) { %>
  <% if(request.getParameter("authorId") == null) { %>
    <jsp:forward page="/ch10/login.jsp"/>
  <% } else { %>
    <jsp:useBean
         id="authors"
         class="com.awl.jspbook.ch10.AuthorBean"/>
    <jsp:setProperty name="authors" property="*"/>
    <%-- If the name does not match the password, no rows
         will match the where clause --%>
    <% authors.select(); %>
    <% if(!authors.next()) { %>
      <jsp:forward page="/ch10/login.jsp"/>
    <% } else { %>
      <jsp:setProperty name="authorvalid"
         property="valid" value="true"/>
    <% } %>
  <% } %>
<% } %>
</jsp:useBean>
```

If an ID and password have been provided, the JSP will use `AuthorBean` to see if they match. If so, `AuthorValidBean` is marked as valid; otherwise, the user is sent back to the login screen. The result is that if someone tries to access a page without valid access, she will be repeatedly sent to the login screen, but once she has logged in the bean will remain in her session and she will not need to log in again. This provides a quick and easy way to protect a page. All that is needed is to add this include at the top.

The Story Creation Page

Once a story has been entered at the newsdesk, the JSP shown in Listing 10.13 will store it in the database. This page is also protected by *authorvalid.jsp*. As might be expected, it uses `ArticleBean`, with properties set from the form parameters, to access the database.

Listing 10.13   A JSP That Stores a New Story

```
<%@ include file="global/dbconnect.jsp" %>
<%@ include file="global/authorvalid.jsp" %>
<HTML>
<HEAD><TITLE>Newsdesk: Story created</TITLE></HEAD>
<BODY>
  <jsp:useBean
    id="article"
    class="com.awl.jspbook.ch10.ArticleBean"/>
  <jsp:setProperty name="article" property="*"/>
  <% article.insert(); %>
  <jsp:setProperty name="article" property="*"/>
  <% article.select(); %>
  <P>Story created with id=<jsp:getProperty
                             name="article"
                             property="articleid"/></P>
  <% article.updateKeywords(); %>

  <P>Return to the<A HREF="newsdesk.jsp">Editor's Desk</A>.</P>
</BODY>
</HTML>
```

The only complex issue here concerns keywords. The `ArticleKeyword` table uses the article's ID, so that ID must be known before the keywords can be obtained. The story creation page uses an interesting trick to get it. Once the insert has been performed, the bean properties are set a second time and an SQL select is done. This retrieves the row whose title matches the provided title and whose body matches the current body, which will be the row that was just inserted. When the select is done it sets allfields of the bean, including the ID.

Once the ID has been obtained, a special method is called to add data to the `ArticleKeyword` table, and a short message is returned to the user to indicate that all went well.

Summary

This completes a full working version of the Java News Today site. The developers started by defining the tables they would need; then they built beans to simplify access to these tables, which made it easy to create pages that display articles, sections, and the JNT home page. These same beans were then used to build pages for the site editors, allowing them to create new pages.

As with any site, there is always more that can be done. Although the keywords are being captured, they are not used anywhere. A small change to the article page can be made to add the keywords in meta-data, which will help search engines index the site. The keywords can also be used for an internal search engine. To do this, one page lists all available keywords in a form. The form then goes to a page that is similar to the index page, except that it filters based on a keyword instead of the section ID.

Similarly, more functionality can be added to the editing features. At some point the reporters will probably want to make changes to old stories. This they can easily do with a slightly modified version of the newsdesk page that retrieves the article based on ID, populates the form with the current values, and then sends it to a page that does an update. The ability to delete articles can be handled similarly.

There is also no page where a new reporter, section, or keyword can be added. Such a page is straightforward, but since these additions happen infrequently it is not too much of a burden to require that they be done through SQL commands.

No doubt hundreds of other additions can be made to this basic setup, but then that will always be true. A web site should always be considered a work in progress, and JSPs make it easy to continually add new features or pages. Even so, the current JNT site is sufficiently useful. The next step is to allow users to customize it and to enable it to dynamically adjust itself to user's interests. This is the subject of the next chapter.

CHAPTER 11

Personalization

In the last chapter, Java News Today was able to build a functioning site by placing all of the content into a database. Now that the basics are working, the next step is to offer some enhanced functionality that will attract and keep users. One of the most significant things JNT can do in this area is allow each user to tailor the site to his or her own tastes. This works on two levels. First, allowing users to make the site exactly what they want means that they are more likely to come back. Second, this is an excellent way to collect valuable information about users, which can provide feedback to the site maintainers about which areas are successful and which can stand to be altered.

Designing the Database

The key to personalization is, once again, the use of a database, and the first step in designing the database is deciding what data will be stored. One relatively simple possibility is to allow the user to customize some of the site's visual elements, including color scheme and general layout. To start with, three major variations of the site will be offered, one with the navigation on the right, one with the navigation on the left, and one with text only, no tables. In addition, four color schemes, based on greens, reds, blues, and greys, that can be selected independently of the layout will be provided.

The next area of customization will allow allow users to filter out elements that do not interest them. The JNT staff figure that they have enough content so that everyone will like some of it, but it's unlikely that anyone will like all of it. Filtering will allow users to turn the general site into one filled only with things that interest them, and who would not want to come back to a site like that? For the time being, filtering will be based on sections and authors. The option will also be offered to remove the quiz on the navigation bar.

All these options will be *explicit*, meaning that users will have to enter their choices in a form. It is also possible to tailor a site with *implicit* data, which is collected by recording how the user interacts with the site. Implicit data collection will be covered later in this chapter.

Now that JNT knows what data they will be collecting, a database schema can be designed. This schema is presented in Listing 11.1. The user table simply assigns each user a unique ID and records a name and password. In addition, it stores simple single-valued, or *scalar*, data, including the style, color scheme, and quiz option.

Listing 11.1   The Table Definitions for Personalization

```
CREATE SEQUENCE userid_seq;
CREATE TABLE users (
        userid      integer
                    default
                    nextval('userid_seq')
                    primary key,
        name        char(30),
        password    char(30),
        email       char(50),
        style       char(10),
        color       char(10),
        wantsquiz char(1)
);

CREATE TABLE usersections (
        userid      int,
        sectionid   int
);
CREATE TABLE userauthors (
        userid      int,
        authorid    int
);
```

The user's selection of authors and sections will have many values. For that reason the values are stored in separate tables joined to the user table through userid. These tables now present an interesting dilemma for the JNT programmers—should they store the sections and authors the user wants or those the user does not want? The advantage of the former is that a new user has no entries in these tables and so gets all sections and authors by default. Likewise, when a new section or author is added, all users see it by default. The complication in this scheme is that it is more intuitive for users to select which elements they do want rather than those they do not. In the end, the designers decide to store the elements users do not want and let the page and the underlying bean worry about presenting this in a user-friendly way.

The UserInfoBean

Almost all the personalization features will be driven by a single ultra-powered version of UserInfoBean, which so far has just gotten the user's name. This bean will need to support a lot more functionality than any bean we have seen up to now, which will make it pretty large. The full source code can be found on the companion CD-ROM, but Listing 11.2 shows all the methods and properties the bean will make available to JSP authors.

Listing 11.2 Properties and Methods in UserInfoBean

- `String style`: the user's selected style
  (navleft, navright, or navtext)
- `String color`: the user's selected color scheme
  (blues, reds, greens or greys)
- `String bgColor`: Color for the page background
- `String textColor`: Color for the text
- `String linkColor`: Color for links
- `String vlinkColor`: Color for visited links
- `String headBgColor`: Background color for the header
- `String vavBgColor`:
  background color for the navigation
- `HttpServletRequest request`:
  Write-only property, used to get a default
  name for the user if they have not logged in.
- `String name`: The user's name
- `String password`: The user's password
- `String email`: The user's email
- `boolean wantsQuiz`:
  true if the user wants the daily quiz
- `boolean loggedIn`:
  True if the user is logged in. If this
  is true, it implies name and password are valid.
- `int authors[]`: The authorIds that the user does NOT want.
- `String sections[]`: The sectionIds that the
  user does NOT want.

- boolean nameInUse():
  returns true if the current name exists
  in the user database.
- boolean wantsSection(int section): Returns true
  if the user wants the indicated section.
- boolean wantsAuthor(int authorId): Returns true
  if the user wants stories by the indicated authorId
- boolean wantsArticle(int sectionId,int authorId):
  Returns true if the user wants an article from the
  given section written by the given author.
- void insert(): Inserts the current user into
  the database
- void select(): Retrieves information from the
  database that matches the current name and password
- void update():
  Updates all attributes of the user.

Creating a New Account

There are many ways to create a new account. Users can send mail to the JNT staff requesting one, or mail or flyers can be sent out offering users pre-created accounts, for example. However, the easiest and most flexible scheme is to allow users to create their own accounts on the site. The account creation page is shown in Listing 11.3.

Listing 11.3 The New Account Page

```
<%@ include file="global/dbconnect.jsp" %>
<%@ include file="global/userinfo.jsp" %>
<HTML>
<HEAD>
  <TITLE>
    Java News Today: Account creation
  </TITLE>
</HEAD>
<BODY BGCOLOR="#FFFFFF">
<TABLE BORDER="0" WIDTH="100%">
  <TR>
    <TD BGCOLOR="#0000FF" ALIGN="CENTER" COLSPAN="2">
      <jsp:include page="/ch11/global/header.jsp"
        flush="true"/>
    </TD>
  </TR>
  <TR>
    <TD ALIGN="TOP" WIDTH="20%" BGCOLOR="#000077">
      <jsp:include page="/ch11/global/navigation.jsp"
        flush="true"/>
```

```
      </TD>
      <TD>
        <%-- Content goes here --%>
<% if(request.getParameter("name") != null) { %>
  <jsp:setProperty
    name="user"
    property="*"/>
  <% if(user.nameInUse()) { %>
  Sorry, that name is already in use.  Please choose another.
  <FORM ACTION="createacct.jsp" METHOD="POST">
    <P>Username:
    <INPUT TYPE="TEXT" NAME="name"></P>
    <P>Password:
    <INPUT TYPE="PASSWORD" NAME="password"></P>
    <P>Email address
    <INPUT TYPE="TEXT" NAME="email"></P>
    <P><INPUT TYPE="SUBMIT" NAME="Login" VALUE="Login"></P>
  </FORM>
  <% } else { %>
    <% user.insert(); %>
    <P>Account created!</P>
    <P>Return to the Java News Today
    <A HREF="index1.jsp">home page</A> or set your
    <A HREF="userprefs.jsp">preferences</A></P>
  <% } %>
<% } else { %>
  <P>Create a new account:</P>
  <FORM ACTION="createacct.jsp" METHOD="POST">
    <P>Username:
    <INPUT TYPE="TEXT" NAME="name"></P>
    <P>Password:
    <INPUT TYPE="PASSWORD" NAME="password"></P>
    <P>Email address
    <INPUT TYPE="TEXT" NAME="email"></P>
    <P><INPUT TYPE="SUBMIT" NAME="Login" VALUE="Login"></P>
  </FORM>
<% } %>
        <%-- end content --%>
      </TD>
    </TR>
</TABLE>
</BODY>
</HTML>
```

If this page is called with a name and password, it will first check the database to see if the name is in use via the bean's nameInUse() method. If the name is not yet in use, the new account will be created; otherwise, the user will be notified that the name he has selected is not available, and he will be given another opportunity to choose one. If the page is called without a name and password, the form will be presented.

Although this is a perfectly adequate first step, much more can be done with this page. The user might be prompted to enter her password twice to ensure that she has typed it correctly. Alternatively, many sites also allow the user to specify a challenge consisting of a question and the correct response. If a user forgets her password, the site can issue her the challenge; if she responds properly the password is shown. JNT will handle the problem of forgotten passwords by allowing a user to request that her password be emailed to the address she has provided, although this has not been implemented yet.

Many sites also offer a weekly email newsletter, which might use some of the sites's highlights to lure users back to the site. When a site offers such a newsletter, the option to receive it is usually presented when the account is created. JNT has decided against a newsletter, at least for now, but by collecting email addresses up front they have made it easy to add such a feature later.

Logging in a User

When an account is first created, the user is automatically logged in. On subsequent visits, he will need to go to a login page, which is shown in Listing 11.4. This page works much like the account creation page. If a user name and password have been provided, the bean will check whether that combination exists in the database. If so, the bean will set the user's `loggedIn` flag and retrieve all the user's preferences. If not, the user will be asked to log in again. If no name has been provided, the user will get the initial login form.

Listing 11.4   The User Login Page

```
<%@ include file="global/dbconnect.jsp" %>
<%@ include file="global/userinfo.jsp" %>
<HTML>
<HEAD>
  <TITLE>
    Java News Today: Login
  </TITLE>
</HEAD>
<BODY BGCOLOR="#FFFFFF">
<TABLE BORDER="0" WIDTH="100%">
  <TR>
    <TD BGCOLOR="#0000FF" ALIGN="CENTER" COLSPAN="2">
      <jsp:include page="/ch11/global/header.jsp"
        flush="true"/>
    </TD>
```

```
      </TR>
      <TR>
        <TD ALIGN="LEFT" WIDTH="20%" BGCOLOR="#000077">
          <jsp:include page="/ch11/global/navigation.jsp"
          flush="true"/>
        </TD>
        <TD>
          <%-- Content goes here --%>
<jsp:setProperty name="user" property="*"/>
<% user.select(); %>
<% if (request.getParameter("password") != null) { %>
    <% if (user.isLoggedIn()) { %>
      <P>Thank you, you are now logged in!</P>
      <P>Return to the Java News Today
      <A HREF="index1.jsp">home page</A> or set your
      <A HREF="userprefs.jsp">preferences</A></P>
    <% } else { %>
      <P>Sorry, that login is incorrect.  Please try again.
        or <A HREF="createacct.jsp">create a new account</A>.</P>
      <FORM ACTION="/jspbook/ch11/userlogin.jsp" method="post">
        <P>Username:
        <INPUT TYPE="TEXT" NAME="name"></P>
        <P>Password:
        <INPUT TYPE="PASSWORD" NAME="password"></P>
        <P><INPUT TYPE="SUBMIT" NAME="Login" VALUE="Login"></P>
      </FORM>
    <% } %>
<% } else { %>
    <P>Please login:</P>
    <FORM ACTION="/jspbook/ch11/userlogin.jsp" METHOD="POST">
      <P>Username:
      <INPUT TYPE="TEXT" NAME="name"></P>
      <P>Password:
      <INPUT TYPE="PASSWORD" NAME="password"></P>
      <P><INPUT TYPE="SUBMIT" NAME="Login" VALUE="Login"></P>
    </FORM>
<% } %>
          <%-- End Content --%>
        </TD>
      </TR>
    </TABLE>
  </BODY>
</HTML>
```

Setting Properties

Once a user has logged in, he can customize the site. The code for the user preferences page is shown in Listing 11.5, and the page itself is shown in Figure 11.1.

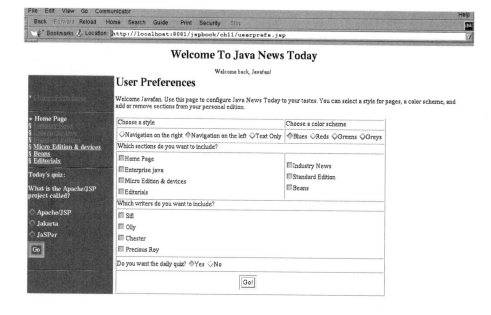

Figure 11.1   The User Preferences Page

Listing 11.5   The User Preferences Page

```
<%@include file="global/dbconnect.jsp" %>
<%@include file="global/userinfo.jsp" %>
<jsp:useBean id="sections"
     class="com.awl.jspbook.ch11.SectionHolder"
     scope="application"/>
<HTML>
<HEAD>
  <TITLE>
    Java News Today: User preferences
  </TITLE>
</HEAD>
<BODY BGCOLOR="#FFFFFF">
<TABLE BORDER="0" WIDTH="100%">
  <TR>
    <TD BGCOLOR="#0000FF" ALIGN="CENTER" COLSPAN="2">
      <jsp:include page="/ch11/global/header.jsp"
      flush="true"/>
    </TD>
  </TR>
```

```
    <TR>
      <TD ALIGN="LEFT" WIDTH="20%" BGCOLOR="#000077">
        <jsp:include page="/ch11/global/navigation.jsp"
         flush="true"/>
      </TD>
      <TD>
        <%-- Content goes here --%>
<H1>User Preferences</H2>
<P>Welcome <jsp:getProperty
              name="user"
              property="name"/>.  Use this page to
configure Java News Today to your tastes.  You can select
a style for pages, a color scheme, and add or remove sections
from your personal edition.</P>
<FORM ACTION="setprefs.jsp" METHOD="POST">
<TABLE BORDER="1">
  <TR>
    <TD><FONT="+1">Choose a style</FONT></TD>
    <TD><FONT="+1">Choose a color scheme</FONT></TD>
  </TR>
  <TR>
    <TD>
      <INPUT TYPE="RADIO" NAME="style" VALUE="navright"
      <% if(user.getStyle().equals("navright")) { %>
       CHECKED
      <% } %>>Navigation on the right
      <INPUT TYPE="RADIO" NAME="style" VALUE="navleft"
      <% if(user.getStyle().equals("navleft")) { %>
       CHECKED
      <% } %>>Navigation on the left
      <INPUT TYPE="RADIO" NAME="style" VALUE="textonly"
      <% if(user.getStyle().equals("textonly")) { %>
       CHECKED
      <% } %>>Text Only
    </TD>
    <TD>
      <INPUT TYPE="RADIO" NAME="color" VALUE="blues"
      <% if(user.getColor().equals("blues")) { %>
       CHECKED
      <% } %>>Blues
      <INPUT TYPE="RADIO" NAME="color" VALUE="reds"
      <% if(user.getColor().equals("reds")) { %>
       CHECKED
      <% } %>>Reds
      <INPUT TYPE="RADIO" NAME="color" VALUE="greens"
      <% if(user.getColor().equals("greens")) { %>
       CHECKED
      <% } %>>Greens
      <INPUT TYPE="RADIO" NAME="color" VALUE="greys"
      <% if(user.getColor().equals("greys")) { %>
       CHECKED
      <% } %>>Greys
    </TD>
```

```
</TR>
<TR>
  <TD COLSPAN="2">Which sections do you want to include?</TD>
</TR>
<TR>
  <% String sectionNames[]  = sections.getNames(); %>
  <% int         sectionIds[] = sections.getIds(); %>
  <TD>
    <% for (int i=0;i<sectionIds.length;i+=2) { %>
      <INPUT TYPE="CHECKBOX" NAME="sections"
      VALUE="<%= sectionIds[i] %>"
      <% if(user.wantsSection(sectionIds[i])) { %>
      CHECKED
      <% } %>><%= sectionNames[i] %><BR>
    <% } %>
  </TD>
  <TD>
    <% for (int i=1;i<sectionIds.length;i+=2) { %>
      <INPUT TYPE="CHECKBOX" NAME="sections"
      VALUE="<%= sectionIds[i] %>"
      <% if(user.wantsSection(sectionIds[i])) { %>
      CHECKED
      <% } %>><%= sectionNames[i] %><BR>
    <% } %>
  </TD>
 </TR>
<TR>
  <TD COLSPAN="2">Which writers do you want to include?</TD>
</TR>
<jsp:useBean
  id="authors"
  class="com.awl.jspbook.ch11.AuthorBean"/>
<% authors.select(); %>
<TR>
  <TD COLSPAN="2">
  <% while (authors.next()) { %>
    <INPUT TYPE="CHECKBOX" NAME="authors"
     VALUE="<%= authors.getAuthorId() %>"
        <% if(user.wantsAuthor(authors.getAuthorId())) { %>
        CHECKED
        <% } %>>
    <jsp:getProperty
        name="authors"
        property="firstName"/> <jsp:getProperty
                                  name="authors"
                                  property="lastName"/><BR>
  <% } %>
  </TD>
</TR>
<TR>
  <TD COLSPAN="2">
```

```
                 Do you want the daily quiz?
                 <INPUT TYPE="RADIO" NAME="wantsQuiz" value="true"
                  <% if (user.getWantsQuiz()) { %>CHECKED<% } %>>Yes
                 <INPUT TYPE="RADIO" NAME="wantsQuiz" value="false"
                  <% if (!user.getWantsQuiz()) { %>CHECKED<% } %>>No
                 </TD>
              </TR>
              <TR>
                 <TD COLSPAN="2" ALIGN="CENTER">
                  <INPUT TYPE="SUBMIT" NAME="Go!" VALUE="Go!">
                 </TD>
              </TR>
           </TABLE>
        </TABLE>
     </BODY>
  </HTML>
```

The most complex feature of this page is its ability to present the user's current options, but even this is accomplished in a straightforward way by getting the relevant data from UserInfoBean. The section list is pulled from SectionHolder, as in the previous chapter, and each section is passed to wantsSection() to determine if the corresponding box should be checked. The author list works the same way, except that the data is pulled directly from the database.

For both sections and authors the user will select the items wanted, and the bean will take this information and generate and store the items the user does not want. It does this by getting the full section and author lists and removing everything the user has selected, leaving only those elements not chosen.

When the user submits this form he will be taken to another JSP that will actually change the values. There is no dynamic content on this page; the only interesting portion is

```
<jsp:setProperty name="user" property="*"/>
<% user.update(); %>
```

The first line changes the values in the bean, and the second updates the database.

No check is made on either of these pages to determine if the user has logged in. This is not a problem, since if the user has not logged in the update() method will silently fail. The result will be that the user will have changed her preferences for as long as the UserInfoBean stays active. This bean is in the session scope, so the changes will remain in effect until the user leaves the site. Currently JNT does not advertise this feature, but they could use it as a way to show users the benefits of getting an account.

Handling Properties in the Header

Almost every JSP will have to change in order to support customization, but the changes are all pretty minor. For example, up to now the header has always shown the user name, although the best it has been able to do is `User from` and the user's computer. It makes more sense to show this only if the name is known, which will only be true if the user has logged in. The new version of the header is shown in Listing 11.6.

Listing 11.6   The New Header

```
<jsp:useBean
 id="user"
 class="com.awl.jspbook.ch11.UserInfoBean"
 scope="session"/>
<jsp:useBean id="pageInfo"
    class="com.awl.jspbook.ch11.PageInfo"
    scope="request"/>
<%-- Begin Header --%>
<H1>Welcome to Java News Today</H1>
<H2>
<jsp:getProperty name="pageInfo" property="sectionName"/>
</H2>
<P>
<jsp:getProperty name="pageInfo" property="sectionDescription"/>
</P>
<% if (user.isLoggedIn()) { %>
<CENTER>
  <FONT SIZE="-1">
    Welcome back,
    <jsp:getProperty name="user" property="name"/>!
  </FONT>
</CENTER>
<% } %>
<%-- End Header --%>
```

Handling Properties in the Navigation

The changes to the navigation are somewhat more extensive, since in addition to the changes necessary to present only the sections of interest, the navigation is a logical place to put the login form. The new version of the navigation is shown in Listing 11.7.

Listing 11.7   The New Navigation

```
<%@include file="dbconnect.jsp" %>
<%@include file="userinfo.jsp" %>
<jsp:useBean id="sections"
```

```
             class="com.awl.jspbook.ch11.SectionHolder"
             scope="application"/>
<jsp:useBean id="pageInfo"
      class="com.awl.jspbook.ch11.PageInfo"
      scope="request"/>
<% String sectionNames[] = sections.getNames(); %>
<% int       sectionIds[] = sections.getIds(); %>
<%-- Begin Navigation --%>
<FONT COLOR="FFFFFF">
<% if(user.isLoggedIn()) { %>
  * <A HREF="userprefs.jsp">Change Preferences</A><P>
<% } else { %>
  <P>Login!</P>
   <FORM ACTION="userlogin.jsp" METHOD="POST">
     <P>Username:
     <INPUT TYPE="TEXT" NAME="name"></P>
     <P>Password:
     <INPUT TYPE="PASSWORD" NAME="password"></P>
     <P><INPUT TYPE="SUBMIT" NAME="Login" VALUE="Login"></P>
   </FORM>
  <P>If you don't have an account yet,
  you can <A HREF="createacct.jsp">create one</A> free!
  </P>
<% } %>
<HR>
<% for (int i=0;i<sectionNames.length;i++) { %>
   <% if (user.wantsSection(sectionIds[i])) { %>
     <% if (sectionIds[i] == pageInfo.getSectionId()) { %>
       <FONT COLOR="#FF0000"><B>&raquo;<B></FONT>
       <%= sectionNames[i] %><BR>
     <% } else { %>
       <FONT COLOR="#FF0000"><B>&sect;<B></FONT>
       <A HREF="../section.jsp?sectionId=<%= sectionIds[i] %>">
       <%= sectionNames[i] %></A><BR>
     <% } %>
   <% } %>
<% } %>
<% if (user.getWantsQuiz()) { %>
<HR>
Today's quiz:<BR>
<jsp:include page="/ch11/global/quiz.jsp"
 flush="true"/>
<% } %>
<HR>
<%-- End Navigation --%>
```

As in the user preferences page, each section is passed to the bean's `wantsSection()` method to determine whether or not to show it. The quiz is shown only if the user wants it, and if the user has not logged in she will be shown a form from which she can do so. If the user has already logged in, this form will be replaced by a link to the customization page.

Handling Properties in the Content Pages

The most extensive changes are on the section, index, and article pages. The first issue to be dealt with is how the multiple layouts will be supported. It would be possible to include all three versions on each page, with a conditional pulling out only the appropriate one. However, this would result in very ugly and difficult to maintain code. A better solution is to replace each of the content pages with a page that dispatches to a page with the correct format but that does not contain any content itself. The new index page is shown in Listing 11.8.

Listing 11.8 The New Index Page

```
<%@include file="global/userinfo.jsp" %>
<% if(user.getStyle().equals("navright")) { %>
<jsp:forward page="index1r.jsp"/>
<% } else if(user.getStyle().equals("textonly")) { %>
<jsp:forward page="index1t.jsp"/>
<% } else { %>
<jsp:forward page="index1l.jsp"/>
<% } %>
```

All this page does is ask `UserInfoBean` which layout to use; the request is then sent to a version of the page with the proper one. A similar page will also be constructed for the section and articles pages, variations of which will also be created.

Within each variation the changes are somewhat simpler. First, the colors will no longer be hard-coded into the page, but will come from `UserInfoBean`. Second, no article will be shown to a user unless it meets that user's criteria for sections and authors. The text-only version of the index page is shown in Listing 11.9; the other variations and the article and section pages are included on the CD-ROM.

Listing 11.9 The Text-Only Version of the Index Page

```
<%@include file="global/dbconnect.jsp" %>
<%@include file="global/userinfo.jsp" %>
<%-- Set up the section holder --%>
<jsp:useBean id="sections"
     class="com.awl.jspbook.ch11.SectionHolder"
     scope="application"/>
<jsp:useBean id="pageInfo"
     class="com.awl.jspbook.ch11.PageInfo"
     scope="request">
```

```
<jsp:setProperty name="pageInfo" property="*"/>
</jsp:useBean>
<jsp:useBean
 id="allBoards"
 class="com.awl.jspbook.ch11.AllBoardsBean"
 scope="application"/>
<jsp:useBean
 id="board"
 class="com.awl.jspbook.ch11.BoardProxyBean"
 scope="page"/>
<%-- This connects the proxy bean to the AllBoardsBean --%>
<jsp:setProperty
 name="board"
 property="allBoards"
 value="<%= allBoards %>"/>
<HTML>
<HEAD>
  <TITLE>
    Java News Today:
    <jsp:getProperty name="pageInfo" property="sectionName"/>
  </TITLE>
</HEAD>
<BODY BGCOLOR="<jsp:getProperty
                  name="user"
                  property=bgColor/>"
      TEXT="<jsp:getProperty
                  name="user"
                  property=textColor/>"
      LINK="<jsp:getProperty
                  name="user"
                  property=linkColor/>"
      VLINK="<jsp:getProperty
                  name="user"
                  property=vlinkColor/>">
<jsp:include page="/ch11/global/header.jsp"
 flush="true"/>
<HR>
      <%-- Content goes here --%>
      <%-- get the last ten articles --%>
      <jsp:useBean
          id="articles"
          class="com.awl.jspbook.ch11.ArticleBean"/>
      <%-- Search in reverse order, to get latest
           stories first --%>
      <% articles.setOrderBy("articleId desc"); %>
      <% articles.select(); %>
      <%-- Get a maximum of ten stories --%>
      <% int count = 0; %>
      <% while (articles.next() && count < 10) { %>
          <% if(!user.wantsArticle(articles.getSectionId(),
                                   articles.getAuthorId()))
                               continue; %>
```

```
<% String URL="article.jsp?sectionId=" +
            articles.getSectionId() +
            "&articleId=" +
            articles.getArticleId(); %>
<FONT SIZE="+1">
  <A HREF="<%= URL %>"><jsp:getProperty
                          name="articles"
                          property="headline"/></A>
</FONT>
<BLOCKQUOTE>
  <jsp:getProperty name="articles" property="summary"/>
</BLOCKQUOTE>
<!-- top three comments from board go here. -->
<%-- This will create the board if it
  doesn't exist yet --%>
<jsp:setProperty name="allBoards"
  property="newBoardName"
  value="<%= articles.getArticleIdString() %>"/>
<%-- This sets the board bean to the specific board
      we're interested in --%>
<jsp:setProperty
  name="board"
  property="boardId"
  value="<%= articles.getArticleIdString() %>"/>
<%-- Get up to three messages --%>
<UL>
<% while(board.hasMoreMessages()) { %>
  <LI>
    <jsp:getProperty name="board" property="subject"/>
<% } %>
</UL>
<HR>
<% } %>
<%-- end content --%>
<jsp:include page="/ch11/global/navigation.jsp"
  flush="true"/>
</BODY>
</HTML>
```

The heart of the index page is the call to wantsArticle(), which determines whether or not the current article should be presented to the user. If this method returns false, the continue will jump back to the start of the loop, which will retrieve the next article.

As formidable as personalization may seem from the outside, that's it. This completes the explicit portion of JNT's personalization.

Implicit User Properties

Useful though the information provided by users may be, it is often not the whole story. There are many reasons for this. Perhaps the most obvious is that a user may not want to create an account, so sometimes the best way to gather information about him is to watch how he actually uses the site. Some of this will be done by examining the web site's log files, but this tends to give only aggregate behavior. In addition, because log files are processed offline, there is no way to use this information to customize a particular user's experience.

Java News Today could derive sections and authors of interest to a user by simply recording the section and author of each article read. However, the keywords that were included in the site in Chapter 9 can give more detail. If a user always reads stories about Linux, regardless of what section the story is in, it is a pretty safe bet that future Linux stories are likely to be of interest. Relevant stories can then be highlighted or listed first on the section or article pages.

Once again, the first step in making this a reality is to design the database schema to hold this new information. The new table is shown in Listing 11.10. It will be joined to the user and keyword tables by the *userid* and *keywordid* fields. The score will be incremented each time that user reads a story tagged with that keyword, allowing `UserInfoBean` to compute how important each topic is to him.

Listing 11.10   The Table Definition for Recording Derived Information

```
CREATE TABLE userinterests (
        userid     int,
        keywordid  int,
        score      int
);
```

The next step is to add a method to the bean to gather this information and to add the appropriate code to the article page. Because this code will be relevant regardless of which style the user has selected, it will be placed on the top-level article page, as shown in Listing 11.11.

Listing 11.11   The Article Page, with a Call to Collect Data

```
<%@include file="global/userinfo.jsp" %>
<jsp:setProperty
 name="user"
 property="articleId"/>
<% if(user.getStyle().equals("navright")) { %>
<jsp:forward page="/jspbook/ch11/articler.jsp"/>
<% } else if(user.getStyle().equals("textonly")) { %>
```

```
<jsp:forward page="/jspbook/ch11/articlet.jsp"/>
<% } else { %>
<jsp:forward page="/jspbook/ch11/articlel.jsp"/>
<% } %>
```

When the bean's `articleid()` method is called, it will look up the relevant keywords and add them to the running tally; the bean will also need to load this information from the database when the user first logs in. This data will not be saved each time the user reads a new article, which would be severely detrimental to performance. Instead, it will be pushed out to the database only when the session expires, which can be accomplished by adding support for `HttpSessionBindingEvent` to `UserInfoBean`, as discussed in Chapter 7.

Once obtained, there are many ways to use this information. For example, stories of interest could be moved to the top of the list, but this would be fairly complex, since the list of articles would now have to come from `UserInfoBean` instead of `ArticleBean`; it could also cause the site to appear too static, since a new story would be featured lower on the list than an old one that happens to be of interest. One remedy would be to keep track of which stories a user has read, but this adds another layer of complexity.

Instead, JNT has decided to change the color of headlines of stories of interest. If they later discover that this is not sufficiently capturing users' attention, it can be easily replaced by something else. One version of the new section page that uses this information is shown in Listing 11.12.

Listing 11.12   The Section Page, Highlighting Stories of Interest

```
<%@include file="global/dbconnect.jsp" %>
<%@include file="global/userinfo.jsp" %>
<%-- Set up the section holder --%>
<jsp:useBean id="sections"
    class="com.awl.jspbook.ch11.SectionHolder"
    scope="application"/>
<jsp:useBean id="pageInfo"
    class="com.awl.jspbook.ch11.PageInfo"
    scope="request">
<jsp:setProperty name="pageInfo" property="*"/>
</jsp:useBean>
<jsp:useBean
 id="allBoards"
 class="com.awl.jspbook.ch11.AllBoardsBean"
 scope="application"/>
<jsp:useBean
 id="board"
 class="com.awl.jspbook.ch11.BoardProxyBean"
 scope="page"/>
<%-- This connects the proxy bean to the AllBoardsBean --%>
```

```
<jsp:setProperty
 name="board"
 property="allBoards"
 value="<%= allBoards %>"/>
<HTML>
<HEAD>
  <TITLE>
    Java News Today:
    <jsp:getProperty name="pageInfo" property="sectionName"/>
  </TITLE>
</HEAD>
<BODY BGCOLOR="<jsp:getProperty
                 name="user"
                 property=bgColor/>"
      TEXT="<jsp:getProperty
                 name="user"
                 property=textColor/>"
      LINK="<jsp:getProperty
                 name="user"
                 property=linkColor/>"
      VLINK="<jsp:getProperty
                 name="user"
                 property=vlinkColor/>">
<TABLE BORDER="0" WIDTH="100%">
  <TR>
    <TD BGCOLOR="<jsp:getProperty
                   name="user"
                   property=headBgColor/>">"
        ALIGN="CENTER" COLSPAN="2">
      <jsp:include page="/ch11/global/header.jsp"
       flush="true"/>
    </TD>
  </TR>
  <TR>
    <TD>
      <%-- Content goes here --%>
      <%-- Content goes here --%>
      <%-- get the last ten articles --%>
      <jsp:useBean
          id="articles"
          class="com.awl.jspbook.ch11.ArticleBean"/>
      <%-- restrict the search to this section --%>
      <jsp:setProperty
          name="articles"
          property="*"/>
      <%-- Search in reverse order, to get latest
           stories first --%>
      <% articles.setOrderBy("articleId desc"); %>
      <% articles.select(); %>
      <%-- Get a maximum of ten stories --%>
      <% int count = 0; %>
      <% while (articles.next() && count < 10) { %>
```

```
<% count++; %>
<% String URL="article.jsp?sectionId=" +
            pageInfo.getSectionId() +
            "&articleId=" +
            articles.getArticleId(); %>
<% if(user.interestedIn(articles.getArticleId)) { %>
  <FONT COLOR="#FFFF00">
<% } %>
  <A HREF="<%= URL %>"><jsp:getProperty
                          name="articles"
                          property="headline"/></A>
<% if(user.interestedIn(articles.getArticleId)) { %>
  </FONT>
<% } %>
<BLOCKQUOTE>
  <jsp:getProperty name="articles" property="summary"/>
</BLOCKQUOTE>
<!-- top three comments from board go here. -->
<%-- This will create the board if it
 doesn't exist yet --%>
<jsp:setProperty name="allBoards"
 property="newBoardName"
 value="<%= articles.getArticleIdString() %>"/>
<%-- This sets the board bean to the specific board
      we're interested in --%>
<jsp:setProperty
 name="board"
 property="boardId"
 value="<%= articles.getArticleIdString() %>"/>
<%-- Get up to three messages --%>
<UL>
<% while(board.hasMoreMessages()) { %>
  <LI>
  <jsp:getProperty name="board" property="subject"/>
<% } %>
</UL>
<HR>
<% } %>
</TD>
<TD ALIGN="LEFT" WIDTH="20%"
    BGCOLOR="<jsp:getProperty
                name="user"
                property=navBgColor/>">
  <jsp:include page="/ch11/global/navigation.jsp"
   flush="true"/>
</TD>
</TR>
</TABLE>
</BODY>
</HTML>
```

The final issue to be resolved is how `isInterestedIn()` will make its decision. There are lots of ways it can do this, but for the time being JNT will show an article as being "of interest" by marking it with the keyword that currently has the highest score.

Summary

This chapter presented ways to customize the JNT experience for each user. The process started with the definition of the database and the beans that simplify access to it. This methodology is exactly the same one used to build the JNT site initially in Chapter 10.

. Two kinds of data are used to personalize the site. The first is information the user provides explicitly, by choosing a color scheme and general layout and eliminating articles and sections that are not of interest. The second is information figured out implicitly by watching the way a user uses the site. Stories similar to ones the user has found interesting are highlighted.

There is nothing especially difficult or complex about personalization. It all comes down to another application of a database to store information about users, whether provided by them or inferred. Pages can use this information to alter themselves.

Of course, there may be performance issues to deal with when the site starts getting a lot of traffic and needs to store data about many users. Some can be addressed by optimizing the code, such as waiting for the session to expire before storing the updated user information. However, at some point as the site continues to grow, there will be a need to buy new computers for the site as well as for the database. To do this, a large web site must have some way of supporting itself, and Java News Today hopes to build two sources of income: selling banners to advertisers and various T-shirts, mugs, and other items with the Java News Today logo directly to consumers. Both of these topics will be discussed in the next chapter.

CHAPTER 12

Dynamic Ads and E-Commerce

Money does not really make the world go around; gravity and momentum take care of that quite nicely. However, money can keep a web site running, which at times may seem almost as important. There are many ways a web site can make money, and more are showing up daily. This chapter will focus on two of the most common, advertising and merchandising.

Neither of these is fundamentally at odds with a user-centric site, such as Java News Today. No one enjoys the endless repetition of ads for items they do not care about or constant plugs to buy shoddy or uninteresting goods. However, the Web can make shopping very easy and convenient, and if an advertisement informs a user of an item he or she might like but did not know about, it is a win for the user, the vendor, and the site.

The secret here is to show users only items that actually appeal to them and filter out the advertising noise that most people find so irritating. In other words, the key is personalization, just as it is with content. With customized ads users will not be bothered with irrelevant advertising, and advertisers are generally willing to pay much more to ensure that their ads are seen only by people who might actually buy their products. Again, everybody wins.

The same is true for merchandise that a site might offer on its own, such as T-shirts and mugs with the site logo. If users really like a site and feel part of it, and if the merchandise is well constructed and clever, users will want to buy these things. All a site has to do is make them easy to obtain and be subtle in selling them.

Advertisements

Since personalization will be the driving force behind JNT's ads, it should not be surprising that the ads will be held in the database. Once again, this means that the first step will be to design the tables according to what information needs to be stored.

The first and most obvious element is the ad text. In order to match ads with users, the ads will need to be weighted according to relevant keywords, so an auxiliary table will be needed that maps ad IDs to keyword IDs. This will work in much the same way that keywords were associated with articles in Chapter 9. Also important is that most ads are sold based on a number of *impressions;* in other words, an advertiser may pay a specified amount to ensure that its ad is seen a certain number of times. Thus the database will need to store the number of impressions sold as well as the number of times the ad has been seen so far. The database schema is shown in Listing 12.1.

Listing 12.1   The Table Definitions for Ads

```
CREATE SEQUENCE adid_seq;
CREATE TABLE ads (
        adid                        integer
                                    default
                                    nextval('adid_seq')
                                    primary key,
        impressions                 int,
        impressionssofar            int,
        adbody                      text
);
CREATE TABLE adkeywords (
        adid                        int,
        keywordid                   int
);
```

The next step, as always, is to define the beans. There will be an ad on every page of the site, so there is good reason to minimize the calls to the database. This is accomplished with an `AdHolder` bean that works much like the `SectionHolder` bean used in the last two chapters. Some additions will also be made to the `UserInfo` bean, which will be discussed shortly.

Once the beans have been written, a page can be built to put new ads into rotation. It will closely resemble the article creation page from Chapter 10 and is shown in Listing 12.2. Like the newsdesk, this page starts by including *authorvalid.jsp* to ensure that the user is a valid author and has logged in. In a large site ads are not created by the reporters but by a staff dedicated to ad sales and management. When JNT gets large enough to hire an ad sales department, it will be easy enough to create a new table for people who will be entering ads.

Listing 12.2 The Ad Creation Page

```
<%@ include file="global/dbconnect.jsp" %>
<%@ include file="global/authorvalid.jsp" %>
<HTML>
<HEAD><TITLE>Ad Desk</TITLE></HEAD>
<BODY>
  <H1>Ad Creation Page</H1>
  <P>Create a new ad:</P>
  <FORM ACTION="adcreate.jsp" METHOD="POST">
  <TABLE>
  <TR>
    <TD>Ad text:</TD>
    <TD><TEXTAREA NAME="body"></TEXTAREA></TD>
  </TR>
  <TR>
    <TD>Number of Impressions:</TD>
    <TD><INPUT TYPE="TEXT" NAME="impressions"></TD>
  </TR>
  <TR>
    <TD>Provide a weight for all keywords:</TD>
    <TD>
      <jsp:useBean
          id="keyword"
          class="com.awl.jspbook.ch12.KeywordBean"/>
      <% keyword.select(); %>
      <% while (keyword.next()) { %>
        <INPUT TYPE="TEXT" NAME="keyweight"
        VALUE="1" SIZE="3"><jsp:getProperty
                               name="keyword"
                               property="keyword"/><BR>
      <% } %>
      </SELECT>
    </TD>
  </TR>
  <TR>
    <TD COLSPAN="2">
      <INPUT TYPE="SUBMIT" NAME="Submit" Value="Submit">
    </TD>
  </TR>
  </TABLE>
  </BODY>
  </HTML>
```

The only major change between this page and the newsdesk is the text field, which allows the ad to be weighted according to how relevant it is to each keyword. For example, an ad for an integrated development environment that runs on Linux and Solaris will have a high number for the IDE, Linux, and Solaris keywords and low or zero scores for the others. If this IDE also supports a custom Java compiler, the compiler keyword may also be given a larger weight. This scheme allows ads to be matched against users through a more sophisticated scheme than the simple single-value comparison used to match articles to users.

When all the values have been entered, the ad will actually be created by *adcreate.jsp,* which is shown in Listing 12.3.

Listing 12.3   The JSP That Enters a New Ad into the Database

```
<%@ include file="global/dbconnect.jsp" %>
<%@ include file="global/authorvalid.jsp" %>
<%@ include file="global/ads.jsp" %>
<HTML>
<HEAD><TITLE>News Desk: Ad created</TITLE></HEAD>
<BODY>
   <jsp:setProperty name="ad" property="*"/>
   <% ad.insert(); %>
   <P>Ad created</P>
   <P>Return to the<A HREF="addesk.jsp">Ad Desk</A>.</P>
</BODY>
</HTML>
```

Again, note the similarity between this example and the corresponding *storycreate.jsp* from Chapter 10. This page uses a bean called ad, defined in *ads.jsp,* which is included at the top. This JSP contains the definition for the AdHolder bean, simply as a convenience, since it is easier to do the include than to type the following in each page:

```
<jsp:useBean
  id="ad"
  class="com.awl.jspbook.ch12.AdHolder"
  scope="application"/>
```

Everything is now in place to start serving ads to users. However, in order for the customization to work, there must be some interaction between the UserInfo bean and the AdHolder bean. The two can be connected in many ways; but since the UserInfo object is already being passed the request object on most pages, it can use the request to obtain AdHolder from the application scope. The UserInfo bean can then export a new property, ad, which will contain an ad relevant to the user. The ad will appear in the header, as shown in Listing 12.4.

Listing 12.4 The Header with an Ad

```
<%@ include file="ads.jsp" %>
<%@ include file="userinfo.jsp" %>
<%-- Begin Header --%>
<H1>Welcome to Java News Today</H1>
<HR>
<jsp:getProperty name="user" property="ad"/>
</HR>
<H2>
<jsp:getProperty name="pageInfo" property="sectionName"/>
</H2>
<P>
<jsp:getProperty name="pageInfo" property="sectionDescription"/>
</P>
<% if (user.isLoggedIn()) { %>
<CENTER>
  <FONT SIZE="-1">
    Welcome back,
    <jsp:getProperty name="user" property="name"/>!
  </FONT>
</CENTER>
<% } %>
<%-- End Header --%>
```

The getAd() method will need to do quite a lot. Most obviously, it will need to select an ad, based on the keyword weights for each ad and the user's keyword scores, as discussed in Chapter 11. These numbers will be matched up using what is called a "least squares" distance, computed by subtracting the user's value for each keyword from the corresponding value for the ad, squaring the result, and adding all these results together. For example, if there were only two keywords called A and B, this computation would result in

```
(Ad value for a - user's value for a)^2 +
(Ad value for b - user's value for b)^2
```

Once this has been computed, the ad that results in the smallest value will be the closest fit to the user's interests. To see this, consider what would happen in the case of a perfect match between ad and user. The values for each keyword would be the same, giving a result of zero when subtracted.

This computation may be time consuming, so it will only be done once, the first time an ad is requested. This means that the ads will not change as a user moves around the site and changes the keyword count, but this is acceptable since over a long enough period of time the changes made during any one session will be small compared to the bulk of accumulated data.

Even though there may be one ad that fits a user better than any other, if the same ad appears on every page the user may soon start to ignore it. To avoid this problem, after the least squares computation is done the `UserInfo` bean holds onto the ten closest matches and rotates through each.

If a user has not logged in, or for new users who do not yet have an extensive profile, ten ads will be chosen at random. The best thing to do in this case is to match the ad profiles against the current article profile, but that may take time to compute and may also leave open the question of which ad to show on the section and index pages. JNT expects that most users will log in and quickly build up useful profile data. If this assumption later turns out to be incorrect, they will move to a content-based targeting system instead of the current user-based scheme.

Finally, each time the `UserInfo` bean shows an ad, it will notify the `AdHolder` bean, allowing it to keep track of how many impressions have been served so that an ad can be taken out of rotation once enough people have seen it.

E-Commerce

Virtually everything that can be sold can be sold online. E-commerce sites like CDnow and Amazon are huge success stories and clearly point the way to the future of shopping. Java News Today is not quite in a position to do this kind of site, since their main focus is information, not goods. However, it will be fairly easy for them to sell site-related merchandise like T-shirts, mugs, stuffed animals, and so on. Many businesses specialize in manufacturing such items in small or midsized lots, so obtaining the goods is not difficult. It is just necessary to construct pages that allow users to order these items. Once again, these pages will be based on a database and will follow the development patterns we have now seen several times.

The first step is to define the tables. Clearly one will be needed to hold the catalog, with descriptions of each item to be sold. Also needed is a table for multiple variations of an item, such as T-shirts in a variety of sizes and colors. Yet another table will be needed to record orders that have been placed and each order's status.

The schema for the e-commerce database is shown in Listing 12.5. The descriptions table holds the descriptions and a unique ID for the major classes of items, such as mugs. The catalog table includes minor variations of the items, such as color and size, the price for each variation, and the number currently available. The new information associated with users will be made available through the `UserInfo` bean; the other tables will also have corresponding beans, as in previous examples.

Listing 12.5   The Schema for the E-Commerce Tables

```
CREATE SEQUENCE itemid_seq;
CREATE SEQUENCE catid_seq;
CREATE SEQUENCE orderid_seq;
CREATE TABLE ads (
CREATE TABLE descriptions (
        itemid          integer
                        default
                        nextval('itemid_seq')
                        primary key,
        name            text,
        shortdesc       text,
        fulldesc        text
);
CREATE TABLE catalog (
        catid           integer
                        default
                        nextval('catid_seq')
                        primary key,
        itemid          int,
        variation       text,
        price           float,
        inventory       int
);
CREATE TABLE orders (
        orderid         integer
                        default
                        nextval('orderid_seq')
                        primary key,
        userid          int,
        catid           int,
        status          int
);
CREATE TABLE usershipinfo (
        userid          int,
        billaddress     text,
        shipaddress     text,
        creditcardnum   char(30),
        expmonth        int,
        expyear         int
);
```

Since the catalog will not be changed that often, JNT will not create screens to update it or add new items but will accomplish this through SQL commands. Therefore, the first pages to be built will present the catalog to users. The entry page is shown in Listing 12.6.

Listing 12.6   The Catalog Entry Page

```
<%@include file="global/dbconnect.jsp" %>
<%@include file="global/userinfo.jsp" %>
<jsp:useBean id="pageInfo"
    class="com.awl.jspbook.ch12.PageInfo"
    scope="request">
<jsp:setProperty name="pageInfo" property="*"/>
</jsp:useBean>
<HTML>
<HEAD>
  <TITLE>
    Java News Today: The store
  </TITLE>
</HEAD>
<BODY BGCOLOR="<jsp:getProperty
                name="user"
                property=bgColor/>"
      TEXT="<jsp:getProperty
                name="user"
                property=textColor/>"
      LINK="<jsp:getProperty
                name="user"
                property=linkColor/>"
      VLINK="<jsp:getProperty
                name="user"
                property=vlinkColor/>">
<TABLE BORDER="0" WIDTH="100%">
  <TR>
    <TD BGCOLOR="<jsp:getProperty
                name="user"
                property=headBgColor/>">
        ALIGN="CENTER" COLSPAN="2">
      <jsp:include page="/ch12/global/header.jsp"
        flush="true"/>
    </TD>
  </TR>
  <TR>
    <TD ALIGN="LEFT" WIDTH="20%"
        BGCOLOR="<jsp:getProperty
                name="user"
                property=navBgColor/>">
      <jsp:include page="/ch12/global/navigation.jsp"
        flush="true"/>
    </TD>
    <TD>
      <%-- Content goes here --%>
      <H1>The JNT Online store!</H1>
      <P>
      Thank you for visiting our store.  The items listed
      below have been carefully designed and hand-crafted to
      be fun, cool, and durable.  Click on an item for more
```

```
information, or you can take a look at the current
contents of your <A HREF="shoppingcart.jsp">shopping cart</A>.
</P>
<jsp:useBean
  id="catalog"
  class="com.awl.jspbook.ch12.DescriptionBean"/>
<% catalog.select(); %>
<DL>
<% while catalog.next() { %>
<DT><A HREF="item.jsp?itemid=<jsp:getProperty
      name="catalog" property="itemid"/>
      <jsp:getProperty name="catalog" property="name"/></A>
<DD><jsp:getProperty name="catalog" property="shortdesc"/>
<% } %>
</DL>
    </TD>
  </TR>
</TABLE>
</BODY>
</HTML>
```

Note that this page employs the user's color preferences and still includes the full navigation. This will help the store integrate better with the rest of the site. This version does not use the user's choice of left or right side navigation or text only, but these can easily be added.

The heart of this page is the loop through the items in the catalog. Each item is linked to another page where details can be read, variations examined, and items ordered. This latter page, without the surrounding navigation, is shown in Listing 12.7. Here is another classic example of a database- and bean-driven page. CatalogBean is passed the itemID of interest through the setProperty() call; it then loops through all the variations, showing the price of each and linking to the shopping cart page.

Listing 12.7 The Item Information Page

```
<jsp:useBean id="item"
  class="com.awl.jspbook.ch12.CatalogBean"/>
<jsp:setProperty name="item" property="*"/>
<H1><jsp:getProperty name="item" property="name"/></H2>
<P>
<jsp:getProperty name="item" property="longdesc"/>
</P>
<P>Variations:</P>
<UL>
<% item.select(); %>
<% while(item.next()) { %>
<LI><jsp:getProperty name="item" property="variation"/> -
```

```
$<jsp:getProperty name="item" property="price"/>.
<A HREF="shoppingcart.jsp?additem=<jsp:getProperty
name="item" property="catid"/>"Buy it!</A>
<% } %>
</UL>
```

The shopping cart page is, of course, based on a shopping cart bean, which lives in the session scope and contains all the items the user has selected. It also contains methods for adding or removing items, as well as a method to check out all items and place the order. The page is shown in Listing 12.8; once again the navigation and surrounding elements have been left out.

Listing 12.8   The Shopping Cart Page

```
<jsp:useBean id="cart"
 class="com.awl.jspbook.ch12.ShoppingCartBean"
 scope="session">
<jsp:setProperty
  name="cart"
  property="userId"
  value="<%= user.getUserId() %>/>
</jsp:useBean>
<jsp:setProperty name="cart" property="*"/>
<% if (cart.isEmpty()) { %>
<P>Your shopping cart is currently empty.</P>
<P><A HREF="catalog.jsp">Continue shopping</A></P>
<% } else { %>
<P>Your shopping cart currently contains the following:</P>
<TABLE>
  <TR>
    <TH>Item</TH>
    <TH>Version</TH>
    <TH>Price</TH>
    <TD></TD>
  </TR>
<% cart.select(); %>
<% while (cart.next()) { %>
  <TR>
    <TD><jsp:getProperty name="cart" property="name"/></TD>
    <TD><jsp:getProperty name="cart" property="variation"/></TD>
    <TD><jsp:getProperty name="cart" property="price"/></TD>
    <TD><A HREF="shopingcart?delitem=<jsp:getProperty
                name="cart" property="catId"/>">delete</A></TD>
  </TR>
<% } %>
  <TR>
    <TD COLSPAN="2" ALIGN="RIGHT"><B>Total:</B></TD>
    <TD><jsp:getProperty name="cart" property="totalPrice"/></TD>
    <TD></TD>
```

```
    </TR>
</TABLE>
<P>
You can now <A HREF="catalog.jsp">continue shopping</A>
or <A HREF="checkout.jsp">check out</A>.
</P>
<% } %>
```

There is nothing fundamentally new on this page. When the bean is first created, its `userId` is set from the `UserInfo` bean, which links the two beans together. It is also possible to make the shopping cart a member of `UserInfo` or even to do away with the shopping cart entirely and add its methods to `UserInfo` directly. However, since the two beans do conceptually different things, it makes more sense to keep them separate.

The most interesting feature of this page is the delete links, which send the user back to the shopping cart page. When the `delitem()` method is set as part of the call to `setProperties()`, the item is removed and the remaining items in the cart, if any, are shown. Also note the special `totalPrice` method, which computes the total cost of all items in the cart.

Almost done. The last page needed is the checkout page, which ensures that all necessary shipping and credit card information is available and places the order in the orders table. This page is shown in Listing 12.9.

Listing 12.9 The Checkout Page

```
<jsp:useBean id="cart"
 class="com.awl.jspbook.ch12.ShoppingCartBean"
 scope="session"/>
<%-- If we were called with shipping info,
     process it here. --%>
<jsp:setProperty name="user" property="*"/>
<% if (user.canOrder()) { %>
<% cart.order(); %>
<P>Thank you!  Your order has been placed, and should
be delivered within 5 business days.</P>
<% } else { %>
<P>Please provide the following information, so we can
process your order:</P>
<FORM ACTION="checkout.jsp">
<P>Billing Address:</P>
<P><TEXTAREA NAME="billAddress"></P>
<P>Shipping Address (if different):</P>
<P><TEXTAREA NAME="shipAddress"></P>
<P>Credit Card Number:
<INPUT TYPE="TEXT" NAME="creditCardNum"></P>
```

```
<P>Month of credit card expiration:
<SELECT NAME="expMonth">
<OPTION>1
<OPTION>2
<OPTION>3
<OPTION>4
<OPTION>5
<OPTION>6
<OPTION>7
<OPTION>8
<OPTION>9
<OPTION>10
<OPTION>11
<OPTION>12
</SELECT>
</P>
<P>Year of credit card expiration:
<SELECT NAME="expYear">
<OPTION>1999
<OPTION>2000
<OPTION>2001
<OPTION>2002
<OPTION>2003
<OPTION>2004
</SELECT>
</P>
<P><INPUT TYPE="SUBMIT" NAME="SUBMIT"></P>
</FORM>
<% } %>
```

Conceptually, the checkout page is a simple one. It checks the `UserInfo` bean to determine whether the user has provided enough information to process the order. If not, the user is prompted for billing, shipping, and credit card information. This information is sent back to the same page, where the `setProperty()` tag at the top stores it in the database if necessary.

Once the user has provided all the necessary information, the shopping cart's `order()` method is called. This copies the order to the order table, clears the cart, and decrements the inventory in the catalog table.

The two remaining steps in the process are charging the user's credit card and sending the merchandise. There are many services available to handle the credit card processing tasks. Hell's Kitchen Systems, at *http://www.hks.net*, even offers a Java module that can be called from a servlet or JSP page. This module handles contacting the credit card service and doing the charge, and reports back on whether or not the charge has been accepted either online when the user places the order or offline through another process that scans the order database.

Once the charge has been accepted, someone at Java News Today needs to manually ship the merchandise. If JNT ever gets so large that it is no longer feasible to do it themselves, they can look into hiring a professional service to handle the process, called *fulfillment*.

The database as constructed stores the credit card information unencoded, which is something no real site would do. Even if the database is completely secure from outside users, the fact that anyone on the JNT staff can access it makes that information insecure. This is not a question of trusting the employees but simply one of users demanding protection for their most sensitive data.

Users can enter their credit card number each time they order, but while this eliminates the problem of storing the information securely, it also eliminates some of the convenience. A better option is to store an encrypted form of the credit card information using passwords. A password can be stored in the `UserInfo` object and used to decrypt the credit card information at the time the order is placed. Of course, this means that the password also needs to be stored in the database in an encrypted form, which, although possible, complicates the login page and the `UserInfo` bean somewhat.

These topics are beyond the scope of this book, but any site that is going to deal with credit cards should make every effort to ensure that it is secure from crackers and that sensitive data is well encrypted so that even if a hostile person breaks into the system, he will find nothing of value. There are numerous good books on web site security. We recommend *Web Security: A Step-by-Step Reference Guide* by Lincoln Stein.

Summary

To a large extent ads and e-commerce are simply two more examples of using a database with JSPs. They both follow the now familiar pattern: tables are designed, beans are written, and the beans are used in pages. Beyond this basic template for building dynamic pages, ads can be targeted to users' interests in a number of ways, including the keyword-based matching shown in this chapter.

There are many other ways to target ads, including geographically, where ads are shown to users based on location. For example, a store in San Francisco might want their ads to be seen only by users who have specified a San Francisco shipping address when ordering something. Other possibilities include targeting based on browser or domain.

Most of what makes e-commerce interesting—credit card processing and fulfillment—is best handled by an external service. The basics of presenting a catalog of merchandise, maintaining a shopping cart, and placing the orders are all straightforward applications of the same standard database techniques used for ads and, for that matter, articles and other content.

This concludes the last major component of the Java News Today site, which is not to say that the site is finished, since no site is every truly complete. However, this should be sufficient information to start building any web site that is dynamic, customizable, and frequently updated.

The final chapter of this book deals with some of the more advanced features of JSPs. However, before we can jump into this topic we must better understand the servlets that form the basis for JSPs. This is the topic of the next chapter.

CHAPTER 13

Servlets

From time to time throughout this book we have made references to *servlets*. In particular, we have noted that a JSP file is turned into a servlet at translation time, which then is run at request time. This means that JSPs and servlets are really the same thing.

As discussed in Chapter 1, a servlet is a small class that may be thought of as a dynamic extension to a web or application server. This is in sharp contrast to traditional CGIs, which are external programs started by the web server. The change from external to internal extensions has a number of advantages, chief of which is performance. Since a servlet is loaded only once, the first time it is needed, and after that resides in the same Java Virtual Machine in which the web server or application server resides, the large overhead of starting a new program for each request is avoided.

This chapter is not meant to be a comprehensive study of servlets, as this topic could fill a book itself. In fact, it has filled several such books, of which we recommend *Inside Servlets: Server-Side Programming for the Java™ Platform* by Dustin R. Callaway for a much more detailed look at servlets and the servlet API. Even so, since JSPs ultimately are servlets, it makes sense for JSP authors to know at least a little about what is going on behind the scenes if for no other reason than to appreciate how much easier it is to write JSPs.

The Servlet Life Cycle

A CGI has a pretty simple life. When a user makes a request the web server runs the CGI program. For a Perl program, this means starting up the Perl interpreter, which then reads the file comprising the program and starts executing instructions, beginning at the top of the file and moving down. For a CGI written in C or C++, the program starts at its main() method, which may then call other procedures, create classes, and so on. In either case, the web server communicates all the information about the request through environment variables and possibly some data written to the program's input. The program generates a response by printing some headers, followed by the body of the response. It then exits, vanishing from system memory as if it had never existed. If there are many requests for the same CGI, either all at once or one after the other, a new instance of the CGI is created each time.

In principle a servlet follows the same pattern. It can consist of nothing more than a class with a service() method, which handles a request. Each time a request comes in, a new instance of the servlet is created and then its service() method is called. Inside this method, the class can make calls to get request information and can return results by printing the headers and the resulting HTML page, just as a CGI does.

This process saves the overhead of loading the class each time, but it is still very inefficient. The actual servlet API can best be understood by starting from this model and seeing what improvements can be made.

First, it is unnecessary to create a new instance for every request—the web server only needs to create a single instance and can then call this instance's service() method. For this to be possible, the service() method cannot use any global data or write to a common output stream. If global data were used to hold the request, input would be jumbled if two or more requests came in at the same time. Likewise, if a single output stream were used, the output of multiple simultaneous requests would be intermingled.

The solution to this problem is to have the web server pass in unique instances of a request and response object each time it calls the service() method. In other words, instead of constructing a new instance of a servlet each time, the server constructs new objects representing the request and response. This might seem even worse than just constructing a new servlet, but in fact there are advantages to doing it this way. For one thing, the web server probably needs to do this work anyway, since there will have to be some way to isolate different requests. For another, the request and response objects are typically much simpler than the servlet object, so it is easier to build them. By the way, if the notion of a request object sounds familiar, it should. This is exactly the same request object that JSPs use to get form variables and other data.

Now that the servlet will only be constructed once, a further optimization can be made. Consider a CGI that uses a database. Each time it is started, it needs to reconnect to the database because it has no way to hold onto a connection between the time it shuts down and the time it starts up again. However, since a servlet never goes away after it is started, it needs to open this connection only once. The same is true for many other kinds of initializations, such as building some auxiliary classes or setting some variables to known defaults. This means that all the initialization code can be taken out of the `service()` method and put into a separate method called `init()`. The web server will call `init()` once, when the servlet is first loaded; after that it may call `service()` multiple times.

If servlets lasted forever, these two methods would be the only ones needed. However, there are a number of ways a servlet may be retired. Sooner or later the web server will need to shut down, and when it does it should give all its servlets a chance to clean up after themselves, close database connections, and so on. A servlet might also be replaced by a newer version, in which case the old version should also be given the opportunity to close any resources it has opened. Servlets handle this with a `destroy()` method, called by the web server when it knows that the servlet will not be asked to service any more requests. The servlet then has the chance to undo anything it did in the `init()` method.

These three methods define the servlet life cycle, which is illustrated in Figure 13.1.

The Servlet Class Hierarchy

The most basic servlet definitions live in the `javax.servlet` package and consist of a number of interfaces.

The `ServletContext` interface provides a means for servlets to communicate with the surrounding web or application server. This communication can take the form of requests for system resources, reports written by the servlet to a log file, and so on. Indirectly `ServletContext` also allows servlets to communicate with each other, primarily by sending requests to other pages. This is how the `jsp:forward` and `jsp:include` tags are implemented, as we will see shortly. `ServletContext` is implemented by the writers of the web or application server; servlet authors seldom need to use it directly and never need to extend it.

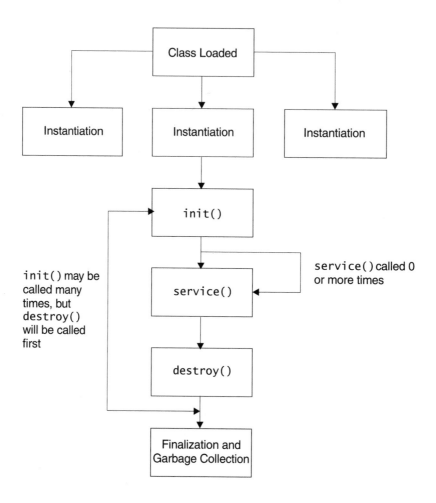

Figure 13.1   The Servlet Life Cycle

The ServletConfig interface is a way for the web server to pass initialization information to the servlet's init() method. This information takes the form of pairs of names and values, which a site administrator typically sets by editing a file or using an administration GUI. For example, if a servlet is going to open a connection to a database, it does not make sense to hard-code the name of the driver class and the database URL; doing so would make the servlet harder to change if a new database were ever installed. Instead, this information is sent to the servlet as parameters and the servlet uses ServletConfig to retrieve these values and act accordingly. Like ServletContext, this interface is implemented by the authors of the web server.

Finally we come to the `Servlet` interface itself. This interface defines the three lifecycle methods as well as a handful of others.

Also residing in the `javax.servlet` package are the `ServletRequest` and `ServletResponse` interfaces, which encapsulate a request to and a response from the servlet. Objects that implement these interfaces are passed to the servlet's `service()` method, which provides the servlet with all the information about the request and with a means to return the generated page as well as auxiliary information.

Finally, the `javax.servlet` package defines three classes. Two of these, `ServletInputStream` and `ServletOutputStream`, read and write data respectively. The third, `GenericServlet`, implements both the `Servlet` and `ServletConfig` interfaces and forms the basis for almost all real servlets.

Note that so far none of this has been specific to the Web or HTTP. This is deliberate. There are many kinds of servers on the web, including FTP, mail, chat rooms, games, and so on, and many of these want the same kind of dynamic extensibility that web servers can use. Thus, it makes sense for each of them to have a corresponding servlet. A multiuser dungeon game might have a "character" servlet and a "weapon" servlet, and as new characters and weapons are introduced these can be written as servlets and loaded as needed.

The Web-specific versions of the servlet classes are included in a package called `javax.servlet.http`, the heart of which is the `HttpServlet` class, which extends `GenericServlet`. This class's `service()` method takes `HttpServletRequest` and `HttpServletResponse` objects instead of the generic versions from the `javax.servlet` package. These variations contain a great deal of HTTP-specific information, such as cookies, remote user names, and authentication schemes.

`HttpServlet` also has a built-in `service()` method, which looks at the request received and calls an appropriate method to handle it. For example, if the request is an HTTP GET, `doGet()` will be called. There are also `doPost()`, `doDelete()`, and so on. These methods free a servlet writer from worrying about handing specific requests properly. He or she can just override the appropriate DO method or methods, and if any other kind of request comes in the servlet will report that it does not handle it.

Listing 13.1 depicts a very simple servlet that shows these methods in use. After the servlet is loaded, its `init()` method is called to look for a parameter to display as a response to a request. If no such parameter is provided, a default is used. Note that `init()` starts by calling `super.init()`, which ensures that all the "behind the scenes" setup is done properly.

Listing 13.1   A Simple Servlet

```
package com.awl.jspbook.ch13;
import javax.servlet.*;
import javax.servlet.http.*;
import java.io.*;
public class HelloServlet extends HttpServlet {
  private String message;
  public void init(ServletConfig sc)
    throws ServletException
  {
    super.init(sc);
    message = sc.getInitParameter("message");
    if (message == null)
      message = "Hello, world!";
  }
  public void doGet(HttpServletRequest req,
                  HttpServletResponse res)
    throws IOException,ServletException
  {
    handle(req,res);
  }
  public void doPost(HttpServletRequest req,
                  HttpServletResponse res)
    throws IOException,ServletException
  {
    handle(req,res);
  }

  public void handle(HttpServletRequest req,
                  HttpServletResponse res)
    throws IOException,ServletException
  {
    res.setStatus(res.SC_OK);
    res.setContentType("text/html");

    PrintWriter out = res.getWriter();
    out.println("<HTML>");
    out.println("<HEAD><TITLE>A servlet</TITLE></HEAD>");
    out.println("<BODY>");
    out.println(message);
    out.println("</BODY>");
    out.println("</HTML>");
    out.close();
  }
  public void destroy() {
    return;
  }
}
```

This servlet does not override the service() method, so the default is used.
Consequently, any GET or POST requests are handled by the corresponding

method, and any other kind of request results in an error. In this case the response to GET and POST requests will be identical, so both call `handle()`, which is responsible for actually handing the request.

`Handle()` first sets some information about the response it is returning—in particular, that the request succeeded, by setting the status code to `SC_OK`, and that the data to be returned is HTML. It then obtains a `Writer` object, which it uses to actually print the page. Even on a page as simple as the one in Listing 13.1, all those print statements can be a burden, which is one reason it is so much easier to write JSPs.

This servlet has nothing to clean up when it is decommissioned, so the `destroy()` method simply returns. In fact, this method is not needed here at all, but it is included for completeness.

Two exceptions are declared by the methods in this servlet. `IOException` is thrown whenever there is a problem with IO, which can happen if the user hits the stop button on her browser before receiving the full page or if there is some kind of network problem. `ServletException` indicates that the servlet has run into a problem while processing. The servlet in Listing 13.1 never actually throws this exception, but if the servlet author decides that failing to provide a message is a critical error, `init()` can throw `ServletException` instead of setting the message to a default value. This exception can be constructed with a message describing the problem, which will end up in a log file.

A servlet can provide additional information by throwing `Unavailable Exception`. This is a subclass of `ServletException` that comes in two flavors, permanent and temporary. The permanent version tells the web server that this servlet cannot continue, so the web server will never call the servlet's `init()` or `service()` methods again. The temporary version may include a time interval in seconds during which the web server will wait and then call the method that threw the exception. This is useful if a servlet discovers that some resource it needs, such as a database, has become unavailable. The chances are good that the database will be restarted shortly, at which point the servlet can reconnect and continue working. In the meantime, however, there is no need for the servlet to try to handle requests, which will only put a lot of unnecessary burden on the network.

The HttpServletRequest Interface

By now most of the common methods of `HttpServeletRequest` should be familiar, as we have been using them since Chapter 3, where the implicit request object was introduced. In the broadest sense this interface defines everything there is to know about a request. Some of this information is fairly straight-forward, such as the name of the machine from which the request was issued or the browser that is being used. However, there are a few types of information provided by the request object we have not yet examined.

One important type of data provided by the request object is the list of *cookies*. Cookies are small pieces of data that a web site can send to a browser and that the browser is expected to send back to the web site on subsequent requests. They have a number of properties, including the *domain*, which indicates what system the cookie should be sent to; the *path*, which indicates the URLs within that domain to which the cookie should be sent; and a *maximum age*, which indicates how long the cookie has to live—once the time has passed the cookie will no longer be sent back to the web site and will probably be deleted from the browser's cookie repository.

In the servlet APIs, cookies are represented by the `javax.servlet.http.Cookie` class, which contains all the preceding information and possibly additional fields. When the request object calls its `getCookies()` method an array of all the cookies the browser sent with the current request is returned.

JSPs and servlets also use a special cookie internally to keep track of sessions, since HTTP is by nature a *stateless* protocol, meaning that no information is preserved between each request. All the information about each session is stored somewhere in memory and a special key is used to look it up. This key is passed in a cookie, so each time the user makes a request the key is sent along. The JSP Engine can then retrieve this cookie and use it to access the relevant session data.

Some users distrust cookies, so the servlet application programming interface provides an alternate way to pass the key back and forth by rewriting each URL so that it includes the key. For example, if a user without cookies tries to access *http://somesite.com/apage.jsp*, he might be redirected to something else where the additional information contains the session key such as, *http://somesite.com/To1010mC0673157862957708/apage.jsp*. Any links on the page should be relative, such as . . . */something/another page.jsp*, so that when the user follows the link the portion of the URL that contains the session key will be preserved.

The request object can tell a servlet or JSP if the user's session is stored in a cookie or a URL by using the `isRequestedSessionIdFromCookie()` and `isRequestedSessionIdFromURL()` methods. The request object can also provide access to the session itself, which we will discuss further when we look at using scopes from servlets.

Listing 13.2 shows a servlet that prints all its cookies as well as some information about the current session. Structurally this servlet closely resembles the servlet from Listing 13.1; the major difference is that this one has no `init()`

or `destroy()` method. Inside the handler, the cookies are obtained from the request object and printed. The servlet then checks whether there is a current valid session and if so determines whether it came from a cookie or was written into the URL.

Listing 13.2   A Servlet That Gets Cookie and Session Information

```
package com.awl.jspbook.ch13;
import javax.servlet.*;
import javax.servlet.http.*;
import java.io.*;
public class CookieServlet extends HttpServlet {
  public void doGet(HttpServletRequest req,
                    HttpServletResponse res)
    throws IOException,ServletException
  {
    handle(req,res);
  }
  public void doPost(HttpServletRequest req,
                     HttpServletResponse res)
    throws IOException,ServletException
  {
    handle(req,res);
  }

  public void handle(HttpServletRequest req,
                     HttpServletResponse res)
    throws IOException,ServletException
  {
    res.setStatus(res.SC_OK);
    res.setContentType("text/html");

    PrintWriter out = res.getWriter();
    out.println("<HTML>");
    out.println("<HEAD><TITLE>Cookies</TITLE></HEAD>");
    out.println("<BODY>");
    Cookie cookies[] = req.getCookies();
    if(cookies == null || cookies.length == 0) {
      out.println("You have no cookies");
    } else {
      out.println("<TABLE>");
      out.println("<TR>");
      out.println("<TH>Name</TH>");
      out.println("<TH>Domain</TH>");
      out.println("<TH>Path</TH>");
      out.println("<TH>Value</TH>");
      out.println("<TH>Max Age</TH>");
      out.println("</TR>");
      for(int i=0;i<cookies.length;i++) {
        out.println("<TR>");
        out.println("<TD>" + cookies[i].getName() + "</TD>");
```

```
                out.println("<TD>" + cookies[i].getDomain() + "</TD>");
                out.println("<TD>" + cookies[i].getPath() + "</TD>");
                out.println("<TD>" + cookies[i].getValue() + "</TD>");
                out.println("<TD>" + cookies[i].getMaxAge() + "</TD>");
                out.println("</TR>");
            }
        }
        out.println("</TABLE>");
        if(req.isRequestedSessionIdValid()) {
          if(req.isRequestedSessionIdFromCookie()) {
           out.println("This session is from a cookie");
          }
          if(req.isRequestedSessionIdFromURL()) {
           out.println("This session is from the URL");
          }
        } else {
          out.println("There is no session associated");
          out.println("with this request");
        }
        out.println("</BODY>");
        out.println("</HTML>");
        out.close();
    }
}
```

When this example is first run the user will not have any cookies, so the output will be rather sparse. It can be made more interesting by creating a servlet that will issue cookies. This is covered in the next section.

The HttpServletResponse Interface

HttpServletResponse is in some ways the mirror image of the request object, which holds information about the request that the servlet is meant to read but cannot change. The response object is where the servlet can write information about the data it will send back. Whereas the majority of the methods in the request object start with get, indicating that they get a value, many of the important methods in the response object start with set, indicating that they change some property. Note how even these interfaces adhere to the usual naming conventions for beans.

We have already seen two of these SET methods: status code and content type. The status code indicates the status of the response, which hopefully will usually be SC_OK to indicate that the request succeeded normally and the page data will follow. Another code is SC_INTERNAL_SERVER_ERROR, which indicates a problem internal to the web server. This is the code that turns into all those error 500 messages encountered when a JSP runs into problems. A complete list of codes supported by the HTTP protocol is included in the HttpServlet Response interface.

The content type indicates what kind of data will be sent back to the user. In every example we have seen so far, this has been text/html. However, a servlet could also send out plain text by setting this type to text/plain, or it could even generate an image by using something like image/bmp. We will see some examples of creating different kinds of data in the next chapter, when we discuss advanced topics.

In addition to these two methods, a servlet can use the setContentLength() method to indicate how much data is coming back. This attribute is seen in relatively few pages these days, but whenever possible its use is encouraged because it tells the browser when it can close the connection to the server and stop showing the throbbing *N* or spinning *e*.

The request object can also add new cookies by calling the addCookie() method. This method can take as an argument a brand new cookie, or it can obtain an existing cookie from the request, modify it, and send it back to the user.

The other important method in the request class is getWriter(), which returns a PrintWriter that the servlet uses to send its data. This is normally the preferred way to send data back to the user, since the PrintWriter class is convenient to use and automatically handles some internationalization issues. However, if the servlet is going to be sending back binary data, it may instead use the ServletOutputStream class, which can be obtained via getOutputStream(). This class contains a write(byte[]) method, which is ideal for sending bytes of data that should not be interpreted or altered in any way by either the browser or the server.

Note that all of the header information, such as content type and length, must reach the browser before any of the data does. Otherwise, the browser will not know what to do with the data. For this reason, under most circumstances all the response's SET methods must be called before anything is printed to either ServletOutputStream or PrintWriter. To be completely accurate, the output from the servlet is *buffered*; that is, it is held in memory until a certain amount has accumulated, then it is sent to the user all at once.

Efficiency is the goal here, since sending data across the network incurs a lot of overhead and is best done as infrequently as possible. This means that new headers can be set until the buffered content is transmitted, determined via the isCommitted() method, which returns true if any data has been sent to the user. To be on the safe side, though, we recommend always setting all headers before starting to print data.

Listing 13.3 shows how a servlet can use HttpServletResponse to add a new cookie and set a variety of other information.

Listing 13.3   A Servlet That Sets Cookies

```
package com.awl.jspbook.ch13;
import javax.servlet.*;
import javax.servlet.http.*;
import java.io.*;
public class ResponseServlet extends HttpServlet {
  public void doGet(HttpServletRequest req,
                    HttpServletResponse res)
    throws IOException,ServletException
  {
    handle(req,res);
  }
  public void doPost(HttpServletRequest req,
                    HttpServletResponse res)
    throws IOException,ServletException
  {
    handle(req,res);
  }

  public void handle(HttpServletRequest req,
                    HttpServletResponse res)
    throws IOException,ServletException
  {
    StringBuffer text = new StringBuffer();
    String name  = req.getParameter("name");
    String value = req.getParameter("values");
    if(name == null) {
      name = "Acookie";
    }
    if(value == null) {
      value = "AcookieValue";
    }
    text.append("<HTML>");
    text.append("<HEAD><TITLE>A servlet</TITLE></HEAD>");
    text.append("<BODY>");
    text.append("<P>Added a cookie whose name is: ");
    text.append(name);
    text.append(" with a value of: ");
    text.append(value);
    text.append("</P>");
    text.append("<FORM ACTION=ResponseServlet METHOD=GET>");
    text.append("<P>Name: <INPUT TYPE=TEXT NAME=name></P>");
    text.append("<P>Value: <INPUT TYPE=TEXT NAME=value></P>");
    text.append("<P><INPUT TYPE=SUBMIT></P>");
    text.append("</FORM>");
    text.append("</BODY>");
```

```
                      text.append("</HTML>");
                      String html = text.toString();
                      res.setStatus(res.SC_OK);
                      res.setContentType("text/html");
                      res.setContentLength(html.length());
                      Cookie cookie = new Cookie(name,value);
                      cookie.setMaxAge((int) System.currentTimeMillis() +
                                  1000 * 60 * 10);
                      res.addCookie(cookie);

                      PrintWriter out = res.getWriter();
                      out.print(html);
                      out.close();
                  }
              }
```

Cookie creation itself is straightforward: The cookie is constructed and sent to the user with the addCookie() method; it is set to last for ten minutes by setting its maximum age to the current time plus ten minutes, expressed in milliseconds.

This servlet also sets the content length, by buffering the output internally using StringBuffer. The code would have been a little cleaner if it had used a string and the + operator, but the StringBuffer class is generally much more efficient.

The final thing illustrated in this servlet is the getParameterValues() method. It is used, much as it was in Chapter 4, to obtain an array of values that is then checked to ensure that it is neither null nor empty.

Convenience Methods in HttpServletResponse

Since most of the time servlets send out formatted HTML, they set the status to SC_OK. However, there are two other common status response a servlet might generate, errors and redirects. Error pages are all too common; they contain a numeric code indicating the kind of error and usually some short, cryptic message telling the user that something went wrong. Rather then setting the status to the appropriate code and printing the error text, a servlet can simply use the sendError() method, which takes an integer representing the error code and a string to use as the error text. The text is enclosed by <body></body> tags, making things a little easier for the servlet programmer. A typical use might look something like

```
      res.sendError(res.SC_INTERNAL_SERVER_ERROR,
          "Yikes, something went awry!  Please check back later.");
```

Redirects tell a browser that the page it has asked for has moved to a new URL; the browser responds by asking the appropriate server for that URL. This is a common technique for preventing links from going stale, but it is also used to send a user to a different page based on some condition. For example, if a user tries to access a page she does not have permission to read, a page can be sent explaining what she needs to do to obtain this permission.

HttpServletResponse provides a method called sendRedirect() to make redirects easier to use. This method takes a single string argument containing the URL to which the user should be sent. Unlike sendError(), sendRedirect() does not takes a string describing why the user is being sent elsewhere, since in practice the user will never have a chance to read this message before his browser loads the new page. SendRedirect() also does not need a status argument, since the status is assumed to be SC_MOVED_TEMPORARILY. A typical use for this method looks like this:

```
res.sendRedirect("http://www.brunching.com");
```

The URL should be complete and cannot be relative, unlike an HREF. Most browsers correctly handle a relative redirect, but this is not part of the official HTTP specification.

The RequestDispatcher Class

Many examples throughout this book have sent a user to some other page, but they have used a very different technique from the redirects discussed above. The jsp:forward tag is a sort of "server-side" redirect, since the server generates a different page instead of telling the browser to load one. This is related to the jsp:include tag, which includes the body of one JSP, HTML page, or servlet in another. There is no corresponding way to do this on the client side, at least not one that works on all browsers.

Both of these tags are handled internally by the RequestDispatcher class, which, as the name implies, can dispatch a request to another resource in the system. It does this through two methods called, appropriately enough, forward() and include(). Both take as arguments the request and response objects that were passed to the calling servlet. As might be expected, these objects end up being passed to the target servlet's service() method. Listing 7.2 showed a JSP that used a jsp:forward tag and input from the user to send the user one of three pages. Listing 13.4 shows how a servlet accomplishes the same thing.

Listing 13.4 A Servlet That Forwards Requests

```
package com.awl.jspbook.ch13;
import javax.servlet.*;
import javax.servlet.http.*;
import java.io.*;
public class DispatchServlet extends HttpServlet {
  public void doGet(HttpServletRequest req,
                    HttpServletResponse res)
    throws IOException,ServletException
  {
    ServletContext sc = getServletContext();
    RequestDispatcher rd;
    String which = req.getParameter("which");
    if(which != null) {
      if(which.equals("red")) {
      rd = sc.getRequestDispatcher("/ch06/red.jsp");
      rd.forward(req,res);
      } else if(which.equals("green")) {
      rd = sc.getRequestDispatcher("/ch06/green.jsp");
      rd.forward(req,res);
      } else if(which.equals("blue")) {
      rd = sc.getRequestDispatcher("/ch06/blue.jsp");
      rd.forward(req,res);
      } else {
      res.sendError(res.SC_INTERNAL_SERVER_ERROR,
                  "A page was requested that does exist!");
      }
    } else {
      res.sendError(res.SC_INTERNAL_SERVER_ERROR,
                  "No destination page was specified!");
    }
  }
}
```

It is important to realize that once the target page finishes, the forward()
method returns and the calling servlet regains control. However, the output
stream will have been closed, so the servlet should not try to set new headers or send new data, although it can clean up any global resources if necessary. The calling servlet also cannot print any data before calling forward(),
because the target page will likely set one or more headers and, as we observed previously, this may not work if data has already been sent. A similar restriction applies to the include() method. The page it includes cannot
set any headers because the servlet calling include() may have already
printed data.

Using Scopes from Servlets

Chapter 6 discussed the various scopes in which objects can live. Although these scopes are usually accessed by setting the *"scope="* field in a useBean tag, they can also be accessed through scriptlets or through code in a servlet. Listing 13.5 shows a servlet with a counter that works much like the JSP in Listing 6.3.

Listing 13.5   A Servlet with a Page Counter

```
package com.awl.jspbook.ch13;
import javax.servlet.*;
import javax.servlet.http.*;
import java.io.*;
public class Counter1 extends HttpServlet {
  private int count;

  public void init(ServletConfig sc)
    throws ServletException
  {
    super.init(sc);
    count = 0;
  }
  public void doGet(HttpServletRequest req,
                HttpServletResponse res)
    throws IOException,ServletException
  {
    handle(req,res);
  }
  public void doPost(HttpServletRequest req,
                HttpServletResponse res)
    throws IOException,ServletException
  {
    handle(req,res);
  }

  public void handle(HttpServletRequest req,
                HttpServletResponse res)
    throws IOException,ServletException
  {
    res.setStatus(res.SC_OK);
    res.setContentType("text/html");

    PrintWriter out = res.getWriter();
    out.println("<HTML>");
    out.println("<HEAD><TITLE>A Counter</TITLE></HEAD>");
    out.println("<BODY>");
    out.println("This page has been accessed");
    out.println(count);
    out.println("times");
```

```
        out.println("</BODY>");
        out.println("</HTML>");
        count++;
        out.close();
    }
}
```

The count variable here is in the instance scope, just as it would be if it had been created in a JSP declaration. This example does not actually use any servlet features, since the "instance scope" is really just the set of nonstatic fields in the class. Listing 13.6 shows how a similar counter can be used from the session scope so the page will count how often each user has visited it.

Listing 13.6   A Servlet with a Session-Based Counter

```
package com.awl.jspbook.ch13;
import javax.servlet.*;
import javax.servlet.http.*;
import java.io.*;
public class Counter2 extends HttpServlet {
  private static final Integer ONE = new Integer(1);
  public void doGet(HttpServletRequest req,
                    HttpServletResponse res)
    throws IOException,ServletException
  {
    handle(req,res);
  }
  public void doPost(HttpServletRequest req,
                    HttpServletResponse res)
    throws IOException,ServletException
  {
    handle(req,res);
  }

  public void handle(HttpServletRequest req,
                    HttpServletResponse res)
    throws IOException,ServletException
  {
    HttpSession theSession = request.getSession();
    Integer count = theSession.getValue("count");
    res.setStatus(res.SC_OK);
    res.setContentType("text/html");

    PrintWriter out = res.getWriter();
    out.println("<HTML>");
    out.println("<HEAD><TITLE>A Counter</TITLE></HEAD>");
    out.println("<BODY>");
    if(count == null) {
      out.println("This is your first visit to this page!");
```

```
        count = ONE;
      } else {
        out.println("You have seen this page");
        out.println(count);
        out.println("times before");
      }
      theSession.putValue("count",
                          new Integer(count.intValue() + 1));
      out.println("</BODY>");
      out.println("</HTML>");
      out.close();
    }
  }
```

The call to getSession() creates a new session if one has not already been given to the current user. This causes a new cookie to be sent along with this page. Once the session has been obtained, the count variable is accessed with the call to getValue(). Sessions can hold only objects, not primitive types like integers, which is why the value is stored as an integer.

The first time count is requested, it is not in the session and so null is returned. Thus the servlet knows that the session is new, so it can print a different message. This corresponds closely to putting special code or text between <useBean> and </useBean> tags to do something special when the bean is first created.

The variable ONE provides a very slight performance improvement, since it saves having to construct a new integer for every new request, which is faster and uses less memory. Technically this means that every session will be sharing the same object, at least for each user's first visit. Since the value of ONE is never changed, this does not present a problem; however, it does hint at some interesting ways different users could share changeable data. For example, two users could have the same hashtable in their sessions, and any values placed in this table by one user could be seen by the other.

The application and request scopes work almost exactly the same way as the session scope; the only difference is in the methods used to store and retrieve objects. For the request scope, objects are retrieved from the request object by calling request.getAtribute(name) and stored using the corresponding request.setAtribute(name,value).

The application scope is stored in the ServletContext object, since there is only one of these in any given server. A servlet can store data in the application scope by calling

```
ServletContext sc = getServletContext();
sc.setAttribute(name,value);
```

Likewise, once the `ServletContext` has been obtained, objects can be retrieved from it with `sc.getAttribute(name)`.

Using Beans from Servlets

Beans are just as useful for servlet authors as they are for JSP authors, although they are not quite as easy to use from a servlet. Obtaining the bean is straightforward, as shown in Listing 13.7, which uses the bean containing album information for Siouxsie and the Banshees's "Tinderbox" from Chapter 4.

Listing 13.7   A Servlet That Uses a Bean

```
package com.awl.jspbook.ch13;
import javax.servlet.*;
import javax.servlet.http.*;
import java.io.*;
import java.beans.*;
import com.awl.jspbook.ch05.AlbumInfo;
public class CDInfo extends HttpServlet {
  public void doGet(HttpServletRequest req,
                    HttpServletResponse res)
    throws IOException,ServletException
  {
    handle(req,res);
  }
  public void doPost(HttpServletRequest req,
                     HttpServletResponse res)
    throws IOException,ServletException
  {
    handle(req,res);
  }

  public void handle(HttpServletRequest req,
                     HttpServletResponse res)
    throws IOException,ServletException
  {
    AlbumInfo tinderbox;
    res.setStatus(res.SC_OK);
    res.setContentType("text/html");

    PrintWriter out = res.getWriter();
    try {
      tinderbox = (AlbumInfo) Beans.instantiate(
                        getClass().getClassLoader(),
                        "tinderbox");
    } catch (Exception e) {
      tinderbox = null;
    }
```

```
out.println("<HTML>");
out.println("<HEAD><TITLE>Album Info</TITLE></HEAD>");
out.println("<BODY>");
if(tinderbox == null) {
  out.println("The bean could not be found or loaded");
} else {
  out.println("<P>Album name: "
              + tinderbox.getName() + "</P>");
  String tracks[] = tinderbox.getTracks();
  out.println("<P>Tracks:</P>");
  out.println("<OL>");
  for(int i=0;i<tracks.length;i++) {
  out.println("<LI>" + tracks[i]);
  }
  out.println("</OL>");
}
out.println("</BODY>");
out.println("</HTML>");
out.close();
  }
}
```

The call to instantiate() does the real magic in this example. Here it is used to load a serialized bean, but if it had been given the name of a class instead of a filename, it would have loaded the class, called its constructor, and returned a new instance. The first argument to instantiate() is ClassLoader, which, as the name implies, loads other classes. Every Java class can get access to the class loader that loaded it by calling getClassLoader(), and any object can get its class by calling getClass().

Once the bean is loaded, it is treated just like any other class. In particular, it is first cast into the appropriate type and then the methods of this class are called directly. The full power of bean introspection, which can dynamically determine the properties and methods of a bean at runtime, is not being employed here. Introspection is what makes things like automatically setting properties from form parameters possible.

Servlets can do introspection, but since that feature is beyond the scope of this book an example will not be provided. More information can be found in a good book on beans or in the Java documentation, starting with the getBeanInfo() method of the java.beans.Introspector class found at

http://java.sun.com/beans/javadoc/java.beans.Introspector.html

Once a bean has been obtained by a call to instantiate(), it may be stored in any of the four scopes, just like any other object. If a bean is placed in a scope by a servlet, a JSP can later retrieve it through the normal useBean tag. The reverse is also true: Any bean placed in a scope by a JSP can be obtained and used by a servlet. For example, if Listing 13.7 had included the following lines:

```
ServletContext sc = getServletContext();
sc.setAttribute("tinderbox",tinderbox);
```

a JSP could access this bean with the following tag:

```
<jsp:useBean id="tinderbox"
    class="com.awl.jspbook.ch05.AlbumInfo"
    scope="application"/>
```

Note that when a servlet or JSP tries to load a serialized bean, it looks for a file with the *.ser* suffix. In this case, the file loaded is *tinderbox.ser.*

The ability to store beans in the various scopes provides a convenient way for servlets and JSPs to share data and makes the transition between them completely transparent to users. This is a very common programming practice. Typically a request will first go to a servlet, which will do some complex processing. Once the processing is complete the data will be stored in a simple bean, which will be placed in the page or request scope. The servlet will then forward the request to a JSP, which will obtain data values from the bean but otherwise be concerned only with presentation. This is illustrated over the next several listings, which show a simple application that takes a list of numbers and computes their sum and average.

Listing 13.8 starts the process off with a servlet that creates a bean called data and places it in the request scope. The bean is shown in Listing 13.9.

Listing 13.8   A Servlet That Passes a Bean to a JSP

```
package com.awl.jspbook.ch13;
import java.util.StringTokenizer;
import java.io.IOException;
import javax.servlet.*;
import javax.servlet.http.*;
public class SumAvgServlet extends HttpServlet {
    public void doPost(HttpServletRequest req,
                  HttpServletResponse res)
       throws IOException,ServletException
  {
    RequestDispatcher rd;
      ServletContext sc = getServletContext();
      String values       = req.getParameter("values");
    SumAvgBean data       = new SumAvgBean();
    int num           = 0;
    int sum           = 0;
    double avg        = 0;
    int count         = 0;
    /* Add the bean to the request scope */
    req.setAttribute("data",data);
    data.setValues(values);
```

```
    if(values == null) {
        rd = sc.getRequestDispatcher (
                "/jspbook/ch13/sumavgform.jsp");
        rd.forward(req,res);
    } else {
        StringTokenizer st = new StringTokenizer(values);
        String token;
        while(st.hasMoreTokens()) {
            token = st.nextToken();
          try {
              num = Integer.parseInt(token);
          } catch (NumberFormatException e) {
              data.setBad(token);
              rd = sc.getRequestDispatcher (
                      "/ch13/sumavgerror.jsp");
              rd.forward(req,res);
              return;
          }
          count++;
          sum = sum + num;
        }
    }
    data.setSum(sum);
    data.setAvg(sum/count);
    rd = sc.getRequestDispatcher("/ch13/sumavgresult.jsp");
    rd.forward(req,res);
  }
}
```

Listing 13.9   A Bean That Contains Sum and Average Data

```
package com.awl.jspbook.ch13;
public class SumAvgBean {
    private int sum;
    private double avg;
    private String bad;
    private String values;
    public void setBad(String bad) {this.bad = bad;}
    public String getBad() {return bad;}
    public void setValues(String values) {
      this.values = values;
    }
    public String getValues() {return values;}
    public void setSum(int sum) {this.sum = sum;}
    public int getSum() {return sum;}
    public void setAvg(double avg) {this.avg = avg;}
    public double getAvg() {return avg;}
}
```

The servlet then checks whether it has been given any values. If not, it sends the request on to *sumavgform.jsp*, which is shown in Listing 13.10. If so, it breaks them up into individual numbers and adds them together. If a non-number is encountered while processing, the servlet places the offending text in the bean's bad property and passes the request to *sumavgerror.jsp*, which is shown in Listing 13.11. Finally, if all goes well the resulting sum and average are placed in a bean, and the values are sent to *sumavgresult.jsp*, which is shown in Listing 13.12.

Listing 13.10   A Form Where Numbers May Be Entered

```
<HTML>
<BODY>
<P>
Enter a list of numbers, seperated by commas.  I will
compute their sum and average.
</P>
<FORM ACTION="/jspbook/ch13/sumavg" METHOD="POST">
<INPUT TYPE="TEXT" NAME="values">
<INPUT TYPE="SUBMIT">
</FORM>
</BODY>
</HTML>
```

Listing 13.11   A JSP That Displays an Error Value from a Bean

```
<jsp:useBean
   class="com.awl.jspbook.ch13.SumAvgBean"
   id="data"
   scope="request"/>
<HTML>
<HEAD><TITLE>Error</TITLE></HEAD>
<BODY>
<P>
I was unable to complete your request, because
<jsp:getProperty name="data" property="bad"/>
is not a number.
</P>
<FORM ACTION="/jspbook/ch13/sumavg" METHOD="POST">
<INPUT TYPE="TEXT" NAME="values"
   VALUE="<jsp:getProperty name="data" property="values"/>">
<INPUT TYPE="SUBMIT">
</FORM>
</BODY>
</HTML>
```

Listing 13.12   A JSP That Displays Results from a Bean

```
<jsp:useBean
   class="com.awl.jspbook.ch13.SumAvgBean"
   id="data"
   scope="request"/>
```

```
<HTML>
<HEAD><TITLE>Results</TITLE></HEAD>
<BODY>
<P>
The sum of your numbers is
<jsp:getProperty name="data" property="sum"/>.
</P>
<P>
The average of your numbers is
<jsp:getProperty name="data" property="avg"/>.
</P>
</BODY>
</HTML>
```

These examples are some of the cleanest JSPs seen since Chapter 3, and they contain no Java code at all. Thus far we have not been able to achieve this level of separation between code and presentation even using beans because beans can only store values and perform computations. Servlets, however, can perform computations and handle redirects.

If this example were written solely as a JSP and a bean, the JSP would need to differentiate between the cases where input is and where it is not provided. It would also need to handle the error conditions. Both situations would need to be dealt with in Java, although the bean could limit the code to relatively simple conditionals. In constrast, the servlet can handle both the *application logic* and what might be called the *page-flow* logic. This leaves the JSPs to do what they do best—presentation.

The JSP Classes

We have often stated that JSPs are servlets, and we are now in a position to clarify what that means. As discussed in Chapter 1, a JSP file is translated to a Java file by the JSP Engine; it is then compiled and run to produce the page output. For a JSP to be a servlet, all that is necessary is for the generated Java file to implement the javax.servlet.Servlet interface. In reality this is accomplished by having the generated Java class implement javax.servlet.jsp.HttpJspPage, which extends javax.servlet.jsp.JspPage, which in turn implements the Servlet interface.

JspPage adds two additional methods to the Servlet interface: jspInit() and jspDestroy(), which act much like a servlet's init() and destroy() methods. The only difference is that jspInit() is not passed a ServletConfig object when it is called, although ServletConfig can be obtained via the getServletConfig() method.

HttpJspPage adds one additional method, _jspService(), which is passed HttpServiceRequest and HttpServiceResponse, just like service().

In the next chapter we will see how jspInit() and jspDestroy() can be used, but it is worth noting here that humans never write a _jspService() method. This method is built by the JSP Engine based on the original JSP file, and if a programmer also provides a method there will be a conflict. In practice this is not a problem, since any code that can be put in a service method can also be put in a scriptlet in the JSP page.

The javax.servlet.jsp package contains a number of classes that provide additional information or that make life easier for a developer. Most of these are used only by the JSP Engine, but page authors may well want to use the PageContext class. An instance of this class is always available in a JSP as an implicit object called pageContext.

The PageContext class provides a number of utility methods for handling scoped data and, in particular, hides the details of how different scopes are implemented. This means that instead of having to know that, say, the request scope is implemented by HttpServletRequest or that the application scope is in ServletContext, a single method can be used to get or set data from any scope. These methods follow the naming conventions we have already seen and are called getAttribute() and setAttribute. They work much like the identically named functions from HttpServletRequest and ServletContext, but take an additional parameter specifying which scope to use. Listing 13.13 shows a JSP that uses these methods to create a per-session counter, just as Listing 13.6 showed this in a servlet.

Listing 13.13   A JSP That Uses PageContext

```
<HTML>
<HEAD><TITLE>Another counter</TITLE></HEAD>
<BODY>
<% Integer count = (Integer)
   pageContext.getAttribute("count",
                            PageContext.SESSION_SCOPE); %>
<% if (count == null) { %>
   <P>This is your first visit to this page!</P>
   <% count = new Integer(1); %>
<% } else { %>
   <P>You have seen this page
   <%= count %> times before </P>

   pageContext.setAttribute("count",
                            new Integer(count.intValue()+1),
                            PageContext.SESSION_SCOPE); %>
<% } %>
</BODY>
</HTML>
```

SESSION_SCOPE is a final integer that indicates that the method should use the session scope. There are similar definitions for the other scopes. This code will turn into a Java class that is almost identical to Listing 13.6, but it is a little easier to write and maintain if for no other reason than that all the calls to `out.println()` are avoided.

Summary

The servlet API provides the foundation on which JSPs are built, and a decent understanding of it can come in handy for page authors. The servlet API defines a life cycle for servlets, starting with an `init()` method called when the servlet first loads, a `service()` method called for each request, and a `destroy()` method called before the servlet is retired. `Init()` may allocate resources that requests will later need, and `destroy()` can free them. `Service()` is passed request and response objects, which it uses to get information about the request, set information about the response, and send the actual data.

Servlets can use all the scopes discussed in Chapter 7. They can also interact with JSPs, using beans as intermediaries. Typically the servlet does the computation, builds a bean with the results, and sends the bean onto the JSP for formatting, all via the `forward()` method. This provides the cleanest separation between logic and presentation.

Since JSPs are ultimately servlets, there is nothing one can do that the other cannot. This means that for pages with any significant amount of HTML, a JSP is almost always the preferred means of creation since JPSs are easier to read and maintain and avoid all the print statements. On the other hand, pages that are mostly dominated by code expressing page logic may be better off created by a servlet, since this will avoid having to put everything in scriptlets.

The next chapter will wrap everything up with look at some advanced topics relating to both JSPs and servlets.

CHAPTER 14

Advanced Topics

Chapters 1 through 13 included more than enough information to build almost any conceivable web site using JSPs, beans, databases, and servlets. That is not to imply that we have said everything there is to say about JSPs. In fact, there is a great deal in the JSP, servlet, JDBC, and bean specifications that we could not include, at least not without turning this book into a 70-pound, 10-volume encyclopedia. Out of that vast quantity of information, however, we have concentrated on the most common features, the ones that will be used 90 percent of the time. In this chapter we will survey a few remaining topics, which should cover another 5 percent.

Declaring Methods

Chapter 4 introduced the declaration tag, which allows new variables to be created and placed in the instance scope. Then in Chapter 13 we saw that variables in the instance scope are simply fields of the servlet class. From this it might be guessed that anything in the <%! %> tag is simply placed, un-changed, into the top level of servlet built by the JSP Engine. This guess would be correct.

The implication is that the declaration tags can define new methods as well as variables. Listing 14.1 shows a JSP page that computes the the nth prime number using a declared method.

Listing 14.1   A JSP with a User-Defined Method

```
<%!
  public int primes(int n) {
    if(n < 2)  return 2;
    if(n == 2) return 3;

    int primes[] = new int[n];
    primes[0]    = 2;
    primes[1]    = 3;

    int candidate = 5;
    int numSoFar  = 2;
    boolean maybePrime;
    while (numSoFar < n) {
      maybePrime = true;
      for(int i=0;i<numSoFar && maybePrime;i++) {
        maybePrime = (candidate % primes[i]) != 0;
      }

      if(maybePrime) {
        primes[numSoFar++] = candidate;
      }
      candidate++;
    }
    return primes[n-1];
  }
%>
<HTML>
<HEAD><TITLE>Primes</TITLE></HEAD>
<BODY>
<P>Here are the first 5 prime numbers:</P>
<UL>
<LI><%= primes(1) %>
<LI><%= primes(2) %>
<LI><%= primes(3) %>
<LI><%= primes(4) %>
<LI><%= primes(5) %>
</UL>
</BODY>
</HTML>
```

Apart from the fact that the method declaration is a lot longer than any variable declaration, the principle is the same. The method itself computes primes in a simple way, starting with the first two primes and computing each one after that by checking every number against the list it has already computed. Thus when checking 9 it first checks 9/2, which does not divide evenly; it then checks 9/3, which does divide evenly, ruling out 9 as a prime number.

Although this method works, it has one major inefficiency. Every time it is called it recomputes the whole array to get to the number it wants, even if it has already computed most or all of that array. Thus Listing 14.1 computes the first four primes when asked to evaluate `primes(4)`; it then recomputes all four in the next step, when it is asked for the fifth.

The solution is to take the primes array out of the method and put it in a separate field in the class. Then each time the method is asked for a prime number it can check the list it has already built and return the number if it has already been computed. If not, it only needs to compute the values between the last one computed and the current one.

It also makes sense to start the array with more than two values, giving the method a bit more of a jump start. The best time to do this is when the JSP is first loaded, placing the initialization code in a `jspInit()` method, as discussed in the previous chapter. Although this method is treated specially by the JSP Engine, it can be declared just like any other method, as shown in Listing 14.2.

Listing 14.2   A JSP with a `jspInit()` Method

```
<%!
   int primes[];
%>
<%!
   public void jspInit() {
      /* Pre-populate the first 100 primes */
      primes(100);
   }
%>
<%!
   public int primes(int n) {
      if(primes != null && n < primes.length) {
         return primes[n-1];
      }

      int oldPrimes[]  = primes;
      primes           = new int[n+1];

      int candidate;
      int numSoFar;

      if(oldPrimes != null) {
         System.arraycopy(oldPrimes,0,primes,0,oldPrimes.length-1);
         candidate = oldPrimes[oldPrimes.length-1];
         numSoFar  = oldPrimes.length;
      } else {
         primes[0] = 2;
         candidate = 3;
         numSoFar  = 1;
      }
      boolean maybePrime;
```

```
      while (numSoFar < n) {
        maybePrime = true;
        for(int i=0;i<numSoFar && maybePrime;i++) {
          maybePrime = (candidate % primes[i]) != 0;
        }

        if(maybePrime) {
          primes[numSoFar++] = candidate;
        }
        candidate++;
      }

      return primes[n-1];
    }
%>
<HTML>
<HEAD><TITLE>Primes</TITLE></HEAD>
<BODY>
<P>Here are the first 5 prime numbers:</P>
<UL>
<LI><%= primes(1) %>
<LI><%= primes(2) %>
<LI><%= primes(3) %>
<LI><%= primes(4) %>
<LI><%= primes(5) %>
</UL>
</BODY>
</HTML>
```

Extending Different Classes

Considering how much Java code is in Listings 14.1 and 14.2, it might as well be a servlet. Of course if it were, there would be the same old difficulty in changing its appearance or other aspects such as the number of primes it should generate. The code could also have been placed in a bean, which might have initialized the array in its constructor. This is normally the recommended approach, but there is an alternative that is preferable in some instances.

In Chapter 13 we mentioned that all JSPs implement the HttpJspPage inter-face. Tomcat does this by making JSPs extend a class called HttpJspBase, which in turn implements HttpJspPage. In principle there is no reason a JSP could not extend a different class, as long as that class also implemented HttpJspPage. This class could define the primes() and jspInit() methods. The JSP Engine would still call jspInit() when it loaded the JSP, and primes() would then be available to the page without the need to define any code in the page itself. Listing 14.3 shows the class containing the prime code.

Listing 14.3 A Base Class with the Prime Methods

```java
package com.awl.jspbook.ch14;
import org.apache.jasper.runtime.*;
public abstract class Primes extends HttpJspBase {
  int primes[];
  public void jspInit() {
    /* Pre-populate the first 100 primes */
    primes(100);
  }
  /**
   * We don't need to do anything when the JSP
   * is destroyed, but we still need to provide
   * this method to satisfy the interface.
   */
  public void jspDestroy() {
    return;
  }
  public int primes(int n) {
    if(primes != null && n < primes.length) {
      return primes[n-1];
    }

    int oldPrimes[]  = primes;
    primes           = new int[n];

    int candidate;
    int numSoFar;

    if(oldPrimes != null) {
      System.arraycopy(oldPrimes,0,primes,0,oldPrimes.length-1);
      candidate = oldPrimes[oldPrimes.length-1];
      numSoFar  = oldPrimes.length;
    } else {
      primes[0] = 2;
      candidate = 3;
      numSoFar  = 1;
    }
    boolean maybePrime;

    while (numSoFar < n) {
      maybePrime = true;
      for(int i=0;i<numSoFar && maybePrime;i++) {
        maybePrime = (candidate % primes[i]) != 0;
      }

      if(maybePrime) {
        primes[numSoFar++] = candidate;
      }
      candidate++;
    }

    return primes[n-1];
  }
}
```

BUG ALERT!   In current versions of Tomcat, a class that serves as the base class of a JSP must
extend `org.apache.jasper.runtime.HttpJspBase`, which is an internal class
used by the JSP Engine. Future versions of Jakarta should allow a base class to
be defined solely in terms of classes and interfaces from `javax.servlet` and
related packages.

Once this class has been defined, using it is quite simple, as shown in
Listing 14.4. Here the JSP is told to use a different base class via the page
directive, which is covered in more detail in the appendix. Apart from this
directive, the rest of the page is straightforward and much cleaner than previous versions.

Listing 14.4   A JSP That Extends a Different Base Class

```
<%@ page extends="com.awl.jspbook.ch14.Primes" %>
<HTML>
<HEAD><TITLE>Primes</TITLE></HEAD>
<BODY>
<P>Here are the first 5 prime numbers:</P>
<UL>
<LI><%= primes(1) %>
<LI><%= primes(2) %>
<LI><%= primes(3) %>
<LI><%= primes(4) %>
<LI><%= primes(5) %>
</UL>
</BODY>
</HTML>
```

Faced with the need to add some functionality to a JSP, we now have three
choices: use a bean, define the methods in the JSP, or put the methods in a separate class. Putting the code in the JSP is ugly and cumbersome, which leaves
the other two possibilities. The final decision almost always falls on the side of
beans. The JSP specification states, in section 3.2, "The extension mechanism
is available for sophisticated users and it should be used with extreme care as
it restricts what [sic] some of the decisions that a JSP engine can take, e.g., to
improve performance."

JSPs and XML

Although it is never safe to make predictions, especially where computers are concerned, it now seems almost certain that XML, the extensible markup language, will play a big part in the Internet's future. XML, like HTML, is descended from SGML, which means that it will look very familiar to HTML authors. However, as its name suggests it was designed to be extensible in a way HTML is not, allowing new tags to be created as needed. *XML and Java: Developing Web Applications* by Hiroshi Maruyama, Kent Tamura, and Naohiko Uramoto, provides an excellent introduction to XML and related technologies.

JSPs help pave the way for XML in two ways. First, the output of a JSP page can be XML just as easily as HTML. Listing 14.5 shows a JSP that generates an XML page containing album info. It uses the "Tinderbox" bean from Chapter 4 as the source of the data.

Listing 14.5 A JSP That Generates an XML Page

```
<% response.setContentType("text/xml"); %>
<jsp:useBean id="album" beanName="tinderbox"
 type="com.awl.jspbook.ch05.AlbumInfo"/>
<RECORD>
  <TITLE>
    <jsp:getProperty name="album" property="name"/>
  </TITLE>
  <ARTIST>
    <jsp:getProperty name="album" property="artist"/>
  </ARTIST>
  <YEAR>
    <jsp:getProperty name="album" property="year"/>
  </YEAR>
  <% String tracks[] = album.getTracks(); %>
  <TRACKS>
    <% for(int i=0;i<tracks.length;i++) { %>
      <TRACKNAME><%= tracks[i] %></TRACKNAME>
    <% } %>
  </TRACKS>
</RECORD>
```

The first thing this example does is change the content type, since by default JSPs set the type to text/html. The first thing this page sends to the user is the location of the Document Type Declaration, or DTD, which specifies which tags will be used to contain record information and how these tags will relate to each other.

The rest of this page is almost an exact copy of Listing 4.5, except that the tags are XML, as specified in the DTD, instead of HTML.

In addition to being able to generate an XML document, a JSP can be written as one. Readers already familiar with XML will have noticed that many of the JSP tags follow XML conventions. The jsp:useBean tag, for example, uses an XML namespace and a slash at the end of the tag when there is no corresponding close tag. Indeed, Listing 14.5 is almost a valid XML document, lacking only a few key elements such as a root tag, DTD, and an XML representation of the scriptlets and expressions.

The JSP specification provides for alternate forms of all the JSP expressions we have seen so far that are not already valid XML, as well as for the other necessary components. Listing 14.6 shows an XML version of Listing 14.5. We can see that the conversion from "standard" JSP to XML is straightforward.

Listing 14.6   A JSP That Is a Valid XML Document

```
<jsp:root
    xmlns:jsp="http://java.sun.com/products/jsp/dtd/jsp_1_0.dtd">
<jsp:scriptlet>
    response.setContentType("text/xml");
</jsp:scriptlet>
<jsp:useBean id="album" beanName="tinderbox"
 type="com.awl.jspbook.ch05.AlbumInfo"/>
<RECORD>
  <TITLE>
    <jsp:getProperty name="album" property="name"/>
  </TITLE>
  <ARTIST>
    <jsp:getProperty name="album" property="artist"/>
  </ARTIST>
  <YEAR>
    <jsp:getProperty name="album" property="year"/>
  </YEAR>
  <jsp:scriptlet>
    String tracks[] = album.getTracks();
  </jsp:scriptlet>
  <TRACKS>
    <jsp:scriptlet>
     for(int i=0;i<tracks.length;i++) {
    </jsp:scriptlet>
      <TRACKNAME>
        <jsp:expression>tracks[i]</jsp:expression>
      </TRACKNAME>
    <jsp:scriptlet>}</jsp:scriptlet>
  </TRACKS>
</RECORD>
</jsp:root>
```

As of this writing, the exact form of the XML version of JSP tags has yet to be finalized. Moreover, no implementation supports the current specification nor are any required to accept these forms. Nevertheless, there is a great deal of interest in how JSPs and XML might interact, so it seems likely that the XML tags will be finalized and included in a forthcoming version of the specification.

Returning Other Kinds of Data

Listing 14.6 used the response object to change the content type, as was discussed in Chapter 13. One of the exciting possibilities arising from this ability is that a JSP can generate binary data, such as an image, as well as different kinds of text. Manipulating binary data is difficult to do directly in a JSP, so a bean is used to do the actual data preparation. Listing 14.7 shows a bean that generates the data for a GIF file containing a small image of an ankh.

Listing 14.7 A Bean That Generates GIF Data

```
package com.awl.jspbook.ch14;
import java.io.*;
public class AnkhBean {
  private final static byte ankhBytes[] = {
    (byte)0x47,(byte)0x49,(byte)0x46,(byte)0x38,
    (byte)0x37,(byte)0x61,(byte)0x12,(byte)0x00,
    (byte)0x1e,(byte)0x00,(byte)0x80,(byte)0x00,
    (byte)0x00,(byte)0x7f,(byte)0x7f,(byte)0x7f,
    (byte)0xff,(byte)0xff,(byte)0xff,(byte)0x2c,
    (byte)0x00,(byte)0x00,(byte)0x00,(byte)0x00,
    (byte)0x12,(byte)0x00,(byte)0x1e,(byte)0x00,
    (byte)0x00,(byte)0x02,(byte)0x3f,(byte)0x8c,
    (byte)0x8f,(byte)0xa9,(byte)0x07,(byte)0xed,
    (byte)0x8b,(byte)0x9e,(byte)0x69,(byte)0x70,
    (byte)0x82,(byte)0x44,(byte)0x57,(byte)0x8e,
    (byte)0x57,(byte)0x77,(byte)0x0e,(byte)0x6d,
    (byte)0xcc,(byte)0xa7,(byte)0x90,(byte)0x56,
    (byte)0x25,(byte)0x06,(byte)0x29,(byte)0x38,
    (byte)0x56,(byte)0xe7,(byte)0x8b,(byte)0x76,
    (byte)0xab,(byte)0xa7,(byte)0x9a,(byte)0x23,
    (byte)0xe5,(byte)0xd8,(byte)0x56,(byte)0xce,
    (byte)0xf3,(byte)0x31,(byte)0xa6,(byte)0x83,
    (byte)0xb9,(byte)0x5a,(byte)0x43,(byte)0x56,
    (byte)0x51,(byte)0x58,(byte)0x9c,(byte)0xfd,
    (byte)0x8e,(byte)0xc8,(byte)0xa1,(byte)0x32,
    (byte)0x14,(byte)0x84,(byte)0x32,(byte)0x9b,
```

```
            (byte)0xae,(byte)0x67,(byte)0x68,(byte)0x3a,
            (byte)0x2c,(byte)0x00,(byte)0x00,(byte)0x3b};
    private String fgColor = "7f7f7f";
    private String bgColor = "ffffff";
    public String getFgColor() {return fgColor;}
    public String getBgColor() {return bgColor;}
    public void setFgColor(String fgColor) {
        this.fgColor  = fgColor;
        byte tmp[]    = toHex(fgColor);
        ankhBytes[13] = (byte) (tmp[0] * 16 + tmp[1]);
        ankhBytes[14] = (byte) (tmp[2] * 16 + tmp[3]);
        ankhBytes[15] = (byte) (tmp[4] * 16 + tmp[5]);
    }
    public void setBgColor(String bgColor) {
        this.bgColor  = bgColor;
        byte tmp[]    = toHex(bgColor);
        ankhBytes[16] = (byte) (tmp[0] * 16 + tmp[1]);
        ankhBytes[17] = (byte) (tmp[2] * 16 + tmp[3]);
        ankhBytes[18] = (byte) (tmp[4] * 16 + tmp[5]);
    }
    public String getAnkh() {
        return new String(ankhBytes);
    }
    public byte[] toHex(String s) {
        byte tmp[] = s.toUpperCase().getBytes();
        for(int i=0;i<tmp.length;i++) {
            if(tmp[i] >= 'A' && tmp[i] <= 'F') {
            tmp[i] = (byte) (tmp[i] - 'A' + 10);
            } else {
            tmp[i] = (byte) (tmp[i] - '0');
            }
        }
        return tmp;
    }
}
```

The GIF data, with a grey foreground and a white background, is held in the ankhBytes array. The setFgColor() and setBgColor methods alter this data by changing the values in the GIF colormap, and the getAnkh method simply returns the data as a new string.

This bean can now be used in a JSP just like any other, as shown in Listing 14.8. The formatting is a little strange, since all the tags are directly adjacent and all the line breaks are inside the tags. This ensures that no whitespace is intermixed with the image data, which would prevent a browser rendering it. For this and numerous other reasons the code in Listing 14.8 is unlikely ever to be seen in the real world, because servlets are much better at manipulating binary data than JSPs, even with the help of beans. However, it does show how a JSP can generate things other than text.

Listing 14.8 A JSP Page That Generates a GIF

```
<% response.setContentType("image/gif"); %><jsp:useBean
id="ankh"
class="com.awl.jspbook.ch14.AnkhBean"/><jsp:setProperty
name="ankh"
property="*"/><jsp:getProperty
name="ankh" property="ankh"/>
```

There is nothing new in the code itself. The content type is set through the response object, the bean is loaded, form parameters are used to set properties, and the ahnk property is obtained.

Finally, Listing 14.9 shows how this JSP might be used from another JSP that allows the user to change the colors and see the resulting image.

Listing 14.9 A JSP That Sets the Colors in the Ankh Image

```
<jsp:useBean
id="ankh"
class="com.awl.jspbook.ch14.AnkhBean"/>
<jsp:setProperty
name="ankh"
property="*"/>
<HTML>
<HEAD><TITLE>A generated image</TITLE></HEAD>
<BODY>
<P>Here is the image!
<IMG SRC="ankh.jsp?fgColor=<jsp:getProperty name="ankh"
property="fgColor"/>&bgColor=<jsp:getProperty name="ankh"
property="bgColor"/>">
</P>
<P>
Set new colors below.  Specify both in standard HTML
color syntax, using all 6 digits.
</P>
<FORM ACTION="ankhform.jsp" METHOD="POST">
<P>Foreground: <INPUT TYPE="text" NAME="fgColor"></P>
<P>Background: <INPUT TYPE="text" NAME="bgColor"></P>
<P><INPUT TYPE="Submit">
</FORM>
</BODY>
</HTML>
```

Threads

Threads are an integral and powerful feature of Java which allow a single program to do many things simultaneously. An obvious example is a web server written in Java that can handle hundreds of user requests at the same time. A traditional web server handles multiple requests by essentially creating a copy of itself for each, but this can be slow and uses lots of memory. Under Java it is just necessary to start a new thread, which uses the same code and same memory as all the other threads.

There are many ways to describe threads, but one analogy is the way people might read this book. One reader might start at page 1 and read straight through to this point. Another may skip around a bit, perhaps checking Chapter 5 to read more about a particular Java construct. In any case, each reader would define his or her own path through the text.

Now consider two or more people reading this book simultaneously. In real-world terms this might mean that pages would need to be torn out and passed around, but conceptually there is no reason that several people could not all read at the same time. A given reader might define her own path through the material, based on her interests and familiarity with some of the topics. Sometimes two or more readers might find themselves at the same words at the same time; at other points all readers would be off on their own.

Java threads work much like this, except that they read Java instructions instead of words. A new thread can be created at any time and given a method to start with, which will usually be the run() method of a class that implements the Runnable interface. Once a thread has started it may take a different path through the code based on user input, time of day, database contents, or anything else that can be expressed in a conditional.

So far there is no problem—multiple readers can go through a book without interfering with each other, and multiple threads can move through a Java program without ever knowing another thread exists. However, consider what would happen if this book had a quiz at the end of each chapter. One reader might start working on a quiz, beginning with the first question; a minute later another reader might start the same quiz, lagging behind the first reader by a few questions. By the time the first reader finished, most of his answers would have been overwritten by the second reader, making the score a meaningless combination.

Threads have an analogous problem, which can be demonstrated by the very simple JSP shown in Listing 14.10. Here machineName is an instance variable, which means that there will be one shared by all the users of this JSP. But consider what might happen if two users, perhaps Tina Root and Susan Wallace from the band Switchblade Symphony, access this page more or less simultaneously. For the sake of discussion, we will say they are using machines called *serpentine.switchblade.com* and *calamity.switchblade.com*, respectively.

Listing 14.10 A JSP with a Potential Thread Problem

```
<%! String machineName; %>
<% machineName = request.getRemoteHost(); %>
<HTML>
<BODY>
<P> You are using a computer called <%= machineName %>.</P>
</BODY>
</HTML>
```

If Susan's request is received first, machineName will be set to *calamity*. If Tina's request is then received before Susan's thread gets to the expression, machineName will be set to *serpentine*. When Susan gets to the expression the JSP will state that she is using *serpentine*, which is incorrect.

The chances of this happening are pretty slim if a page is small and simple, or if it is accessed infrequently. However, as a page gets more complex and takes longer to generate, or as it is used by more people, potential thread problems become much more likely.

The JSP specification provides an easy way to avoid thread problems by allowing a JSP to declare that it is not *thread safe*—that is, it is not able to handle multiple threads—using the page directive. It is just necessary to add the following line at the top of the JSP:

```
<%@ page isThreadSafe="false"%>
```

The same thing can be done in a servlet by having it implement the javax.servlet.SingleThreadModel interface. When the JSP Engine sees that a JSP or servlet is not thread safe, it forces all requests to go through sequentially. Thus if Susan gets to the page first, Tina will have to wait until Susan has gotten the full response back.

This does indeed avoid the thread problem, but the result is that users may have to wait for their turn, making the site seem slower. This may eventually cause users to give up on it in frustration, which is not acceptable for a site that wants to build and hold an audience. Even so, the single-threading technique is useful for tracking down problems. If a page or a whole site is exhibiting strange bugs that appear irregularly and are impossible to recreate or track down, it may be worth making all pages single threaded for a while. If the problems go away, it is a safe bet that some threading issue is the cause.

Avoiding Thread Problems

Avoiding any thread problems can be quite difficult and is a science unto itself. *Concurrent Programming in Java™: Design Principles and Patterns* by Doug Lea provides much more information for those who want to understand the issues, and *The Developer's Guide to the Java™ Web Server™* by Dan Woods, Larne Pekowsky, and Tom Snee has a chapter on threads in a servlet context.

With a little care it is not difficult to avoid the most common thread problems in a JSP. The first step is knowing what may potentially cause.

As Listing 14.10 showed, instance variables can definitely cause bugs. However, local variables cannot. When a thread calls a method, a private copy of all that method's variables are created so that each thread is working with its own copy. Thus if the declaration in Listing 14.10 were replaced with a scriptlet creating a local variable, as in

```
<% String machineName; %>
```

the problem would vanish.

Each request and response object is also private to each thread, so if Listing 14.10 had just skipped the intermediate variable altogether and called

```
<%= request.getRemoteHost() %>
```

the problem would never have arisen.

This applies to objects in the request scope as well. Since each thread has its own request, each request scope is separate from all others, which means that beans or other objects placed in it will not normally be available to any other thread. Of course, if some object is already available to multiple threads, simply placing it in the request scope will not protect it. Moreover, if several threads all place the machineName instance variable in their own request scopes, it will still be the same variable and any change made by one thread will still be visible to all others.

Objects in the session scope are also safe, since only one user, and hence one thread, access a given session at any moment. This, after all, is the whole point of the session scope. The same is true of the page scope.

That leaves the application scope, which is clearly not thread safe. Anything in this scope may be used by several pages and several users simultaneously. Although a powerful mechanism for sharing data across pages, this means that thread safety may need to be carefully considered.

Usually the application scope contain beans created by the useBean tag. Thus the issue of thread safety resides in the Java code within the bean. The easiest way to ensure that a bean is thread safe is for each of its methods to be written as

```
public int someMethod(...) {
    synchronize(this) {
        ... method code ...
    }
}synchronize
```

In fact, not all methods of a bean need to be synchronized, which further decreases the chances that any user will have to wait for another. This is where the science of threading comes in, and interested readers are referred to *Concurrent Programming in Java™* for the details.

Using Threads

So far threads have seemed only to be potential sources of bugs, but they can be powerful allies as well. Any time a user request requires some action on the server side but does not need to wait for it to be completed, the action can be handled by creating a new thread. For example, when placing an order at an e-commerce site, the user needn't wait for the order to reach the shipping center; it is enough for him to know that the order has been entered into the system. Once that has been done, a page can show the user that the order is being processed, and a separate thread can start that will handle the back-end processing, including contacting the shipping center.

Threads can also be used to ensure that data is updated or that data in memory and in a database is synchronized. For example, recall the bean that contained advertising information for Java News Today in Chapter 12. We stated that it would load data from the database when it was first constructed. This data would include the number of impressions the advertiser had purchased and the number delivered so far, and each time the ad was shown to a user the count would be incremented. However, it would be extremely inefficient to have this bean update the count each time an ad was shown, since that would entail a constant stream of writes to the database, which would slow down the whole site.

A better solution is to have the ad bean keep the counts in memory and once every 10 minutes or so update all the counts in the database. The outline of the code that does this is shown in Listing 14.11. (The full code is included on the CD-ROM.)

Listing 14.11   A Bean That Periodically Saves Itself to a Database

```
public class AdHolder implements Runnable {
    private thread runner;
    public AdHolder() {
      // load the data from the database
      runner = new Thread(this);
      runner.start();
    }
    public void run() {
      while(true) {
```

```
            try {
                Thread.sleep(1000 * 60 * 10);
            } catch (Exception e) {}
            update();
        }
    }
}
```

When the bean is first constructed it creates and then starts a new thread. The `Thread` class calls the `run()` method of the object it is created with, which in this case is the same object. `Run()` simply sleeps for 10 minutes and then calls the bean's `update()` method, which saves any new data to the database.

Custom Tags

With beans almost all code can be removed from JSPs, letting page authors concentrate on presentation. However, there is a point where the boundary between beans and presentation is strictly delineated, requiring some control to be put in scriptlets. Consider, for example, the database beans for the CD tables from Chapter 9. A typical page that displays track data might look something like Listing 14.12.

Listing 14.12   A JSP That Uses Scriptlets

```
<jsp:setProperty name="tracks" property="*"/>
<% cd.select(); %>
<UL>
<% while db.next() { %>
  <LI><jsp:getProperty name="tracks" property="name"/>
<% } %>
</UL>
```

It would be nice to eliminate the scriptlets with the select as well as the while loop and closing brace to make this page completely free of Java code. With a bean, such a thing would be possible only if the bean were to generate the entire output of this code, including the list tags, and export it all as a property, as shown in Listing 14.13. However, this goes too far, moving HTML into the bean. If it were later decided that this information should be in a table instead, the bean programmer would need to make changes to the source code.

Listing 14.13   A JSP That Leaves All the Formatting in a Bean

```
<jsp:setProperty name="tracks" property="*"/>
<jsp:getProperty name="tracks" property="wholeList"/>
```

What is really needed here is a new tag that will do the looping and also create and modify new variables to hold the values. This might look something like Listing 14.14, which is the perfect blend. The tags are simple to use, understand and modify, and all the presentation is in the page where it belongs. In fact, this listing is a complete, functional JSP.

Listing 14.14   A JSP with Custom Tags

```
<HTML>
<BODY>
<%@ taglib
  uri="http://java.apache.org/tomcat/examples-taglib"
  prefix="awl" %>
<H1>Tracks</H1>
<TABLE BORDER="1">
  <TR><TH>Name</TH><TH>Length</TH></TR>
  <awl:tracks CD="Liquid">
    <TR>
      <TD><%= name %></TD>
      <TD><%= length %></YD>
    </TR>
  </awl:tracks>
</TABLE>
</BODY>
</HTML>
```

The ability to define new tags is part of the JSP 1.1 specification, which also includes the mechanism by which new tags can be added and many of the classes programmers can use to create them. Current versions of Tomcat provide an implementation.

A custom tag starts with an XML specification describing it. This is called a *tag library*, which explains the *taglib* directive in Listing 14.14. The tag library may reside anywhere on the Internet or on the local machine. The library description for the tracks tag is shown in Listing 14.15.

Listing 14.15   The *taglib* Specification for the TrackTag

```
<?xml version="1.0" encoding="ISO-8859-1" ?>
<!DOCTYPE taglib
        PUBLIC "-//Sun Microsystems, Inc.//DTD JSP Tag Library
               1.1//EN"
      "http://java.sun.com/j2ee/dtds/web-jsptaglibrary_1_1.dtd">
            <taglib>
```

```
<tlibversion>1.0</tlibversion>
<jspversion>1.1</jspversion>
<urn></urn>
<info>
    A tag that reads tracks from a database
</info>
<tag>
  <name>tracks</name>
  <tagclass>com.awl.jspbook.ch13.TrackTag</tagclass>
  <teiclass>com.awl.jspbook.ch13.TrackTagExtraInfo</teiclass>
  <bodycontent>JSP</bodycontent>
  <info>
      Provided with the CD name, returns track info
  </info>
  <attribute>
    <name>CD</name>
    <required>true</required>
  </attribute>
</tag>
</taglib>
```

In addition to providing a lot of descriptive information, this specification describes the parameters to the tag and states which are mandatory. Here we have one parameter called CD, which is required. This information will be used at translation time to determine if the tag is formatted properly.

The taglib also contains the names of the classes used to implement the tag. The teiclass class extends javax.servlet.jsp.tagext.TagExtraInfo. It can provide a wide variety of information about what the tag will do. Listing 14.16 shows the teiclass for the tracks tag.

Listing 14.16   The Class That Provides Extra Information

```
package com.awl.jspbook.ch14;
import javax.servlet.jsp.tagext.*;
public class TrackTagExtraInfo extends TagExtraInfo {
    public VariableInfo[] getVariableInfo(TagData data) {
        return new VariableInfo[]
            {
                    new VariableInfo("name",
                                     "String",
                                     true,
                                     VariableInfo.NESTED),
                    new VariableInfo("length",
                                     "Integer",
                                     true,
                                     VariableInfo.NESTED)
            };
    }
}
```

This class overrides only one method, `getVariableInfo`, which tells the JSP Engine what variables the tag will create. Note that the JSP in Listing 14.14 used two variables, `name` and `length`, which are created and maintained by the tag. The system is notified of these variables by `TrackTagExtraInfo`.

That leaves only the implementation class of the tag itself, which is shown in Listing 14.17. This class will be used at request time.

Listing 14.17   The Class That Implements the New Tag

```
package com.awl.jspbook.ch14;
import javax.servlet.jsp.*;
import javax.servlet.jsp.tagext.*;
import java.util.Hashtable;
import java.io.Writer;
import java.io.IOException;
import java.sql.*;
public class TrackTag implements Tag, BodyTag {
  private BodyContent bodyOut;
  private PageContext pageContext;
  private Tag parent;

  private Connection theConnection;
  private Statement  theStatement;
  private ResultSet  results;
  private String     cd;
  private boolean anyRows = false;

  public void setCD(String cd) {this.cd = cd;}

  public void setParent(Tag parent) {
    this.parent = parent;
  }

  public void setBodyContent(BodyContent bodyOut) {
    this.bodyOut = bodyOut;
  }

  public void setPageContext(PageContext pageContext) {
    this.pageContext = pageContext;
  }

  public Tag getParent() {
    return this.parent;
  }

  public int doStartTag() {
    try {
      Class.forName("postgresql.Driver");
      theConnection = DriverManager.getConnection (
                      "jdbc:postgresql:jspbook",
                      "dbuser",
                      "dbuser");
```

```
      theStatement   = theConnection.createStatement();
      results        = theStatement.executeQuery(
                       "SELECT track.name,track.length " +
                       "FROM track,cd " +
                       "WHERE cd.albumid=track.albumid " +
                       "AND cd.name = '" +
                       cd + "'");
    } catch (Exception e) {
      System.err.println("Unable to connect to DB");
      e.printStackTrace();
      return SKIP_BODY;
    }
    return EVAL_BODY_TAG;
  }

  public int doEndTag() throws JspException {
    return EVAL_PAGE;
  }


  public void doInitBody() throws JspError {
    try {
      if(results.next()) {
       pageContext.setAttribute(
                   "name",
                   results.getString("name"));
       pageContext.setAttribute(
                   "length",
                   new Integer(results.getInt("length")));
       anyRows = true;
      }
    } catch (Exception e) {
      e.printStackTrace();
      throw new JspError("Unable to get data");
    }
  }

  public void release() {
    bodyOut      = null;
    pageContext  = null;
    parent       = null;
    try {
      results.close();
      theStatement.close();
      theConnection.close();
    } catch (Exception e) {}
    results       = null;
    theStatement  = null;
    theConnection = null;
  }
```

```
public int doAfterBody() throws JspError {
  try {
    if(!results.next()) {
if (anyRows)
  bodyOut.writeOut(bodyOut.getEnclosingWriter());
return SKIP_BODY;
    } else {
pageContext.setAttribute(
                "name",
                results.getString("name"));
pageContext.setAttribute(
                "length",
                new Integer(results.getInt("length")));
anyRows = true;
return EVAL_BODY_TAG;
    }
  } catch (Exception e) {
    return SKIP_BODY;
  }
 }
}
```

A detailed explanation of these methods is available in the JSP specification, but the ones to notice at the moment are setCD, doStartTag(), doInitBody(), release(), and doAfterBody(). Each is called at a specific point during the tag processing.

SetCD() is called when the tag is first encountered, and it is automatically called with the value of the CD parameter in the tag, much as a bean's SET methods are called when handling user input from a form. If the tag library declares other parameters, the corresponding SET methods are also called.

DoStartTag() is called next, when the tag processing begins. It is used here to set up the connection to the database and do the query. If all goes well, this method will return EVAL_BODY_TAG, indicating that the tag's body should be processed. If something goes awry, SKIP_BODY is returned, and the final page will contain nothing from the tag.

Next comes doInitBody(), when the body first starts processing. It sets values for the name and length variables and indicates that at least one row is available.

DoAfterBody() is called when the end of the body has been reached. If there are any more rows, it sets the next values for name and length and indicates that the body should be processed again by returning EVAL_BODY_TAG. If all the rows have been exhausted, this method writes out the contents of the body that has been built by calling bodyOut.writeOut(). If no rows are available, this method is not called, and so the tag simply vanishes from the final page. Finally, doAfterBody() returns SKIP_BODY, indicating that the body should be processed again. The JSP Engine then calls release(), which gives the tag a chance to clean up any resources it has allocated.

Summary

The topics covered in this chapter are not everyday concerns, but they are included here on the theory that no knowledge is ever wasted. There may be times when it is easier for a JSP to define a utility method than to use a bean, and this method might used so often that it makes sense to put it in a base class. Sooner or later the highest-volume sites will have to start worrying about thread issues, and there is enough information in this chapter to avoid most of the common problems that may be encountered in a multithreaded environment. Finally, XML and custom tags are the wave of the future, so there is no reason that JSP authors should not start preparing for them now.

That concludes our introduction to the wonderful world of JavaServer Pages, but hopefully it is just the beginning of your exploration of this exciting and powerful technology. The CD-ROM contains the complete set of Java News Today pages. A good place to start experimenting might be to take the site as it is and turn it into something with a design that might actually attract users. Or try creating new sections, authors, or keywords, or perhaps even drop all the existing ones and create a brand new set. You might start from scratch and create a news site about Linux or childcare or anything else.

For every dynamic web site that exists today there are an infinite number of ideas that have yet to be explored. Let JavaServer Pages be the technology that turns your great idea into a dynamic and compelling web site that might just be the Internet's Next Big Thing.

APPENDIX

Summary of JSP 1.1 Tags

This appendix outlines all the tags in version 1.1 of the JSP specification.

Comments

```
<%-- ... text ... --%>
```

JSP comments are stripped out by the JSP Engine at translation time. Consequently, they never appear in the final servlet and are never sent to the user. Comments are useful for indicating to page maintainers what a region of HTML or code is used for. They were first seen in Chapter 2.

Declarations

```
<%! type varname;  %>
<%! returntype methodname(argument1, argument2 ...) {} %>
```

Declarations may be used to add variables or methods to a JSP. Anything in a declaration is added to the resulting servlet at the class level. For variables, this means that there will typically be one instance of the variable shared across all requests. Declarations were first seen in Chapter 6.

Expressions

```
<%= expression %>
```

The expression tag places the printable form of a Java expression into the output of a page. Expressions may be anything from a simple variable to a method call to a complex mathematical form involving multiple terms. They were first seen in Listing 3.1.

Scriptlets

```
<% ...java code... %>
```

Scriptlets allow arbitrary Java code, and eventually other languages, to be placed in a JSP. For the most part such code should reside in beans and other classes, but there are times when placing it in a page is unavoidable. Complex logic can be added to pages by surrounding regions of text with scriptlets, where one scriptlet ends with an opening brace and a second one provides the matching close. Scriplets were first seen in Listing 6.2

Include Directive

```
<%@ include file=""%>
```

The include directive adds the text of one JSP or other file to another file at translation time. The effect is exactly as if the author had used an editor to paste the included file into the primary one. The include directive was first seen in Listing 2.4.

Page Directive

```
<%@page options... %>
```

The page directive specifies a large number of options that affect the entire page. Each of these options may be used independently. They may all appear in the same page directive, or each may be placed in a separate one.

```
language="java"
```

This code specifies what language will be used in scriptlets. Currently only Java is supported.

```
extends="base class"
```

This code can force the generated servlet to extend a specific class. This should be used very rarely. See Chapter 13 for more details.

```
import="package.class"
import="package.*"
```

Import parameters within a page directive turn into import statements in the generated Java file. Multiple import statements can be used.

```
session="true|false"
```

By default, the first time a user accesses any JSP on a site, a session is started for that user and the user will be issued a cookie. This behavior can be disabled by setting the session flag to false.

```
buffer="none|sizekb"
```

This flag sets the amount of data that will be buffered before being sent to the user. The default is 8 Kbytes. None indicates that all output should be sent directly.

```
autoFlush="true|false"
```

If buffering is turned on and this value is set to true, data will automatically be sent to the user when the buffer is full. If buffering is on and this value is set to false, an exception will occur when the buffer is full. If buffering is not on, this value has no effect. The default is true.

```
isThreadSafe="true|false"
```

This value indicates whether it is is safe for the JSP Engine to send multiple requests to a page simultaneously. The default is true. Setting it to false is equivalent to declaring that the generated servlet will implement `SingleThreadModel`.

```
info="text"
```

This value sets a description of the page's purpose, its author, or any other information. Anything placed here will be accessible through the resulting servlet's `getServletInfo()` method.

```
errorPage="pathToErrorPage"
```

This value customizes the page sent to the user when an error occurs at runtime. By default in such a situation, the user sees a standard `Error 500` page; but if this value is set to the path of another JSP page, the contents of that page are sent instead.

```
isErrorPage="true|false"
```

This value indicates that a JSP will be used as an error page. When this is true, the JSP will have access to an additional implicit value called *exception,* which will be an Exception or Throwable representing the error that occurred. The default for this value is false.

```
contentType="mime-type"
```

This value changes the content type of the page. In current implementations, it is equivalent to `request.set("mime-type")`. The default is text/html.

The page directive was first seen in Chapter 14.

taglib Directive

```
<%@taglib uri="..."  prefix="tagPrefix" %>
```

This directive loads a set of custom tags. It was first seen in Listing 14.14.

Request forward

```
<jsp:forward page="target">
<jsp:forward page="target">
  <jsp:param name="name" value="value"/>
  ...
</jsp:forward>
```

This tag may be used to send the request to another page. The calling page cannot send any data to the user before invoking this tag, although if buffering is on and the buffer has not yet been flushed, the pending output will be discarded before the request is forwarded. If buffering is not on or data has already been flushed from the buffer, an exception will be thrown.

The target URL may be a string, or it may be an expression that produces a string.

In the second form of this tag, one or more `jsp:param` tags may be used. These provide name/value pairs that are carried into the requested page. If a forward tag includes

```
<jsp:param name="color" value="#FF0000"/>
```

the forwarded page may call

```
request.getParameter("color");
```

The request forward was first seen in Chapter 7.

Request-Time include

```
<jsp:include page="target" flush="true">
<jsp:include page="target" flush="true">
  <jsp:param name="name" value="value"/>
  ...
</jsp:include>
```

This tag may be used to include a JSP or HTML page within another page. Unlike the include directive, this include is done at request time, so if the included page changes, the next request picks up the new version.

The originating page may send any data to the user before or after this tag appears. However, the called page may not set any headers. If it does, an `IllegalStateException` will be thrown.

The `flush="true"` parameter indicates whether the output should be flushed before the included page is called. Currently this value must appear, and it must be set to true.

As with the `jsp:forward` tag, additional parameters may be passed to the called page through the use of `jsp:param` tags.

The request-time include was first seen in Listing 7.6.

Plugin

This tag generates the code for an applet or an embedded object, depending on what the browser can handle. Its use is beyond the scope of this book.

useBean

```
<jsp:useBean name="id" parameters.../>   [first form]
<jsp:useBean name="id" parameters>   [second form]
...jsp code...
</jsp:useBean>
```

This tag makes a bean available for use later in the page. The name provided here is used in the ID field in later tags. In the second form, the code between the opening and closing tags is executed when the bean is first constructed but not on subsequent uses of the bean.

Several parameters may be used in both forms to modify the way the bean is created or other aspects of the bean. These are described on the next page.

```
scope="page|request|session|application"
```

This parameter places the bean in the specified scope or accesses it from that scope if it already exists. The default is page. See Chapter 6 for more on scopes.

```
beanName="name"
```

This parameter tells the useBean tag to load a serialized bean named name instead of constructing a new one. If this parameter is used, type must be present as well.

```
class="package.class"
```

This parameter tells the useBean tag which class to use when constructing the bean. It must not be used if a serialized bean is being loaded; type must be used instead.

```
type="package.class"
```

This parameter indicates the type the bean should be treated as. If this parameter is used in conjunction with class and a newly constructed bean, the bean is cast to the specified type. If type is used with beanName and a serialized bean, it specifies the type of the bean.

The jsp:useBean tag was first seen in Listing 4.1.

setProperty

```
<jsp:setProperty name="name" property="propName" value="value"/>
   [first version]
```

```
<jsp:setProperty name="name" property="propName"/>
   [second version]
```

```
<jsp:setProperty name="name" property="propName"
   param="param_name"/>
   [third version]
```

```
<jsp:setProperty name="name" property="*"/>
   [fourth version]
```

This tag sets one or more bean properties. The first version sets the named property to a specified value, which may be either a constant such as 3 or string or an expression tag.

The second version sets the property from a form parameter of the same name. If no form parameter with that name was provided, the action does nothing.

The third version sets the property from a form parameter with possibly a different name. Again, if the named parameter is not present, the action does nothing.

The last version sets all properties for which a matching form parameter is provided.

See Chapter 4 for more information on the connection between beans and forms. The jsp:setProperty tag was first seen in Listing 4.2.

getProperty

```
<jsp:getProperty name="id" property="propName"/>
```

This tag places the current value of a property on the output page. In current implementations it is equivalent to

```
<%= beanName.getPropName() %>
```

although this may not be true in future versions. GetProperty was first seen in Listing 4.1.

INDEX

Java™ Technology from
Addison-Wesley

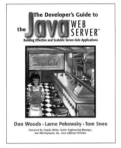

ISBN 0-201-37949-X

ISBN 0-201-37963-5

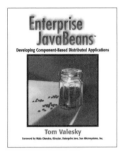

ISBN 0-201-60446-9

ISBN 0-201-43329-X

ISBN 0-201-48543-5

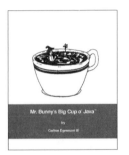

ISBN 0-201-61563-0

ISBN 0-201-30972-6

ISBN 0-201-59614-8

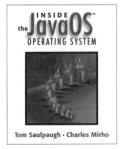

ISBN 0-201-18393-5

ISBN 0-201-32573-X

ISBN 0-201-32582-9

http://www.awl.com/cseng
∿ Addison-Wesley

Addison-Wesley Professional

How to
Register
Your Book

Register this Book

Visit: **http://www.aw.com/cseng/register**

Enter the ISBN*

Then you will receive:

- Notices and reminders about upcoming author appearances, tradeshows, and online chats with special guests
- Advanced notice of forthcoming editions of your book
- Book recommendations
- Notification about special contests and promotions throughout the year

*The ISBN can be found on the copyright page of the book

Visit our Web site

http://www.aw.com/cseng

When you think you've read enough, there's always more content for you at Addison-Wesley's web site. Our web site contains a directory of complete product information including:

- Chapters
- Exclusive author interviews
- Links to authors' pages
- Tables of contents
- Source code

You can also discover what tradeshows and conferences Addison-Wesley will be attending, read what others are saying about our titles, and find out where and when you can meet our authors and have them sign your book.

We encourage you to patronize the many fine retailers who stock Addison-Wesley titles. Visit our online directory to find stores near you.

Contact Us via Email

cepubprof@awl.com

Ask general questions about our books.
Sign up for our electronic mailing lists.
Submit corrections for our web site.

mikeh@awl.com

Submit a book proposal.
Send errata for a book.

cepubpublicity@awl.com

Request a review copy for a member of the media interested in reviewing new titles.

registration@awl.com

Request information about book registration.

Addison-Wesley Professional
One Jacob Way, Reading, Massachusetts 01867 USA
TEL 781-944-3700 • FAX 781-942-3076

CD-ROM WARRANTY